UNIVERSITY OF CAMBRIDGE
DEPARTMENT OF APPLIED ECONOMICS

MONOGRAPHS

6

PRODUCTIVITY AND TECHNICAL CHANGE

UNIVERSITY OF CAMBRIDGE
DEPARTMENT OF APPLIED ECONOMICS

MONOGRAPHS

This series consists of investigations conducted by members of the Department's staff and others working in direct collaboration with the Department.

The Department of Applied Economics assumes no responsibility for the views expressed in the Monographs published under its auspices.

PRODUCTIVITY AND TECHNICAL CHANGE

BY

W. E. G. SALTER

With an Addendum

BY

W. B. REDDAWAY

Director, Department of Applied Economics,
University of Cambridge

CAMBRIDGE
AT THE UNIVERSITY PRESS
1969

PUBLISHED BY
THE SYNDICS OF THE CAMBRIDGE UNIVERSITY PRESS

Bentley House, 200 Euston Road, London, N.W.1
American Branch: 32 East 57th Street, New York, N.Y. 10022

This edition © CAMBRIDGE UNIVERSITY PRESS 1966

Standard Book Number:
521 06186 5 *clothbound*
521 09568 9 *paperback*

First published 1960
Second edition 1966
First paperback edition 1969

First printed in Great Britain at the University Press, Cambridge
Reprinted in Great Britain, by photolithography,
by Unwin Brothers Limited,
Woking and London

TO
M.J.S.

CONTENTS

LIST OF TABLES

LIST OF DIAGRAMS

PREFACE TO THE SECOND EDITION

WILFRED SALTER's untimely death in 1963 deprived the world of a first-class economist who had the supreme gift of combining theoretical insights and the power to apply his ideas; of all the research students whose work I have supervised he certainly taught me the most, and made me do the greatest amount of hard work.

So far as I know the comments evoked by the path-breaking analysis in this book had not led him to plan any serious revisions for the second edition: the original text has therefore been left exactly as it was. The passage of time has, however, made possible the inclusion of an addendum, in which Salter's scheme of analysis has been applied to the statistics for the period 1954 to 1963. Like his own independent test through the use of American data, this one adds strength to one's belief in the fundamental rightness of his ideas.

Miss T. Seward, of the Department of Applied Economics deserves the credit for the patient work needed to deal with the statistical discontinuities and other problems encountered in conducting this test. The Board of Trade kindly made available in January 1966 some preliminary results of the 1963 Census of Production, which were not due for publication until considerably later in the year.

W. B. REDDAWAY

CAMBRIDGE, 1966

PREFACE TO THE FIRST EDITION

THE ideas on which this book is based were developed at Cambridge between 1953 and 1955. Among the many persons who assisted in shaping them, W. B. Reddaway and the late Dr L. Rostas were prominent. The statistical analysis which forms the foundation of Part II was planned in conjunction with Rostas shortly before his death. My debt is thus not only the general one owed him by all workers in the field of productivity, but is also personal and direct. W. B. Reddaway has provided advice, criticism, and encouragement at every step; in the early stages of the development of the theory he often provided the clue which ultimately resolved many problems; in the later stages he painstakingly criticised innumerable drafts. Others who assisted in many different ways are A. D. Roy, C. Christ, A. R. Prest and F. E. A. Briggs. I am particularly indebted to Frank Briggs who rescued me from a rather tricky statistical dilemma; his contribution forms the basis of Appendix C.

During 1956, I was fortunate in being able to spend some time at Johns Hopkins University. Fritz Machlup and Edith Penrose commented on earlier drafts of chapter II, while Tom E. Davies provided a stimulating sounding-board in working out the analysis of chapters IV, v and vi. Here at the Australian National University, T. W. Swan and I. F. Pearce have provided valuable criticism and much-needed encouragement in the actual labour of writing.

I also wish to pay tribute to the very valuable productivity studies of the United States Bureau of Labor Statistics. The Bureau has been investigating productivity ever since 1890, and the very considerable number of extremely careful studies accumulated since then have greatly influenced my thinking.

W. E. G. S

CANBERRA, 1959

CHAPTER I

INTRODUCTION

As an almost inevitable consequence of full employment, the post-war decade has witnessed an upsurge of interest in productivity. With resources fully employed, productivity has taken the centre-place of discussion, as the new economic problem becomes one of increasing the yield of available resources. One consequence has been an increasing volume of empirical material concerning productivity: time-series of output per man-hour at both industry and national levels, inter-national comparisons, and inter-plant and inter-firm studies have all contributed to an extensive factual knowledge of productivity. Of this empirical effort, one pioneer in the field[1] has remarked that far too little interpretive analysis has been attempted. This is a pertinent comment, for to measure is not to understand, and many pressing problems demand an understanding of both the causes and consequences of increasing productivity. It is the declared aim of governments to raise the productivity of industry; but there can be little certainty of the most appropriate policy measures without an understanding of the basic causes of increased productivity. References to productivity are increasingly frequent in wage discussions; yet there is little agreement as to how far it is relevant, or who is entitled to share in the 'gains' of increasing productivity, or in the manner in which they should be distributed. Empirical measures can only assist in providing insight into such problems when we are able adequately to interpret their significance. The difficulty, however, is that the interpretation of even the simplest measures of productivity raises a host of very complex problems. For behind productivity lie all the dynamic forces of economic life: technical progress, accumulation, enterprise, and the institutional pattern of society. These are areas where our understanding remains rudimentary. But, if we are to progress beyond the stage of sheer measurement to more fruitful interpretive analysis, then it is essential that we make some attempt to understand the relationships between productivity and these dynamic forces for change.

In this book I have attempted to analyse one small part of the problem: the relationship between productivity and technical change. I have begun from the premise that to understand productivity movements we must see them as one part of an economy in the process of change, and that the problem is basically to fit productivity and technical change into a context of prices and costs. For reasons which will be made clear subsequently, I have approached the problem from two directions. The first is a theoretical analysis of the relationships between

---

[1] W. Duane Evans in a contributory chapter to *Employment and Wages in the United States*, by W. S. Woytinsky and associates (New York, 1953).

movements of productivity, prices, costs, wages and investment in industries experiencing a continuous flow of new techniques. This analysis attempts to integrate productivity movements, particularly those arising out of technical change, with conventional theory. The second approach is empirical and examines the relationships between movements of productivity, prices, costs, etc., in a number of British and American industries. Both approaches are primarily concerned with productivity in individual industries and are only incidentally aggregative. This, I recognise, is unfashionable; but I also believe that the common procedure of hiving-off the level of output as a separate problem from the composition of output can be taken too far; in fact, one of the points which the statistical analysis seeks to establish is the extreme variety of growth between industries, and the complexity of the relationships between the level and composition of output. It is important, therefore, that we extend our understanding of these problems, both because they are significant in their own right, and as a step towards a less over-simplified aggregative analysis.

One of the reasons why interpretive analysis of productivity has been slow to develop has been the interminable controversy over what is productivity and what do we really wish to measure. The word now carries a multitude of meanings; to some it measures the personal efficiency of labour; to others, it is the output derived from a composite bundle of resources; to the more philosophic, it is almost synonomous with welfare; and in one extreme case it has been identified with time. I personally believe that much of this discussion has proved fruitless and only served to confuse the issues of measurement with the issues of interpretation. Unless there is a revolution in statistical techniques and information, only one type of productivity concept is measurable. This is the concept of output per unit of input. There are as many productivity measures as the number of classes of input we care to distinguish: output per man-hour, output per ton of coal, output per pound's worth of investment. The most common form of measure is that of labour productivity, output per man-hour. Although this measure has a perfectly respectable ancestry—it is no more or less than the average physical product of conventional theory—the critics object that it does not measure anything peculiar to labour and that increased capital or materials may raise labour productivity while labour itself remains passive.

It is important to realise that these objections have nothing to do with the problems of definition and measurement, but rather are relevant to the problems of interpretation. The only questions of definition concern output and man-hours. In this study 'output' has the sense of the volume of saleable goods and services produced by a plant, firm, industry, or economy; and, since the volume of output is an ambiguous term, it must be measured by an appropriate index-number form. 'Man-hours' refers to the total number of man-hours directly required to produce these goods. If we wish it may be divided into categories, such as operative man-hours and salaried man-hours, or direct man-hours and overhead man-hours. Output divided by man-hours yields a measure of output per man-hour, and man-hours divided by output yields the reciprocal concept of unit labour requirements. It is possible to proceed in comparable fashion for any other factor which can be defined and measured.

These are the true problems of measurement. Figures derived in this way are no more than what they are defined to be: output adjusted on a pro-rata basis for changing employment (or vice versa). The interpretive problems begin once we ask what such figures mean. They are not a measure of efficiency, for a high output per man-hour can be produced as inefficiently as a low one. Nobody attempts to maximise labour productivity, nor indeed should they. Businessmen—despite what they say at productivity congresses—are interested in prices, costs and profits, and to them increasing productivity is simply one means of reducing labour costs. The only significance that can be given to such figures is that they are indications of what may be termed '*growth in depth*' as distinct from '*extensive growth*'—growth which merely reproduces a given situation. They are measures which crystallise out changes in content as distinct from changes in amount. But because changes in depth are as highly interrelated as any other forms of economic change, individual productivity measures, such as labour productivity, have little direct significance unless we can relate them to the complex processes of change of which they are a product. From this viewpoint, controversy over the desirability or otherwise of measures such as output per man-hour is as sterile as its nineteenth-century counterpart of whether labour, capital, or land is the more important factor of production. We cannot divorce changes in the productivity of one factor from the productivity of other factors, or indeed, from all the elements in an interrelated economic system. While quantitative information on the productivity of factors other than labour is not always available, it is important that measures such as labour productivity should be interpreted in this spirit—otherwise we run the risk of giving them a significance they do not deserve. Such interpretation is not easy for essentially it involves an appreciation of the workings of an economic system in the process of movement. But progress in this direction is much more likely with the conventional concepts which are firmly rooted in economic theory, rather than some more superficially appealing concept which has pretensions to measuring 'economic efficiency'.

If we adopt this position, there are two possible approaches to the problem of improving our understanding of the productivity concepts which have been defined. The first is to ask the question: what in fact are the observable relationships between changing productivity and other economic variables? This is the rationale of the statistical analysis of Part II, which examines the movements of labour productivity in a number of British industries between 1924 and 1950, and then relates these movements to changes in prices, wages, costs, output, and employment. This investigation does result in certain statistical associations. For example, we find that industries with rapidly expanding output usually record high rates of increase in output per head; that there is no tendency for above-average increases in labour productivity to be accompanied by above-average increases in earnings; that unequal increases in labour productivity are reflected in all costs, non-labour costs as well as labour costs; and that inter-industry differences in movements of labour productivity are closely associated with changes in relative product prices.

By itself, such statistical analysis is not very helpful. All we have are observed facts only a stage advanced beyond sheer measurement. To understand their full significance and to draw out all their implications, we need to relate one 'fact' with another, to distinguish cause from effect, and to isolate the conditions necessary for such relationships to be observed. It is at this point that we are confronted with what, in my opinion, is the major problem of productivity analysis: the absence of a suitable theoretical framework in which to organise our factual knowledge of productivity. This may seem a surprising statement, for productivity is a central theoretical concept and there is a system of analysis dealing with the long period. But, when we are interested in movements through time, a system of analysis is required which not only takes note of all important changes occurring parallel with time but also considers the way in which the present grows out of the past. Long-period theory—and by this term I understand the system of static equilibrium analysis which treats all factors as variable—has only limited application to such problems involving time (and has never purported to claim otherwise in its stricter formulations). Even so, this means that many important problems concerning productivity must be discussed in a theoretical vacuum.

The crux of the difficulty lies in the inability of static equilibrium concepts to analyse continuous processes through time. Let me illustrate this with an example drawn from the theory of production. In discussing the productivity of a factor of production we must obviously take note of its price, and the theory of production provides a convenient apparatus for analysing the effect of changes in relative factor prices on the productivity of different factors. Consider the case where entrepreneurs wish to employ more highly mechanised techniques because of a change in relative factor prices. The change-over is a slow process, for as Professor Hicks has said '...an entrepreneur by investing in fixed capital equipment gives hostages to fortune. So long as the plant is in existence, the possibility of economising by changing the method or scale of production is small; but as the plant comes to be renewed it will be in his interests to make a radical change.'[1] This is the difficulty:

[1] *The Theory of Wages* (London, 1932), p. 183.

certain adjustments to changing conditions take long periods of time to work themselves out, particularly when capital equipment is involved. While static equilibrium analysis tells us the equilibrium which would be reached if no further changes occurred, in fact change is continuous. With the technical knowledge and factor prices ruling today, technique *A* may be most appropriate and is adopted by entrepreneurs currently building new plants or replacing existing ones. But, before even a fraction of industry is equipped with technique *A*, either technical knowledge or factor prices change, and technique *B* becomes appropriate. Some progress is made in installing *B*, and then technique *C* appears on the horizon. In such circumstances, when we measure the output per man-hour of an industry we find it refers to the productivity of labour working with a varied assortment of techniques of production. Techniques *A, B, C, D, ...* are in use because before the adjustment to one technique has worked itself out an even newer technique has appeared; each step towards the equilibrium to which the theory of production refers is nullified by a continuous flow of disturbances.

This is an important problem in productivity analysis, for the two elements in this example—continuous disturbance and slow adjustment—are essential features of technical change. Techniques of production change through time for two reasons: improving technical knowledge and changing factor prices. Both are continuous processes in time and together give rise to a stream of new techniques, each following the other in quick succession. The 'once-over' analysis of comparative statics is only appropriate to changes in technique which are sufficiently great to displace completely all pre-existing methods before they themselves are displaced. It hardly needs to be stressed that such cases are rare; in fact, many experienced observers[1] rate the cumulative effect of small unnoticed modifications and improvements as equally great as the more significant changes normally regarded as innovations.[2] Moreover, factor prices change slowly but continuously through time, and this alone is sufficient to produce a constant stream of new techniques of production.

For these reasons, before the theory of production can be applied to the analysis of productivity movements, the notion of independent

---

[1] See, for example, Boris Stern, 'Employment and Productivity in the Automobile Tire Industry', *Monthly Lab. Rev.* December 1932, and 'Productivity Changes since 1939', *Monthly Lab. Rev.* December 1946.

[2] Two examples may serve to illustrate this: Detailed studies by the United States Bureau of Labor Statistics into the most up-to-date methods available to the cotton textile industry (Boris Stern, 'Mechanical Changes in the Cotton Textile Industry, 1910–1936', *Monthly Lab. Rev.* August 1937) show that improvements in detail but not in basic methods were sufficient to allow a potential increase in labour productivity of 50 % between 1910 and 1936. Larger spinning bobbins, improved design, chain drives and greater speeds, were some of the numerous small improvements which allowed this increase. A more extreme case is that of mechanical methods for the manufacture of electric light bulbs which, when first introduced in 1925, represented a radical break with previous methods. But, in the following six years, improvements in detail alone were sufficient to allow a five-fold increase in output per man-hour (Witt Bowden, *Technological Changes and Employment in the Electric Lamp Industry* (Bulletin 593 of the Bureau of Labor Statistics, 1933)).

'once-over' changes must be rejected, and in its place must be substituted concepts of continuous disturbance. Instead of a given change in technical knowledge, we must think of a rate of improvement; and for a given change in factor prices must be substituted a rate of change. By itself, this substitution raises few technical difficulties: the most important concern the nature of the interaction between new technical knowledge and changing factor prices, as they determine the appropriate technique of production at each date. The real problems arise because this continuous change in techniques is allied to a slow adjustment process caused by durable capital equipment. In such circumstances the flow of new techniques outstrips the ability of the system to adjust, and a gap appears between potential technical change and actual technical change. This distinction may be most conveniently described by means of an empirical example. Table 1 sets out two measures of labour productivity in the United States blast-furnace industry for selected years between 1911 and 1926.

Table 1. *Best and average practice labour productivity in the United States blast-furnace industry, selected years from 1911 to 1926*

Year	Gross tons of pig-iron produced per man-hour	
	Best-practice plants	Industry average
1911	0·313	0·140
1917	0·326	0·150
1919	0·328	0·140
1921	0·428	0·178
1923	0·462	0·213
1925	0·512	0·285
1926	0·573	0·296

Source: U.S. Bureau of Labor Statistics, *The Productivity of Labor in Merchant Blast Furnaces* (Bulletin no. 474, December 1928).

The first column records the output per man-hour of modern plants constructed at each date; it approximates to what will be termed 'best-practice' labour productivity since it relates to the most up-to-date techniques available at each date.[1] The second column records the average performance of the industry, the conventional output per man-hour estimate. In this industry, average labour productivity is only approximately half best-practice productivity. If all plants were up to best-practice standards known and in use, labour productivity would have doubled immediately. In fact, a decade and a half elapsed before this occurred, and in the meantime the potential provided by best-practice productivity had more than doubled. This is not an isolated example; all the available evidence, some of which is presented in later

[1] I have borrowed this term from Anne P. Grosse, 'The Technological Structure of the Cotton Industry', in *Studies in the Structure of the American Economy*, W. W. Leontief and others (New York, 1953).

chapters, points to the crucial importance of this delay in the utilisation of new techniques. This being so, it is obviously impossible to employ the long-period schema for the analysis of technical change and productivity; for, by definition, the long-period approach assumes away the adjustment process which leads to this gap. Moreover, once we admit the existence of continuous disturbance and slow adjustment, the long-period framework is unsuitable for analysis of the cost and price movements accompanying technical change; for its basic tools, such as long-period supply functions, are incapable of application in such circumstances.

These are some of the more important shortcomings of the long-period analysis as a framework for consistent thought about productivity and technical change. I have been extremely conscious of these problems in interpreting the statistical results, and this has led me to develop a system of analysis which at least partly overcomes some of the more important difficulties. This analysis involves few departures from established theory; basically, it is intermediate between the existing long- and short-period frameworks and draws upon elements of both. I am not sure how far it deserves the label dynamic; but it does go some distance in integrating the process of continuous disturbance and adjustment into established theory, and therefore enables us to say something about movements through time.

Although this analysis was initially developed simply as a framework for interpretation of the empirical results of Part II, once the basic framework had been erected many questions quite unrelated to the empirical study could be analysed quite simply. For this reason I have thought it worth while to develop the theoretical analysis in its own right and separate it from the empirical analysis; hence the division into two parts.

Part I covers these theoretical investigations. It deals with two main types of problems: The first group concern the additional complications which must be introduced into the theory of production when both technical knowledge and factor prices change through time and, by their interaction, determine the most appropriate techniques of production at each date—the best-practice techniques of the blast-furnace example. Chapter II attempts to relate improving technical knowledge to production-possibilities and considers the nature of technique decisions in such circumstances. Chapter III examines the problem of classifying technical advances into labour- and capital-saving categories, and analyses the influence of technical progress in the manufacture of capital goods on techniques of production. The remaining chapters of Part I are concerned with the second group of problems: those arising out of the adjustment process to the flow of new best-practice techniques. Chapter IV begins an examination of this process by setting up a highly simplified model based on the theory of rent which relates new techniques to those of past periods inherited in the capital stock. Chapter V employs the model to isolate the strategic factors which determine the extent of the lag in the utilisation of new techniques resulting from the adjustment process. It shows that while quasi-institutional factors, such as lack of competition and enterprise, may have some influence, the extent of this lag is primarily determined by relative factor prices and that the speed of adjustment is a form of factor substitution. Chapter VI considers the relationships between movements of prices, costs, productivity and investment; it suggests that many of the propositions of long-period equilibrium analysis, particularly those concerned with prices, may be sustained without recourse to the assumptions of long-period equilibrium. Chapter VII indicates the means by which the main assumptions of the model may be relaxed, and briefly considers the adjustment to new techniques in non-competitive market situations.

This theoretical analysis makes no attempt to be comprehensive. In general I have shunned the complications of the short period, that is, the factors which determine year-to-year movements. For the purposes of the theory, the most useful analytical division into long- and short-period factors revolves around the nature of decisions. Long-period decisions concern techniques, investment, and replacement, and, being embodied in capital equipment, extend their influence over long periods of time; short-period decisions, such as varying the extent to which capacity is used, are not embodied in capital equipment and do not directly influence the future. While both types of decisions take place at the one point of time and interact with each other, the long-period decisions are more important in shaping 'trend' movements. Short-period decisions, on the other hand, are chiefly responsible for aberrations around this trend. The analysis is therefore primarily long term, in the special sense that it concentrates on the factors determining trend movements (this sense is, of course, quite different to that of formal long-period theory which involves no temporal connotations).

The more institutional aspects of the subject—the efficiency of management, the willingness of labour to adopt new methods, and the whole question of industrial research—have been treated in a highly sketchy fashion. The only justification for this neglect is that Professors Carter and Williams's *Industry and Technical Progress*[1] has already covered this ground with admirable precision and insight.

A word of explanation is necessary concerning the treatment of capital. One cannot discuss labour productivity without reference to capital, and this immediately raises the whole controversy concerning the theory of capital.[2] But, if we are interested in capital only in relation to technique decisions (which can only be relevant to marginal additions or replacements to the pre-existing capital stock), it is possible to

[1] For the Science and Industry Committee (London, 1957).

[2] See Joan Robinson, 'The Production Function and the Theory of Capital', *Rev. Econ. Stud.* no. 55 (1955), p. 81; 'The Production Function', *Econ. J.* vol. LXV, no. 257 (1955), p. 67; and *The Accumulation of Capital* (London, 1956); R. M. Solow, 'The Production Function and the Theory of Capital', *Rev. Econ. Stud.* no. 61, p. 101; T. W. Swan, 'Economic Growth and Capital Accumulation', *Econ. Rec.* no. 68 (1956).

conduct the analysis in terms of investment instead of the ambiguous concept of capital. I have described such an approach elsewhere[1] and, since the question is not fundamental to the analysis, only a brief summary is included in this volume.

In Part II the approach is empirical. The first two chapters are primarily factual reporting. Chapter VIII describes the statistical analysis based on a comparison of the experiences of twenty-eight British industries over the period 1924–50, and briefly examines a number of purely statistical questions (these are treated in detail in Appendices). Chapter IX describes the main results, some of which have already been noted.

The following three chapters are interpretive in the sense that they attempt to probe behind the figures and draw out their implications. In these chapters, I have drawn upon as much of the theory as has appeared relevant, both as a framework for my own thinking and as a vehicle for certain more technical aspects of the interpretation. Despite this, the empirical analysis is in no sense meant as a test of the theory. In fact, I am deeply conscious of the gap between the empirical and theoretical approaches. This is largely unavoidable, both because of the incomplete nature of the theory, and the impossibility of obtaining data for variables which the theory suggests are significant, such as best-practice techniques and costs.

The first step in the interpretation is to suggest an explanation of the regularities found in the comparative inter-industry movements of labour productivity, costs, prices, wages, output and employment. Chapter X seeks such an explanation by examining possible causes of uneven productivity movements between industries with the object of ascertaining which are most consistent with the observed price and cost behaviour. This examination leads to the tentative hypothesis that the pattern of results is largely a reflection of the uneven impact of technical advance and associated economies of scale on different industries. Chapter XI carries this interpretation a stage further by considering the relation between aggregate productivity movements and structural change. It suggests that a number of rapidly growing industries are responsible for a major part of overall productivity gains, and that a flexible structure of production is an important element in a high rate of productivity increase, for it allows an economy to rapidly redistribute its resources so as to take maximum advantage of changing patterns of technical progress. A corollary is that index number ambiguities in the measurement of output and output per head—which are considerable for sample industries—reflect an essential characteristic of the growth process. Chapter XII considers the results from the viewpoint of distribution: it shows that labour (and probably other factors) employed in industries with above-average increases in productivity have not received above-average increases in earnings; and that in the main the

---

[1] 'The Production Function and the Durability of Capital Goods', *Econ. Rec.* no. 70 (1959), p. 47.

gains of increased productivity have been distributed to consumers by means of price changes. In general, the distributive pattern is similar to that which would be expected in a basically competitive economy.

The final chapter is devoted to a similar survey of a number of American industries over the same period. The object of this survey is to provide a check on the British survey, both in the statistical sense of an alternative sample, and to ascertain whether the results lead to similar interpretive conclusions. The results are largely parallel, thereby confirming the important role of productivity and technical change in shaping the structure of relative prices and composition of output.

To facilitate reference, and to aid the reader who may prefer to be selective, summaries have been included at the end of each chapter. These summaries do not, however, necessarily state the conclusions in a fully rigorous form.

PART I

CHAPTER II

TECHNICAL KNOWLEDGE AND BEST-PRACTICE TECHNIQUES

THE first step in the analysis of productivity movements is to consider the behaviour of best-practice productivity. In a growing economy two main forces shape the flow of new techniques which we observe coming into use: improving technical knowledge expands the realm of the technically feasible, and changing factor prices alter the terms of choice between technical alternatives. This chapter considers three questions which are preliminary to the analysis of the effects of this process on best-practice productivity. The first is the relationship between technical knowledge and techniques of production—what do we really mean by the range of alternative techniques implied by a given stock of knowledge? The second is the nature of the interaction between economic choice and technical restraints; and the third is the controversial question of units of measurement for factors of production.

I. TECHNICAL KNOWLEDGE AND PRODUCTION-POSSIBILITIES

At any one time there exists a body of knowledge relating known technical facts and the relationships between them. This knowledge is at a number of levels which differ in their proximity to production. At one level is the knowledge dealing with basic principles of physical phenomena: the properties of fluids, the laws of motion, the principles of metallurgy and, in general, the area of knowledge we associate with pure science. At another level is the knowledge concerned with the application of these principles to production, the field of the applied sciences. Knowledge of this character bridges the gap between principles and practice, such as the transition from the formulae of organic chemistry to the design of an oil refinery, or the application of genetic theory to the breeding of new plants. Finally, there is the knowledge concerned with the day-to-day operations of production: the rules of thumb of the craftsman and the techniques of the production engineer.

The existence of these different levels of technical knowledge raises a number of difficult questions concerning factor substitution. To see these problems clearly, consider the various steps in the transition from a fund of such knowledge to techniques of production. Knowledge is in the form of technical facts and the relationships between them: the properties of steels and alloys, the means of transforming one type of motion into another, the thermal content of different fuels, and so on. Engineers and applied scientists have the task of translating such knowledge, some old and some new, into feasible techniques of production.

The difficulty is that costs impinge upon this process at two points. First, a choice must be made as to which of the countless methods that are technically feasible in principle are sufficiently commercially promising to be worth developing in detail. No engineer goes to the trouble and expense of developing techniques which he is certain will prove uneconomic. The difficulty is that even at this early stage costs, and through them factor prices, intrude to some extent. A method, rejected for detailed development on the grounds that it is commercially impracticable, may have been regarded as promising if factor prices were different. For example, oil-fired locomotives were probably technically feasible fifty years ago but would not have been considered worth developing in view of the relative prices of oil and coal then prevailing. Secondly, in even the simplest designing process there are numerous alternatives which must be decided on the basis of cost: whether a machine should be powered by electricity or diesel power, whether control should be automatic or manual, whether bearings should be of bronze or steel, or whether the flow of materials should be mechanised or not. These, and countless other every-day decisions of engineers, are essentially cost decisions within the framework of technical restraints; they are quasi-economic decisions which precede choice by businessmen.

In addition, the range of techniques available to the individual businessman is very often limited by the range of equipment produced by machine-manufacturers. The interests of such manufacturers lie in producing equipment which meets the needs of their market, that is, equipment which embodies minimum cost techniques. Again, costs and factor prices influence the range of equipment to be designed and marketed, so that the form of equipment actually available implies a substantial degree of pre-selection on the basis of cost.

These three stages in the transition from a fund of knowledge to techniques of production imply that there is no clear dividing line between economic choice and technical restraints. The entrepreneurial function of choice between technical alternatives is not localised in the businessman. By selecting methods to be developed in detail, in the designing process itself, and in the choice of equipment to be designed and marketed, engineers and machine-makers anticipate the needs of businessmen. The analytical problem is not so much this division of labour in the choice of techniques; if all decisions are made according to the same principles the net result will be much the same as if they were centralised. Rather the problem is how we should think of a range of alternative techniques of production. This is a problem that can be expressed in terms of the production function, the traditional means of describing alternative methods of production in terms of the required inputs of factors of production. The above argument implies that there are two ranges of alternative techniques and the production function could refer to either.

The first is the relatively narrow range of developed techniques actually available to businessmen—the range exemplified by the specifi-

2. UNITS OF MEASUREMENT

While the concept of the production function which has been suggested provides a formal description of the alternative techniques implied by the technical knowledge of each date, it does so only in general terms. To give this function concrete content, and to relate it to the productivity of factors of production, units of measurement must be specified for each factor.

The measurement of the labour requirements of each technique is straightforward in principle. Although each class of labour should properly be regarded as a separate factor of production, unless we are particularly interested in specific types of labour, the analysis may be simplified by regarding labour as homogeneous and measuring it in man-hours. Other factors, such as materials, may be measured in their appropriate technical units (tons of coal for example) or, if a greater degree of simplification is appropriate, by an index number aggregate such as the volume of materials.

The major problem is the measurement of capital. As a preliminary to consideration of this complex and controversial question, consider the circumstances in which the production function is relevant. As Schumpeter has said, the production function is 'a planning function in a world of blue-prints where every element that is technologically variable can be changed at will'.[1] This implies it is only relevant to investment decisions for, in general, each technique requires a different outfit of specialised capital equipment. Consequently, the choice between alternative techniques can only take place prior to the act of investment. Once the appropriate technique has been decided and investment has taken place in the necessary equipment, the production function is no longer relevant. From then on, throughout the life of the equipment, factor substitution is of the short-term variety, limited by the nature of the equipment and not by the restraints of technical knowledge. Only when the equipment comes to be renewed does the production function again become relevant. Thus the choice of techniques described by the production function only applies to entrepreneurs who are considering investment, either new investment or replacement investment.[2]

This limited role of the production function is pertinent to the measurement of capital for it implies there is no need to consider part-worn and part-obsolete equipment; such equipment is the result of past investment decisions where the technique of production has already

---

[1] *History of Economic Analysis*, p. 1031.

[2] An alternative way of making this point is: that before the entrepreneur acquires fixed capital equipment, the parameters to his range of production-possibilities are the restraints of knowledge; and after the particular complex of equipment he has acquired. Given such a complex of existing equipment it is possible to derive a short-term production function (which could more usefully be called a utilisation function) that traces out the way output changes as more or less of other factors are employed with this given complex. This is the technical function behind a short-term plant cost curve.

been decided. The problem then becomes one of finding an appropriate means of aggregating and measuring the outfit of equipment required by each technique. Since only new equipment is involved, the appropriate concept is that of investment. For analysis over time, where it is important to avoid the distortions of price changes, each technique may be described by the required 'real' investment or, more precisely, the initial outlay at constant prices of the necessary building, plant, equipment and normal working stocks. This corresponds to general usage and has the sense of the 'quantity' of capital equipment required by each technique.

Complementary to the definition of quantity units for factors is the definition of factor prices. In general these should be: (a) consistent with each other in terms of dimensions, and (b) such that price times quantity for each factor sums to total costs. From this viewpoint, the 'price' of the factor real investment must have the sense of the minimum monetary inducement required to induce investment to be undertaken, that is, the expectation of a return over the life of the investment sufficient to recover the initial outlay and meet interest charges; or, in a form consistent with the wage rate as the price of labour, a gross return per annum sufficient to cover 'capital costs', consisting of amortisation and interest. Thus the price per annum of a unit of capital equipment, or real investment, is a function of the current price of capital goods, the rate of interest, and the life of this investment. Two features should be noted concerning this approach. First, the price of capital goods appears explicitly as a variable. This is essential once we think of capital as something more concrete than uncommitted purchasing power and, as will become apparent, is extremely important in analysing the relationships between productivity and obsolescence. Secondly, by replacing capital in the production function by this less ambiguous concept of investment, we are forced to recognise the time element in technique decisions. This appears in the dependence of capital costs per annum on the expected life of the investment; a short-lived investment requires a high amortisation charge per annum, and a long-lived investment a relatively low charge. Consequently, there are a multiplicity of prices for the factor real investment depending on the expected life of the investment. The time element appears in another form. Techniques requiring the same initial investment may be of a very different character depending on the life of the investment. Moreover, the life of the capital equipment required by a method of production is not technically invariable; a greater investment allows more durable equipment, and while this does not affect output per annum, the period over which the flow of output continues is extended.

The only logically consistent means of treating this time element in technique decisions is to measure capital in two dimensions: an initial real investment and the life of this investment. Technique decisions then involve choosing the optimum combination of capital equipment and other factors of production, and the optimum life of this equipment.

I have described this approach in detail elsewhere,[1] and since the problem is peripheral to the present analysis, only a brief summary is set out below.

When the life of capital equipment is introduced as an additional variable, the production function must describe two kinds of technical restraints: those relevant to combining real investment with other factors of production, and those relating real investment to the durability of capital equipment. In the simple case where labour and capital are the only factors of production, these restraints are described by the function

$$O = f(N, I, l),$$

where O = output per annum, N = man-hours per annum, I = initial investment at constant prices, and l = the life of this investment.

Such a production function describes each possible technique in terms of the labour force and initial investment required to produce a flow of output extending over different periods of time. The function includes each method of production and each possible durability of the necessary capital equipment.

Complementary to this production function is a price for real investment which varies with the life of equipment. The capital costs per annum of the equipment required by each technique depend upon: (i) the initial real investment, (ii) the current prices of capital goods, (iii) the interest rate (or normal profit rate), and (iv) the expected life of this equipment. Thus we may write:

$$G = F(I, P, r, l),$$

where G = capital costs per annum, I = initial real investment, P = the price of capital goods, r = the interest rate, and l = the expected life of the investment.

From the point of view of the individual entrepreneur, the interest rate and the price of capital goods are beyond his control, and are parameters in this function. Thus,

$$G = \phi(I, l),$$

where ϕ is a functional relationship that includes the values of P and r as parameters.

The actual form of this function depends upon the depreciation method. Ideally this should be the theoretically perfect depreciation method where the allowance in each year reflects the reduction in the present value of the expected future gross earnings, or capital value.[2] Straight-line, declining balance, and annuity methods, are more or less approximate versions of this ideal, and which is the more appropriate

[1] 'The Production Function and the Durability of Capital Goods,' *Econ. Rec.* no. 70 (1959), p. 47
[2] See Professor Hotelling's classic paper, 'A General Mathematical Theory of Depreciation', *J. Amer. Statist. Assoc.*, vol. xx (1925), pp. 340–53. Also F. and V. Lutz, *Theory of Investment of the Firm* (Princeton, 1951), pp. 16–48.

depends upon the expected pattern of future earnings. For theoretical analysis the annuity form has obvious attractions since it implies that the sum of interest and amortisation charges are equal in each year, so that capital costs per annum are equal over the life of the investment. Even where the pattern of expected future earnings does not meet this requirement, it may still be employed provided it is regarded as the annual average capital charge, an average of the capital charges appropriate to the theoretically exact depreciation method. In this simplified form

$$G = \frac{IPr}{1 - e^{-rl}}.$$

From this function, the effect on capital costs per annum of marginal changes in initial real investment and the life of the investment may be determined.

For labour we may write w as the wage rate and Nw as labour costs per annum. Total costs of production per annum (U) are then

$$U = Nw + G$$

$$= Nw + \phi(I, l).$$

This equation is in complementary terms to the production function. Given w, P and r, the choice of technique then involves choosing the values of N, I and l which minimise costs of production. As may be expected the solution runs in terms of the familiar marginal productivity conditions:

$$\frac{\partial O}{\partial N} : \frac{\partial O}{\partial I} : \frac{\partial O}{\partial l} = w : \frac{\partial G}{\partial I} : \frac{\partial G}{\partial l}.$$

Two additional features of this approach should be noted. Obsolescence may place a definite limit on the life of capital equipment. In such circumstances the life of investment is not a matter of marginal calculation but is imposed directly by expectations of obsolescence. This has the effect of increasing the capital costs of real investment through reducing the period over which the initial outlay can be amortised, and so results in real investment becoming dearer relative to other factors. Risk plays a similar role through an addition to the interest rate. Thus the factors which determine the capital costs of real investment are a complex of all factors bearing upon the willingness to undertake investment. Some, such as the interest rate and the price of capital goods, are prices in the usual sense; others, such as risk and expectations of obsolescence, are economic factors which operate in the same way as prices by influencing the gross return required before investment is undertaken.

While this approach provides an unambiguous means of treating technique decisions involving capital, it introduces an unnecessary degree of complication into much of the subsequent analysis. Provided this treatment is regarded as underlying the analysis, capital can be measured simply by real investment, and the convention adopted of treating its price as though it were a single quantity. We shall then speak of the price of real investment as the capital costs per annum of a unit of real investment; it may be regarded as a reflection of all the factors bearing upon the willingness to invest: the interest rate, the price of capital goods, risk and expectations of obsolescence.

The problems of definition and measurement also extend to output. One of the most important features of improving technology is the emergence of new products and improvements to existing ones. From the point of view of the purist, comparison between techniques which differ in this way is impossible. If we are not prepared to allow this problem to frustrate all attempts at analysis over time, the artificial convention must be adopted of imagining new products in terms comparable to existing ones; the procedure would be comparable to grafting new commodities into a price index.[1]

3. A FLOW OF NEW KNOWLEDGE

This preliminary groundwork enables the technical knowledge of each date to be related to the production function. A flow of new knowledge leads to continuous change in the production function for each commodity. This may take a variety of forms. Some advances, particularly those which originate in basic science, affect the whole nature of the production function as the basic processes of an industry undergo a radical change. Other advances lead to improvements in existing basic methods. These may apply to only one technique in the range of alternatives—such as the improvements to the bulb-making machine cited earlier—or to a wide range of alternative techniques. Improved standards of engineering design, improved lubrication and new kinds of bearings which allow machines to operate faster, are advances of this character. Some advances, such as electricity, new packing materials and methods of production engineering, apply to the production of many commodities; others are highly specialised—marine turbines and linotype machines for example.

The common characteristics of all such advances is that they lead to a new production function which is superior to its predecessor in the sense that less of one or more factors of production is required to produce a given output, the input of other factors remaining unchanged. This process may be formally represented by a series of dated production functions, one for each time period:

$$O = f_n(a, b, c, \ldots),$$
$$O = f_{n+1}(a, b, c, \ldots),$$
$$\cdots\cdots\cdots\cdots\cdots\cdots$$
$$O = f_{n+t}(a, b, c, \ldots),$$

where O = output; $a, b, c, \ldots$ are inputs of factors of production and n, $n+1, \ldots, n+t$ are consecutive time periods.

---

[1] This problem is examined further in chapter VII, p. 88.

A graphical representation of this series of production functions would involve taking a specified output and, in the elementary but useful case where only labour and capital are considered, drawing schedules of the alternative labour and capital requirements which could produce the given output at different dates. In appearance, this diagram would be similar to the familiar series of iso-product curves of production theory, but time instead of output would be measured on the third axis and each curve would refer to the same output. Variations in output could only be introduced with a fourth dimension. However, if there are no

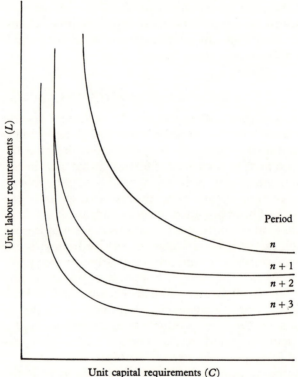

Fig. 1

economies or diseconomies of scale over the range of capacity outputs under consideration, the characteristics of the production function at each date are implicit in the curve for one output, and labour and capital requirements per unit of output are unaffected by changes in output. If we make this assumption it is possible to draw Fig. 1, which relates the series of dated production functions directly to labour and capital productivity.

The vertical axis measures unit labour requirements (L), the reciprocal of output per head, and the horizontal axis measures unit capital requirements (C). Each curve is a snapshot picture of the alternative techniques, described in terms of unit labour and investment requirements, which are available at each date.[1] These curves may run into each other but will not cross—unless we consider special cases such as the retrogression of knowledge, the exhaustion of natural resources, or the imposition of legal or trade union restrictions for safety or other reasons. Apart from such cases, successive curves move inwards towards the origin, reflecting the way in which new technical knowledge opens up successive ranges of alternative techniques which make possible new levels of productivity.

4. BEST-PRACTICE TECHNIQUES OF PRODUCTION

Parallel with improving technical knowledge are changing relative factor prices. Both combine to determine the nature of the flow of new

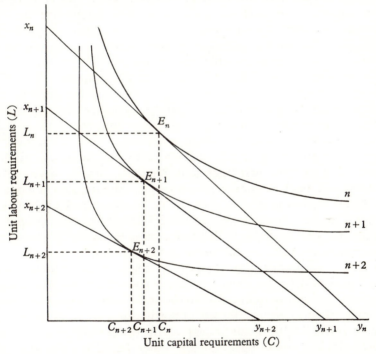

Fig. 2

techniques coming into use—best-practice techniques. The best-practice technique at each date is the appropriate technique having regard to both economic and technical conditions; it is the technique which yields minimum costs in terms of the production function and relative factor prices of each date. Fig. 2 illustrates graphically the determination of successive best-practice techniques.

[1] Mathematically, the procedure is to rewrite the production function in the form $1 = F_n(N/O, I/O)$ and to assume this function is linear and homogeneous so that N/O and I/O do not vary for different values of O. A second system is derived by adding another dimension, time; no assumptions are made as to the form of this derived system.

The lines $x_n y_n$, $x_{n+1} y_{n+1}$, $x_{n+2} y_{n+2}$ have slopes equal to the ratio of factor prices in each period g_n/w_n, g_{n+1}/w_{n+1}, g_{n+2}/w_{n+2}, where g is the 'price' of real investment and w the wage rate. There are innumerable such lines, one for each absolute level of money costs, though only those tangential to the production function at each period have been drawn. These points of tangency E_n, E_{n+1}, E_{n+2} correspond to successive best-practice techniques where the marginal conditions for minimum cost are satisfied. They imply successive unit labour requirements of L_n, L_{n+1}, L_{n+2} and unit investment requirements of C_n, C_{n+1}, C_{n+2}.

From the diagram it is apparent that successive best-practice techniques differ in two respects which, although difficult to distinguish in practice, are analytically quite distinct. First, today's best-practice techniques differ from yesterday's in that they make use of the new knowledge acquired between today and yesterday. This is represented by the shift in the production function; new knowledge by easing technical restraints has opened up a superior range of production-possibilities. Secondly, changed relative prices have altered the technique which is economically appropriate.[1]

Either influence is sufficient to result in a continuous flow of new techniques of production. If knowledge were constant and labour became dearer relative to real investment, best-practice techniques would become increasingly mechanised in the sense that the input of labour would decrease and that of investment increase. This transition would take place in two ways. First, businessmen would find it profitable to employ in new uses machines and methods already developed by engineers and machine-makers; for example, the extension of industrial-type hoists and conveyor systems to building operations. Secondly, engineers and machine-makers would be under pressure to apply the existing fund of knowledge to the design of methods which were labour-saving and investment-using. Such methods would be new only in the sense they were new designs; they would involve little or no new know-ledge but would be largely a rearrangement of existing technological knowledge into forms appropriate to the new factor prices. For example, the small tractors designed for use in horticulture are much more a new design to suit changing factor prices than the result of significant advances in technological knowledge. On the other hand, if knowledge alone were changing, there would also be a flow of new best-practice techniques. These would not necessarily be more or less mechanised than their predecessors. Changes in the extent of mechanisation would depend on whether the knowledge was of a character which tended to save labour more than investment or vice versa.

In fact, both changes take place simultaneously. Consequently, it is extremely difficult to distinguish how far new techniques are the product of new knowledge and how far they are attributable to changed factor prices. For example, how far is automation the result of new knowledge

---

[1] Although it is not possible to illustrate this graphically, we may think of best-practice techniques as also involving optimum plant scale.

or changed factor prices? Ever since the invention of the photo-electric cell in the early thirties, a crude form of automation has been possible.[1] A large degree of automatic control had been achieved in power stations, oil-refineries, and some chemical processes before 1940 and it is probable that automation in the metal-fabricating industries was technically possible although, of course, it would have been an economic monstrosity. During the war and early post-war years, rapid advances in electronics enormously increased knowledge relevant to automation. Whether or not this alone would have been sufficient to induce its use in industry is a matter of speculation. In any case, as will be shown in the next chapter, labour became substantially dearer relative to capital equipment, and this encouraged the use and development of automation. It may be that this change in factor prices was just sufficient to tip the balance in favour of automation, at least in the form we know it today. The engineer who decides in 1950 to incorporate automatic control in a new process may well have reached a different decision if he had employed 1930 prices for labour and capital equipment in his calculations. Without a detailed knowledge of the technical background it is impossible to assess the role of either force in determining the character of best-practice techniques; all we actually observe is the net result.

Changes in best-practice techniques may be described by indexes of labour and real investment requirements per unit of output. There are two methods of deriving such information. The first, which is based on the fact that techniques embodied in newly-constructed plants approximate to the idea of best-practice techniques, is to compare the characteristics of new plants at different dates. This is the method of the initial example of the blast-furnace industry. The second method, which has often been employed by the United States Bureau of Labor Statistics, is to approach firms of consulting engineers for the specification of the most advanced techniques at different dates. An interesting long-run example relating to the shoe industry in the United States is set out below.

Table 2. *Man-hours required by best-practice methods of producing a pair of medium-grade men's shoes at selected dates in the United States*

Year	Man-hours per pair
1850	15·5
1900	1·7
1923	1·1
1936	0·9

Note: Data refer to medium-grade goodyear welt oxford shoes.

Source: Boris Stern, 'Labour Productivity in the Boot and Shoe Industry', Bureau of Labor Statistics, *Monthly Lab. Rev.* (February 1939), p. 271.

[1] See 'Industrial Instruments and Changing Technology', National Research Project Report M-1, WPA (Philadelphia, 1938); 'Automation', Department of Scientific and Industrial Research, H.M.S.O. (London, 1956) and 'Technological Trends and National Policy' (U.S. Government, 1937).

Measures such as this are extremely valuable in productivity analysis, for they give an idea of the potential levels of productivity at each date. If complete and immediate utilisation of new methods were feasible and economic, such levels of productivity could be achieved generally. In fact, the past is always with us so that actual labour productivity always trails behind best-practice labour productivity.

5. SUMMARY

1. Since technical possibilities and restraints originate in technical knowledge which exists at a number of levels ranging from pure science to applied know-how, there are certain ambiguities in the idea of alternative techniques implied by a given state of knowledge. These ambiguities are reflected in the production function concept which could refer either to techniques which have been developed in detail, or to techniques which are feasible in principle but have not been developed because the necessary economic pressures are absent. It is suggested that the latter concept is the most relevant to long-run analysis, although it contains many difficulties.

2. Because technique decisions relate to additions or replacements to the pre-existing capital stock, the appropriate means of measuring capital in the production function is in terms of real investment, and there is no need to consider directly the capital equipment already in existence. The corresponding concept of the price of capital has the sense of capital costs per annum, consisting of amortisation and interest (or normal profits). This is the concept of the price of capital which corresponds to the wage rate as the cost of employing labour, and is consistent with the normal concept of long-run total costs.

3. Production functions defined in these terms describe the alternative techniques at each date, and a series of dated production functions describes the new alternatives opened up by a flow of new technical knowledge. Such a series of production functions may be related to productivity and provide a tool for analysing the way in which technical advances make possible new levels of productivity.

4. Best-practice techniques are defined as the techniques at each date which employ the most recent technical advances, and are economically appropriate to current factor prices. They correspond to the idea of the most up-to-date techniques currently available. Period-to-period changes in best-practice techniques are a product of interaction between the flow of technical advances and changes in factor prices. This interaction may be the result of conscious decisions, or the unconscious product of the process of designing new methods in detail. The importance of best-practice techniques lies in the fact that they represent the potential available if adjustment to new methods were immediate.

CHAPTER III

THE DETERMINANTS OF BEST-PRACTICE PRODUCTIVITY MOVEMENTS

THE previous chapter has shown the flow of new techniques which we actually observe coming into use to be the net result of a complicated interplay between technical advances and changing factor prices. In order to relate this process to movements of best-practice productivity, two questions require examination. The first concerns the many patterns of technical advance: it may be rapid or slow, biased towards labour-saving or capital-saving, or such as to increase or decrease the opportunities for factor substitution. Some apparatus for thinking consistently about these characteristics of technical advance, and their interaction with changing factor prices, is clearly necessary in analysing best-practice productivity movements. The second question is intimately related to the first; it concerns the effects of technical advances in the manufacture of capital goods on the relative prices of labour and capital equipment and the consequent induced changes in best-practice techniques of production.

I. FACTORS SHAPING BEST-PRACTICE PRODUCTIVITY MOVEMENTS

Fig. 3 reproduces the diagram illustrating the determination of successive best-practice techniques. An examination suggests that the total period-to-period change in such techniques may be divided into four components, three of which relate to the characteristics of technical advance, and the fourth to changing factor prices. As a first step, we shall consider these influences in general terms and only attempt to give them some precision in later sections.

The first such influence is represented by the movement towards the origin of successive production functions. In a general sense this corresponds to the improved 'efficiency' which new knowledge makes possible. In absolute terms it is both labour-saving and capital-saving; it leads to a whole new range of alternative techniques within which it is possible to increase the productivity of labour and capital, or both. Speaking loosely, the rate of this movement towards the origin reflects the speed of technical advance; in an industry where technical advance is rapid there would be large differences in the position of consecutive production functions, and in a technically stagnant industry the curves would be bunched together.

Accompanying this type of movement are changes in the shape of the curves—the movement may be greater towards one axis than another. Such changes in shape represent biases which lead to a greater

saving of one factor than the other. For example, the transition from
n to $n+1$ represents a proportionate saving of labour for all techniques,
such as time and motion study. The transition from $n+1$ to $n+2$
represents the converse case of a proportionate saving of capital for all
techniques. Such shifts are special cases of changes in the production
function which tend to raise the productivity of one factor more than
another; they arise solely out of the nature of the technical advance and
are quite distinct from changes in relative factor productivities which
accompany factor substitution. In contrast, the movement from $n+2$
to $n+3$ contains no such bias and does not favour one factor more than
another.

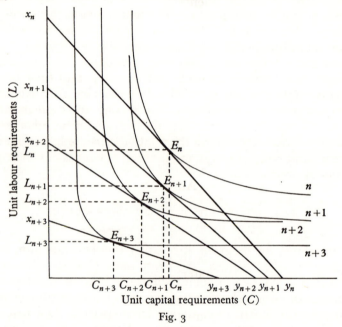

Fig. 3

The third such influence of a technical nature is represented by the
steepness of curvature. This corresponds to the elasticity of substitution,
which measures the ease of substitution and thus the extent to which
changing factor prices influence best-practice techniques. There are two
limiting cases: when the elasticity of substitution is zero the curve
becomes a right angle and changes in factor prices have no effect; when
the elasticity is infinite the curve approaches a straight line and changes
in factor prices have a very large effect on productivity. Period-to-
period changes in the elasticity of substitution also reflect the character
of technical advances. For example, advances which are only applicable
over a small range of the production function, such as improvements
to a particular machine, reduce the elasticity of substitution; while
advances such as electronic control devices increase the elasticity of
substitution by allowing greater freedom in the substitution of capital
for labour.

These three characteristics of technical advance represent the purely technical influences determining period-to-period movement of best-practice productivity. In addition, changing relative factor prices provide a fourth influence which, from the point of view of individual industries, is quite independent of the other three. Its effect is to increase the rate of productivity growth of one factor at the expense of retarding that of another; and, as we have seen, the extent to which such changes in relative factor prices are effective in doing this is dependent on the elasticity of substitution.

Since the observed movements of best-practice productivity are the net resultant of these four influences—broadly represented by the rate of technical advance, biases towards uneven factor saving, the ease of substitution and relative factor prices—it is important to give them some precision in order to distinguish the nature of their separate influences and the interaction between them. But to do so is complicated for two reasons. First, the processes of technical advance and factor substitution are so interwoven that we can only hope to distinguish their separate influences at a highly abstract level. Secondly, the only complete and general description of the characteristics of technical advance is by means of the whole series of dated production functions. Any attempt at a more concise description must necessarily be approximate, and can only hope to summarise the most important features. These difficulties, however, are analogous to those encountered by demand theory in distinguishing between income and price effects, and describing indifference surfaces by their characteristics at particular points. In fact, the whole problem is analogous to that of demand theory in many (but not all) respects;[1] for we wish to divide changes in best-practice productivity into its separate components in much the same way as demand theory attempts to divide changes in consumption into separate components. In the following, the general line of approach is broadly similar to that of demand theory, and the summary concepts which describe the characteristics of technical advance are to some extent parallel.

2. THE CHARACTERISTICS OF TECHNICAL ADVANCE

In isolating the purely technical influences which determine productivity movements—the rate of technical advance, biases towards uneven factor-saving and the elasticity of substitution—the most direct approach is to eliminate those changes in technique caused by factor substitution. Essentially this procedure is analogous to the index-number approach, for it involves asking what changes in technique would take place *if* relative factor prices were constant. In this way

[1] Iso-product curves replace indifference curves and the third dimension is time; instead of budget lines there are unit cost lines; and at any one time innumerable such lines but only one production function. In contrast to indifference curve analysis the advantageous direction of movement is towards the origin.

substitution-type changes in technique may be eliminated and the characteristics of technical advance described by reference to techniques which differ only because of shifts in the production function from one period to another, thus obviating the necessity for the cumbersome device of dated production functions. This approach is set out graphically in Fig. 4. The slope of the parallel lines $x'_n y'_n$ and $x'_{n+1} y'_{n+1}$ is determined by relative factor prices in period n (that is, g_n/w_n), and their position reflects total unit costs. The lines $x''_n y''_n$ and $x''_{n+1} y''_{n+1}$ similarly refer to relative factor prices of period $n+1$. E'_n and E'_{n+1} are the least-cost techniques in terms of the factor prices of period n, and E''_n and E''_{n+1} are the techniques appropriate to the factor prices of period $n+1$.

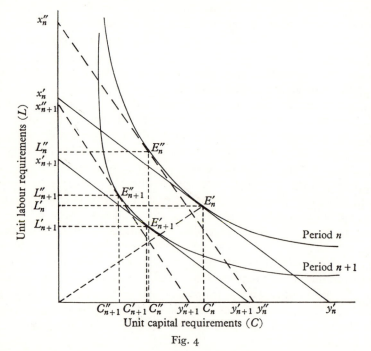

Fig. 4

The first characteristic which is of economic interest is the rate of movement of the production function towards the origin. The most important economic consequence of such movement is the reduction made possible in unit 'real' costs, and it may therefore be defined by reference to such costs. Thus:

The extent of the technical advance from one period to another is defined and measured by the relative change in total unit costs when the techniques in each period are those which would minimise unit costs when factor prices are constant.

If the factor prices of period n are employed to make the comparison, the measure is equivalent to the proportional movement of costs from $x'_n y'_n$ to $x'_{n+1} y'_{n+1}$. In terms of the notation of the diagram this reads

$$T' = \frac{L'_{n+1} w_n + C'_{n+1} g_n}{L'_n w_n + C'_n g_n}.$$

This measure, based on the factor prices of the initial period, corresponds in form to the Lasyperes index-number measure. If the factor prices of period $n+1$ are employed we have the Paasche form which measures the proportional shift of the lines $x_1'' y_1''$ and $x_2'' y_2''$, and is equivalent to

$$T'' = \frac{L_{n+1}'' w_{n+1} + C_{n+1}'' g_{n+1}}{L_n'' w_{n+1} + C_n'' g_{n+1}}.$$

If we think of technical advance as a continuous process rather than a series of discrete jumps, the proportional rate of advance at any one point of time may be defined as

$$T_r = \frac{\dfrac{dL}{dt} w + \dfrac{dC}{dt} g}{Lw + Cg}.$$

Two features of this definition should be noted. First, the measure attempts to give some precision to the broad idea of the rate of technical advance by relating it to the savings in real costs. It does this by asking the question how much would unit costs of production fall if nothing changed except technical knowledge, that is, by assuming factor prices constant. Since the factor prices of either the first or second period may be assumed constant, an index-number ambiguity is involved whenever discrete changes are considered. This is unavoidable; any measure involving costs, or any measure involving savings of more than one factor, must include factor prices and, since these change over time, index-number ambiguities are inevitable. Secondly, although the measure has been framed in terms of costs in order to highlight its economic meaning, it refers to purely technical characteristics of technical advance. This can be seen if the measure is cast in another form. Instead of comparing techniques appropriate to the same factor prices we may compare techniques with the same ratio of the marginal products. Thus:

$$T_r = \frac{\dfrac{dL}{dt} \dfrac{\partial O}{\partial N} + \dfrac{dC}{dt} \dfrac{\partial O}{\partial I}}{L \dfrac{\partial O}{\partial N} + C \dfrac{\partial O}{\partial I}}.$$

Since the ratio of marginal products is equivalent to the ratio of factor prices for least-cost techniques, this form is equivalent to those which involve prices.

The second feature of technical advance which is of economic interest relates to the biases towards uneven factor saving. Such biases are reflected in a relatively greater reduction in labour per unit of output compared to capital per unit of output, or vice versa. They can accordingly be measured by the proportional change in capital per labour unit attributable solely to the technical advance, as distinct from the changes attributable to factor substitution. Thus:

The labour or capital-saving biases of technical advance are measured by the relative change in capital per labour unit when relative factor prices are constant.[1]

In terms of the diagram, the bias (D) is measured by

$$D' = \frac{C'_{n+1}/L'_{n+1}}{C'_n/L'_n} \quad \text{for the Lasyperes form}$$

and

$$D'' = \frac{C''_{n+1}/L''_{n+1}}{C''_n/L''_n} \quad \text{for the Paasche form.}$$

When viewed as a continuous process, the proportional form of the measure is

$$D_r = \frac{d(C/L)}{dt}\left(\frac{L}{C}\right).$$

This measure attempts to isolate those changes in capital per head which arise solely out of technical advance. Thus it is an answer to the question, how much would capital per head change if technical knowledge alone changed? Graphically, it measures the extent to which points on each curve with the same slope move closer to one axis than another. When the ratio D' or D'' is greater than unity, the technical advance has a labour-saving bias in the sense that the proportionate saving in labour is greater than the proportionate saving in capital, and E_{n+1} falls to the right of OE_n; when the ratio is equal to unity, the technical advance is neutral in the sense factors are saved in equal proportions and E_{n+1} falls on the line OE_n; and when the ratio is less than unity, the advances contain a capital-saving bias and E_{n+1} falls to the left of OE_n.

Since the definition of labour-saving and capital-saving is already an overcrowded field, some justification is required for introducing yet another set of definitions. There are, however, two main reasons why these definitions are useful. First, they are complementary to the measure of the most important characteristic of technical change—its rate of growth—and can most usefully be employed in conjunction with it. Secondly, and more important, none of the existing definitions are applicable to productivity analysis at industry level. The class of definition proposed by Professor Hicks[2] and Mrs Robinson,[3] define labour- and capital-saving by reference to relative changes in marginal products. They do this by comparing points on each production function where factor proportions are constant, that is, along the line OE_n in Fig. 4. Such definitions do not, and cannot, provide any guide to the effects of technical advance on productivity; for by assuming fixed factor proportions they automatically assume that the productivity of all factors changes in equal proportions. This inability to provide any information concerning productivity arises, of course, because these

---

[1] The corresponding concept in demand theory is the change in consumption of one good relative to that of another following upon a change in income, relative commodity prices being unchanged.

[2] *The Theory of Wages*, p. 120.

[3] 'The Classification of Inventions', *Rev. Econ. Stud.* vol. v (1937–8), pp. 139–42.

definitions have been framed for aggregative analysis, particularly the question of relative shares. For such purposes it is appropriate to assume factor supplies constant and classify advances according to their effects on marginal products. But, when we are concerned with productivity, price, and cost movements in individual industries where relative marginal products are determined by factor prices external to the industry, it is appropriate to reverse the procedure by assuming marginal products constant and examine the effects on factor requirements, as in the definition proposed above. However, since this definition is the reverse of that of Hicks, they both imply the same definition of neutral technical advance. (Hicks's neutral advance requires an unchanged ratio of marginal products when factor proportions are constant, and the above definition requires that factor proportions are unchanged when the ratio of marginal products is constant.) Thus the two definitions do not differ in their division of technical advances into labour- and capital-saving categories, but only in the measure of the extent to which such advances are labour-saving or capital-saving (and then the difference may not be great). The relationship between this definition and Harrod's is more complex and may conveniently be postponed until later in this chapter.

While the definition proposed above attempts to classify technical advances as closely as possible on the basis of their intrinsic technical characteristics, it is impossible to disregard economic influences in framing such definitions; labour- and capital-saving are at the very heart of factor substitution yet such changes must be excluded. This is one of the reasons why it seems preferable to avoid the terms labour-saving and capital-saving and instead speak of biases which may be offset or accentuated in the observed result through factor substitution. Another reason for avoiding these terms is that they are popularly (and in some economic literature) regarded as mutually exclusive. In terms of absolute savings, this is not so; in fact, the common case seems to be that of technical advances which save all factors simultaneously. For example, the assembly line principle has often been quoted as a highly labour-saving innovation. In absolute terms this is true; but it is also absolutely capital-saving; savings in floor-space, stocks and work-in-progress, are very considerable and the absolute increase in capital productivity may well be as great as that of labour productivity.[1] In the present terminology, the main characteristic of such an innovation is the extent of the technical advance—the extent to which the principle of the assembly line opened up a whole new range of superior techniques—rather than the biases towards uneven factor saving which may be small even though the absolute savings are large.

In fact, to recognise such biases according to the superficial characteristics of technical advances is much more difficult than has been

---

[1] See D. Weintraub, 'The Effects of Technological Developments on Capital Formation', *Amer. Econ. Rev.* (suppl.), vol. xxix, no. 1 (March 1939). Many other similar examples are quoted.

generally realised. For example, consider an advance such as time and motion study which saves labour proportionately for all techniques of production. Superficially such an advance would appear to raise the productivity of labour and leave that of capital unchanged. However, there is another consideration: because such an advance yields the greatest cost-savings in highly labour-using techniques, there is an incentive for the entrepreneur to move from highly mechanised techniques to less mechanised techniques where the advance yields the greatest economies. For example, in Fig. 4, the shift from n to $n+1$ represents a proportionate saving of labour for all techniques; yet, with factor prices unchanged, the proportionate reduction in capital requirements exceeds that for labour in both the cases illustrated. How far this second effect offsets the superficial effect depends upon the elasticity of substitution; when it is zero the second effect cannot operate, and only the productivity of labour is affected; when it is high there is ample scope to move to more or less mechanised techniques where the greatest economies can be realised.[1] The important implication which follows from this argument is that advances which allow absolute savings of only labour or capital are likely to be relatively rare, for they involve the special case of a zero elasticity of substitution. The more general case, at least when such proportional advances are involved, would imply some absolute savings of both factors, though by no means equal savings.

The final characteristic of technical advance which merits attention is its effect on the elasticity of substitution. The elasticity of substitution is important in determining how far changes in relative factor prices are effective in adding to or subtracting from the rates of productivity increase which are established by technical advance alone. Defined precisely, it measures the proportional change in capital per head in response to a small proportionate change in the relative marginal products (or factor prices) of labour and capital; that is,[2]

$$\frac{d(C/L)}{C/L}\cdot\frac{r}{dr}, \quad \text{where} \quad r = \frac{\partial O}{\partial N}\bigg/\frac{\partial O}{\partial I} = \frac{w}{g}.$$

Since the elasticity may change over time, we measure it at the point on each production function appropriate to the measures T and D, that is, the point appropriate to constant factor prices. Advances which tend to make labour and capital more easily substitutable, such as automation, increase the elasticity of substitution, while advances which narrow the possibilities of substitution tend to reduce the elasticity.

These measures—the rate of technical advance, labour- and capital-saving biases, and the elasticity of substitution—represent the minimum description of the economically significant characteristics of technical advance. All are important, and we must know something about each before it is possible to distinguish the effects of technical advance on

[1] For a proof of this proposition see the Appendix to this chapter, p. 47.
[2] See R. D. G. Allen, *Mathematics for Economists*, 1st ed. (London, 1938), p. 341.

productivity. However, it should be recognised that they represent a drastic and approximate summary. This is inevitable, for it is unrealistic to expect to reduce all the information contained in a series of consecutive production functions to three simple measures without a high degree of simplification. One consequence of such simplifications is the index-number problem inherent in the measures. Another is the lack of reference to economies of scale.[1] Such approximations mean that our measures only have value as conceptual constructions for analysing the relationships between technical change and productivity. Before applying them to this purpose it is convenient to consider the changes in relative factor prices which are complementary to technical change.

3. SOURCES OF PRESSURES FOR THE SUBSTITUTION OF INVESTMENT FOR LABOUR

As noted in the previous chapter, when capital has the sense of capital equipment its price is a complex quantity reflecting all influences bearing upon the willingness to invest. Since changes in the relative prices of labour and capital play an important part in subsequent analysis, the question of the influences behind such price changes deserves some consideration, even though this involves an excursion into the field of aggregative analysis. The basic problem is one of the relationships between the three prices which enter into technique decisions; the wage rate, the interest rate, and the price of capital goods. These relationships have been the subject of considerable controversy; this is not so much a question of the relationships between the wage rate and the interest rate, but rather a question of the relationship between the wage rate and the prices of capital goods.[2] It is often argued that because capital goods are produced with labour, a rise in wages results in an equal proportionate increase in the prices of capital goods, and so cannot induce substitution of capital equipment for labour.

This argument, first advanced by Shove,[3] is valid, if at all, only in short-term equilibrium. It is certainly not applicable to a growing economy experiencing technical progress; for then a rise in wage rates is not accompanied by an equal rise in prices. The essence of technical

---

[1] In principle, economies of scale may be introduced into the analysis by employing exactly the same technique as for technical change. Instead of comparing iso-product curves at different points of time, we may compare iso-product curves at different outputs. A measure S_r can be defined which is analogous to T_r, that is, it is the proportionate change in costs per unit (when factor prices are constant) consequent upon a small change in output. The term is therefore a general measure of economies or diseconomies of scale. Similarly, V_r may be defined analogously to D_r, that is, the proportional change in capital per head consequent upon the change in output. This term measures the bias effect of economies of scale.

[2] There is a long literature on the subject beginning with Ricardo, *Principles*, 3rd ed., ch. xxxi. See also the controversy in the *American Economic Review* culminating in the paper by F. D. Graham, 'The Relation of Wage Rates to the Use of Machinery', vol. xvi, no. 3 (September 1926), p. 46; and N. Kaldor, 'Capital Intensity and the Trade Cycle', *Economica* (February 1939), p. 43; and F. A. von Hayek, 'The Ricardo Effect', *Economica* (May 1942), pp. 127–52.

[3] In his review of Hicks's *Theory of Wages* (*Econ. J.*, September 1933, p. 471).

progress is that it enables commodities to be produced with less labour and capital, and so reduces the prices of commodities in terms of labour. This is true of both consumption and capital goods; savings of labour in the consumption goods industries raise the price of labour in terms of consumption goods; and savings of labour in the capital goods industries raise the price of labour in terms of capital goods. Consequently, even though the wage rate and the interest rate may be constant, the cheapening of capital goods which originates in technical progress reduces the capital costs of real investment and so induces substitution of capital equipment for labour. Thus, technical progress in the manufacture of capital goods produces a continuous pressure throughout industry for the substitution of capital equipment for labour. In effect, technical change raises the productivity of labour in two stages: the first is the direct effect of technical advances in each industry; and the second is the substitution of capital equipment for labour, following upon the cheapening of capital goods relative to wages.

The existence of this relationship is one of the main justifications for introducing the price of capital goods as an explicit variable in the analysis of substitution. It cannot be subsumed by measuring wages in real terms except in the special case where technical progress affects the prices of capital and consumption goods equally. Since there is no theoretical or empirical justification for such an assumption, if wages are measured in real terms the ratio of consumption to capital goods prices must be introduced into the analysis. This is a rather devious procedure, and it is much more direct to see the relationship through the eyes of the entrepreneur and simply relate money wages to the prices of capital goods.

When viewed from the stand-point of factor supplies rather than factor prices, this relationship between technical progress and factor substitution simply reflects the fact that technical progress tends to increase the supply of capital goods. Even though the percentage of income saved by an economy may remain constant, the supply of capital goods per worker rises parallel with the increasing productivity of that part of the labour force devoted to the manufacture of capital goods. This increasing supply of capital goods is reflected in a declining price relative to wages which, in the long-run at least, induces their absorption through the substitution of capital equipment for labour.

In order to consolidate our ideas concerning changes in the relative prices of labour and capital (measured as real investment), and to gain some idea of their magnitude, it is helpful to examine some actual figures. Sufficiently comprehensive data are only available for the United States; Table 3 sets out movements of wage rates, consumption goods prices and capital goods prices, over the years 1930–1950.

Since 1930, hourly wages have outstripped consumption prices sufficiently to increase real wages by approximately 80%. Prices of plant and equipment have increased rather more than consumption goods, so that the increase in wages relative to capital goods prices has

Table 3. *Changes in wage rates, consumption prices, and plant and equipment prices, United States, 1930–50*

(1930 = 100)

	Hourly wage rate (1)	Consumption goods prices (2)	Plant and equipment prices (3)	Change in real wages (1) ÷ (2)	Change in ratio of wage rates to plant and equipment prices (1) ÷ (3)
1930	100	100	100	100	100
1950	265	147	167	180	159

Source: Data taken from U.S. Department of Commerce Survey of Current Business, and Historical Statistics of the United States, Bureau of the Census.

been somewhat less, 59 %.[1] This represents a very considerable movement in the relative prices of labour and capital goods.

The dual influences of changes in the price of capital goods and interest rates may be illustrated by combining both into a measure of the capital costs per annum incurred at different dates by a given real investment. This may be achieved by use of the annuity formula. In effect, one calculates the sum of interest plus amortisation charges per annum incurred by the purchase of a given 'machine' in 1930 and 1950, and the movement represents the effect of both changing interest rates and capital goods prices. Because changes in the interest rate are relatively more important for investments with a long life, the extent to which a change in interest rates affects capital costs per annum depends upon the life of the investment. Thus, in making such calculations one must distinguish changes in capital costs for different lives.

In Table 4, items (1), (2) and (4) set out the basic data. The interest rate is the yield on corporate bonds, and even though there is scope

Table 4. *Estimates of changes in the relative costs of employing labour and capital equipment, United States, 1930–50*

		1930	1950
(1)	Plant and equipment prices	100	167
(2)	Interest rates (%)	5·09	2·88
(3)	Capital cost for lives of:		
	5 years	100	163
	10 years	100	156
	20 years	100	141
	30 years	100	116
(4)	Hourly wage rate	100	265
(5)	Ratio of hourly wage rate to capital cost for lives of:		
	5 years	100	162
	10 years	100	170
	20 years	100	188
	30 years	100	228

Source: As for Table 3.

[1] If house-building and other construction were included the rise would be somewhat less.

for opinion whether or not this is appropriate, it serves to illustrate the role played by interest rates. Item (3) combines changes in interest rates and capital goods prices into measures of changes in capital costs per annum for investment of different lives. This is achieved by employing the annuity formula as a means of combining interest and amortisation charges.

An examination of the capital cost item reveals that the considerable fall in interest rates had the greatest effect for investment with long lives. For short-lived equipment the rise in capital costs is only slightly less than the rise in plant and equipment prices, illustrating the minor role played by interest in such investments. Item (5) at the bottom of the table compares these changes in capital cost with the movements of wage rates. Very considerable pressures for substitution are revealed; for short-lived investment this pressure arises almost entirely out of the relative movements of wages and capital goods prices, and for long-lived investments this is substantially augmented by the reduction in interest rates.

As has been noted, risk and obsolescence may also generate important pressures for substitution of labour and investment. By investing in fixed capital equipment an entrepreneur gives 'hostages to fortune'; a decision to employ fixed capital equipment is irrevocable in contrast to labour which can be discharged at will. Consequently, a decrease in risk—because of faith in full employment, for example—favours the substitution of labour by investment by reducing the risk allowance in the interest component of capital costs. Increased obsolescence, on the other hand, is likely to have the reverse effect. Equipment must be amortised over a shorter period, and in so far as this cannot be offset by less durable and cheaper equipment, the capital costs of real investment are increased. Over time we may expect obsolescence to increase, not only because of more rapid technical progress, but also because of the changing ratio between wage rates and the prices of capital goods which, as will be shown subsequently, encourages earlier replacement.[1] However, increased obsolescence is unlikely to provide more than a partial offset to lower relative prices of capital goods; in terms of the United States data, increased obsolescence would need to halve the working life of equipment in only twenty years if the effect of lower relative prices for capital equipment were to be completely offset. Such a substantial increase in obsolescence seems quite unlikely.

In summary, an economy experiencing technical progress automatically generates powerful pressures for the substitution of capital equipment for labour. Of these, the most important is the continuous cheapening of capital goods resulting from technical advances in their manufacture. In addition, risk and obsolescence may modify or accentuate these pressures.

[1] See chapter v, p. 69.

4. COMPONENTS OF BEST-PRACTICE
PRODUCTIVITY MOVEMENTS

We are now in a position to describe the growth of best-practice productivity in terms of the nature of technical advance and changing factor prices. There is a simple relationship between our three measures of the character of technical advance and changing factor prices which provides a convenient basis for the discussion. If all quantities are expressed as proportionate rates of change (denoted by the subscript r) the rate of growth of unit labour and capital requirements may be expressed as[1]

$$L_r = T_r - \pi D_r + \sigma\pi(g/w)_r,$$

and

$$C_r = T_r + (1 - \pi) D_r + \sigma(1 - \pi) (w/g)_r,$$

where L_r and C_r are the proportional rates of change of unit labour and capital requirements, T_r and D_r are the proportional forms of the measures of the rate and bias of technical advance, π is the share of capital costs in total cost, σ is the elasticity of substitution, and $(g/w)_r$ is the proportional rate of change of relative factor prices.

These two relationships enable the main influences determining the growth of capital and labour productivity to be distinguished.[2] The first such influence is the general effect of the rate of technical advance, represented by the term T_r. This reflects the general idea of the speed of technical change and bears equally on both factors. When acting in isolation (that is, the advance is neutral and there is no substitution), savings in labour occur at the same rate as savings in capital, and the productivity of both factors increases at a rate determined by the rate of technical advance.

The second effect is the bias effect, represented by the term D_r. This reflects the divergences from neutral technical advance by measuring changes in capital per head arising solely out of the character of the advances. A labour-saving bias (D_r is positive) leads to additional savings of labour and fewer savings in capital; consequently the rate of growth of labour productivity exceeds the rate of technical advance, and the rate of growth of capital productivity is retarded. Similarly, a capital-saving bias (D_r is negative) retards the growth of labour productivity and adds to that of capital productivity. But, in each case, the extent of this increase or decrease in rates of growth depends upon relative shares in total cost. A high proportion of labour costs implies that a labour-saving bias results in a relatively small increase in the rate of growth of labour productivity beyond that established by the measure of the rate of technical advance (which is related to total costs), and a relatively large retardation in capital productivity. Similar considerations apply to capital-saving biases.

[1] These relationships are derived in the Appendix to this chapter, p. 46.
[2] If the terms S_r and $V_r\pi$ (or $1 - \pi$) are added, the expression then includes the effect of economies of scale. This then gives two additional effects: the general scale effect, and the scale bias effect. The complete relationship is then: $L_r = T_r + S_r - \pi D_r - \pi V_r + \sigma\pi(g/w)_r$.

The third effect is the substitution effect, reflected in the terms $\sigma\pi(g/w)_r$. Such substitution increases the rate of growth of the productivity of one factor at the expense of retarding that of the other factor. Which factor is retarded in its productivity growth and which increased, depends upon the direction of the change in relative factor prices. When labour is becoming dearer relative to capital—the normal case when there is technical progress in the manufacture of capital goods—the rate of growth of labour productivity is increased and the rate of growth of capital productivity is retarded. The extent to which a given rate of change of relative factor prices leads to such a divergence in rates of productivity increase depends upon the elasticity of substitution: a high elasticity leads to a large divergence, and a low elasticity to a small divergence. As with labour- and capital-saving biases, relative shares in total cost determine how far this divergence affects the rates of productivity growth of each factor; a high proportion of capital costs implies that the major part of the divergence comes about through a change in the proportionate rate of growth of labour productivity, and a relatively small amount through a change in the proportional rate of growth of capital productivity.

Finally, technical advances which increase or decrease the elasticity of substitution lead to an acceleration of the rate of productivity growth of one factor, and a slowing down of the rate of productivity growth of the other. For example, if labour is becoming dearer relative to capital, and the elasticity of substitution is increasing, the rate of growth of labour productivity will be accelerating and that of capital productivity will be slowing down; conversely, if the elasticity of substitution is decreasing through time, the rate of growth of labour productivity slows down, and that of capital productivity is accelerated. The situation is reversed if capital is becoming dearer relative to labour.

Harrod's definition of neutral technical progress[1]—that the productivity of capital is unchanged when the rate of interest is constant— is a particular combination of the above three effects. There are two main possibilities. The first is where technical advance has such a strong labour-saving bias there that is no absolute capital-saving, and even with constant factor prices the productivity of capital is constant. The second case (and this is the one Harrod obviously has in mind) is where the pressures for substitution, generated by cheaper capital goods relative to labour because of technical progress in the capital goods industries, are just sufficient to offset the absolute capital-saving tendencies of technical advance and so ensure that the productivity of capital is constant with an unchanged rate of interest. For example, if technical advance is unbiased in both the consumption and capital goods sectors, then the consequent cheapening of capital goods relative to wages leads to substitution of capital equipment for labour. If the net result is to leave the productivity of capital unchanged, then technical progress is neutral in Harrod's sense. In other words, the

---

[1] *Towards a Dynamic Economics* (London, 1948), pp. 24–6.

savings in capital which are achieved directly by new knowledge are cancelled by the indirect effects of technical progress in the manufacture of capital goods. In terms of Fig. 4 this implies that the change in the slope of the line $x'y'$ from period n to $n+1$ caused by a cheapening of capital goods is just sufficient to leave the productivity of capital unchanged, that is, the new equilibrium E'_{n+1} falls on the line $E'_n C'_n$. Thus Harrod's definition is essentially concerned with the net effects of technical change throughout the economy—the net result of technical advances in each industry, and the accompanying substitution induced by the cheapening of capital goods.

It is now clear why Harrod's definition is appropriate for aggregative analysis but not for industry analysis. If we followed Harrod, it would be impossible to distinguish between the direct effects of technical advance in each industry (as described by our three measures) and the indirect effects which work through the cheapening of capital goods. But such a distinction is of critical importance in industry analysis. The pace and character of technical advance varies markedly from industry to industry; in contrast, the cheapening of capital goods is an economy-wide influence which affects all industries, technically progressive and technically backward alike. When we are interested in the impact of technical progress on individual industries, its effects on relative prices and the composition of output, and the causes of inter-industry differences in productivity movements, it is essential to think in two steps: the advances actually taking place in each industry, and the cheapening of capital goods which is common to all industries.

This distinction, between the character of technical progress in individual industries and its character in the economy as a whole, is extremely important in the empirical analysis of Part II, and it is therefore advisable to consider its implications in some detail. There is some evidence to suggest that the character of technical progress is not very different from that implied by Harrod's definition of neutrality. The investigations into movements of the capital–output ratio by Kuznets, Creamer and Goldsmith in the United States, and Redfern and Phelps-Brown in the United Kingdom,[1] point to a constant or very slowly increasing productivity of capital. It is at least certain that the aggregate productivity of labour has increased very much more rapidly than the aggregate productivity of capital. The question which is pertinent to subsequent analysis is the reason for this difference. As has been noted, there are two main possibilities: (i) technical advances

---

[1] S. Kuznets, 'Long-term changes in the National Income of the United States of America since 1870', *Income and Wealth*, series II, Cambridge, England (Bowes and Bowes, 1952). R. W. Goldsmith, 'The Growth of Reproductive Wealth in the United States of America from 1905 to 1950', *Income and Wealth*, series II, Cambridge, England, 1952. D. Creamer, 'Capital and Output Trends in Manufacturing Industries, 1800–1948', *National Bureau of Economic Research*, Occasional Paper 41.

E. H. Phelps-Brown and W. Weber, 'Accumulation, Productivity, and Distribution in the British Economy, 1870–1938', *Econ. J.* vol. LXIII (June 1953), p. 266, and P. Redfern, 'Net Investment in Fixed Assets in the United Kingdom, 1938–1953', *J. Roy. Statist. Soc.* series A, vol. CXVIII, part 2 (1955).

which are highly biased towards labour-saving, and (ii) technical advances which are largely unbiased coupled with a significant amount of substitution induced by technical progress in the manufacture of capital goods. The important difference between these two situations lies in the behaviour of capital productivity in individual industries. In the former case technical advances in each industry contain a highly labour-saving bias so that increases in capital productivity in individual industries would be rare. But in the second case, where the much slower rate of increase of aggregate productivity is the product of factor substitution, we should expect capital productivity to be increasing in some industries but declining in others. For example, consider two industries, one experiencing a rapid rate of unbiased technical advance, and the other a slow rate. Changes in relative factor prices arising out of technical progress in the capital goods industries would bear equally on both industries and increase the rate of growth of labour productivity, and retard that of capital productivity. In considering the net result, we can be sure that labour productivity would continue to increase in both industries, for substitution would add to the rate of growth established by technical advance. But there is no such guarantee that capital productivity would increase in both industries. It is quite possible that substitution could more than offset the rate of growth of capital productivity established by technical advance in the industry where the rate of advance is slow, and not offset it in the industry where the rate of advance is high. Thus, the net result could well be that labour productivity is increasing in both industries, but is accompanied by rising capital productivity in one industry and falling capital productivity in the other. When this case is extended to a number of industries all experiencing different rates of technical advance, it is quite possible for aggregate productivity to remain constant (that is, technical progress is neutral in Harrod's sense) while the productivity of capital is increasing in industries with a rapid rate of technical advance, and declining in industries with a slow rate of technical advance.

There are two main issues in choosing between these two explanations of the behaviour of aggregate labour and capital productivity. The first is the factual question of the behaviour of capital productivity in individual industries; this is considered in Part II where it is shown that the behaviour of costs is most consistent with the explanation based on substitution. The second issue, which is relevant in the present context, is whether there is any *a priori* reason to expect such a strong labour-saving bias. An immediate difficulty which arises in any attempt to assess the likelihood of such biases is that the techniques which we actually observe coming into use are themselves the result of a complex interaction between the character of technical advances and factor substitution. Therefore it is not sufficient to consider recent new techniques in considering this question; the only approach is to ask whether there is anything inherent in the character of technical advance which is likely to lead to such a strong labour-saving bias.

One possible reason for such a bias arises out of energy sources. The first stages of industrialism are characterised by the substitution of mechanical power for human power, and advances which make this possible must have an inherent labour-saving bias. The interesting question, however, is whether or not this is a permanent characteristic. There is some evidence to suggest that the main part of the process of changing over from hand to machine production was completed by the first part of this century. In examining the technological history of the last two or three decades, one is struck by the relatively few revolutionary techniques of production. The period seems to have been characterised by substantial improvements to existing basic methods, a period of unspectacular but nevertheless significant advance. Summarising the findings of the United States Bureau of Labor Statistics, Duane Evans writes: 'the economy has largely passed through the stage of substituting mechanised for hand methods of production. During the earlier period it is obvious that capital per unit of production increased. Today, improved machines are in many cases being substituted for older machines....'[1] Similarly Weintraub writes: '...one difference between the effects of technological change on capital and labour requirements in a particular industry is that labour requirements tend to decrease continually, while capital requirements per unit of product are at first increased as manual operations are progressively mechanised, then tend to decrease when detailed improvements are made to newly established basic processes.'[2] These views, while no more than suggestive, imply that, apart from industries coming late to mechanisation, the inherent labour-saving bias due to energy sources has largely disappeared, or at least become very much weaker.

A second argument for assuming an inherent labour-saving bias arises out of the theory of induced inventions as set out by Hicks.[3] This suggests that when labour becomes dearer relative to capital, the search for labour-saving techniques is stimulated. If one takes this to mean that new labour-saving designs are derived within the fold of existing knowledge, then this process is equivalent to the substitution within the designing process considered in chapter II. It is simply a matter of words whether one terms new techniques of this character inventions or a form of factor substitution. If, however, the theory implies that dearer labour stimulates the search for new knowledge aimed specifically at saving labour, then it is open to serious objections. The entrepreneur is interested in reducing costs in total, not particular costs such as labour costs or capital costs. When labour costs rise any advance that reduces total cost is welcome, and whether this is achieved by saving labour or capital is irrelevant. There is no reason to assume that attention should

---

[1] 'Recent Productivity Trends and their Implications', *J. Amer. Statist. Assoc.* vol. XLII, no. 238 (June 1947), p. 222. See also, 'The Production Economies of Growth', *Amer. Econ. Rev.* vol. XLVI, no. 2, suppl. (May 1956), p. 43.

[2] 'The Effects of Technological Developments on Capital Formation', *Amer. Econ. Rev.* vol. XXIX, no. 1, suppl. (March 1939).

[3] *The Theory of Wages*, p. 125.

be concentrated on labour-saving techniques, unless, because of some inherent characteristic of technology, labour-saving knowledge is easier to acquire than capital-saving knowledge.[1]

Unless there is some such inherent labour-saving bias in the process of acquiring new technical knowledge, there is no justification for the common view that technical advances are essentially labour-saving and only incidentally capital-saving. This view is fostered by three misapprehensions. The first is that new processes actually brought into use appear to show greater evidence of absolute labour-saving than capital-saving. This is to be expected; these techniques are themselves the net result of technical advances and of factor substitution, which offsets absolute capital-saving. The second reason is the view that advances which save labour proportionately over a range of techniques (the time and motion study case) do not also save capital. As we have seen, such advances normally save both labour and capital when factor prices are constant, and only in the special case of zero elasticity of substitution is the productivity of capital not increased. The final reason for an underestimation of absolute capital saving is that savings in labour are much more easily recognised than savings in capital. A new process which allows ten men to do the work of twenty superficially appears to be only labour-saving in character. But if, as one so often finds, the new machinery is working at twice the speed of the old, the process is also absolutely capital-saving. In fact, advances leading to increased speed of machinery are one of the most important avenues of capital-saving. Fifty years ago the average factory was a cumbersome affair involving overhead power-drives which operated crude machinery at a relatively slow speed. Today, electric motors, precision engineering, roller bearings, lubrication systems, tungsten cutting tools and improved control mechanisms, allow machines to work six or seven times faster.[2] Similarly, improvements in organisation and plant layout, faster transport and communication, and fewer breakdowns through improved design, have all made possible substantial absolute economies in capital.

The above arguments make it difficult to accept any *a priori* reason for labour-saving biases sufficiently strong to explain the much greater increases in aggregate labour productivity compared to aggregate capital productivity. It therefore appears reasonable to place primary emphasis on the substitution induced by cheaper capital goods.

---

[1] One cannot say along with Bloom ('A Note on Hicks's Theory of Innovations', *Amer. Econ. Rev.* vol. xxxvi (March 1946), p. 86), that the continuing high cost of labour induces labour-saving inventions. One may as well speak of the continuing high cost of capital for the cost of a factor has no meaning except in relation to product or other factor prices. Bloom's statement then comes to the same thing as saying that high costs stimulate inventions, which is obvious and has no bearing on induced inventions.

[2] S. Lilley, *Men, Machines and History* (London, 1948), gives an account of increases in the speed of machinery.

5. SUMMARY

1. The main influences determining movements over time of best-practice productivity in individual industries are: the rate of technical advance, biases towards uneven factor saving, opportunities for factor substitution, and changes in relative factor prices. Measures which define the first three influences, those concerned with the characteristics of technical advance, are suggested. The rate of technical advance is defined by reference to the rate at which unit costs fall when factor prices are constant; biases are measured by the rate at which factor proportions change when factor prices are constant; and the ease of substitution is defined by the conventional concept of the elasticity of substitution. The measure of biases is closely related to Hicks's definition of labour- and capital-saving and implies the same definition of neutrality. It is suggested that technical advances which lead to absolute savings in labour unaccompanied by absolute savings in capital (both measured per unit of output) are exceptional, and the more usual case is that of advances which involve some absolute saving of both factors.

2. Changes in the relative prices of labour and capital are strongly influenced by the cheapening of capital goods relative to wages resulting from technical progress in the capital-goods industries. This induces substitution of capital equipment for labour throughout the economy even when the rate of interest is constant. Figures, based on United States experience, illustrate such changes in relative factor prices.

3. Movements over time of best-practice productivity may be described in terms of the three measures which summarise the characteristics of technical advance and changing relative factor prices. Three effects are distinguished: (i) the general effect of the rate of technical advance, (ii) the bias effect arising out of technical advances which tend to save more of one factor than another, and (iii) the substitution effect reflecting changes in relative factor prices, including those arising out of technical progress in the manufacture of capital goods. Harrod's definition of labour- and capital-saving is inapplicable to industry analysis since it does not distinguish between the general effect and bias effect of technical advance which vary between industries, and the substitution effects arising out of cheaper capital goods which bears upon all industries.

4. The much greater rate of increase of aggregate labour productivity compared with aggregate capital productivity may be explained either by strong labour-saving biases in the technical advances occurring within each industry, or by the offsetting influence of factor substitution arising out of cheaper capital goods. It is suggested that there is no *a priori* reason for assuming the strong labour-saving bias implied by the former explanation.

MATHEMATICAL APPENDIX TO CHAPTER III

1. The three measures which define the salient characteristics of technical advance are:

$$T_r = \frac{\frac{dL}{dt}w + \frac{dC}{dt}g}{Lw + Cg}, \tag{1}$$

$$D_r = \frac{d(C/L)}{dt} \cdot \frac{L}{C}, \tag{2}$$

$$\sigma = \frac{d(C/L)}{C/L} \bigg/ \frac{g/w}{d(g/w)}. \tag{3}$$

Denote changes in L and C caused by shifts of the production function when w and g are constant by the subscript T; and changes in L and C caused by movements around the production function in response to changes in w and g by the subscript S.

Solving for $(dL/dt)_T$ from (1) and (2) yields

$$\left(\frac{dL}{dt}\right)_T \cdot \frac{1}{L} = T_r - D_r \frac{Cg}{Lw + Cg}.$$

Let $\pi = \dfrac{Cg}{Lw + Cg}$ = share of capital costs in total costs, then

$$\left(\frac{dL}{dt}\right)_T \cdot \frac{1}{L} = T_r - D_r \pi. \tag{4}$$

Similarly solving for $\left(\dfrac{dC}{dt}\right)_T \cdot \dfrac{1}{C}$ from (1) and (2) yields

$$\left(\frac{dC}{dt}\right)_T \cdot \frac{1}{C} = T_r + D_r(1 - \pi). \tag{5}$$

Expanding (3) and simplifying

$$(dL)_S = \sigma \pi L \frac{d(g/w)}{g/w},$$

and

$$\left(\frac{dL}{dt}\right)_S \cdot \frac{1}{L} = \sigma \pi \frac{d(g/w)}{dt} \frac{w}{g}. \tag{6}$$

Similarly

$$\left(\frac{dC}{dt}\right)_S \cdot \frac{1}{C} = \sigma(1 - \pi) \frac{d(w/g)}{dt} \cdot \frac{g}{w}. \tag{7}$$

The total change in L is given by (4) + (6), that is,

$$\frac{dL}{dt} \cdot \frac{1}{L} = \left(\frac{dL}{dt}\right)_T \cdot \frac{1}{L} + \left(\frac{dL}{dt}\right)_S \cdot \frac{1}{L}$$

$$= T_r - D_r \pi + \sigma \pi \frac{d(g/w)}{dt} \cdot \frac{w}{g}.$$

Similarly $\quad \dfrac{dC}{dt}\cdot\dfrac{1}{C} = T_r + D_r(1-\pi) + \sigma(1-\pi)\dfrac{d(w/g)}{dt}\cdot\dfrac{g}{w}.$

Writing $\quad \dfrac{dL}{dt}\cdot\dfrac{1}{L} = L_r, \quad \dfrac{dC}{dt}\cdot\dfrac{1}{C} = C_r \quad$ and $\quad \dfrac{d(g/w)}{dt}\cdot\dfrac{w}{g} = \left(\dfrac{g}{w}\right)_r,$

$$L_r = T_r - D_r\pi + \sigma\pi(g/w)_r$$

and $\qquad C_r = T_r + D_r(1-\pi) + \sigma(1-\pi)(w/g)_r.$

2. Proportional shifts in the production function may be represented by a term λ which is less than unity. The production functions for successive periods are accordingly:

$$O = f(L, C), \tag{1}$$

$$O = f(L\lambda, C). \tag{2}$$

Let L_1C_1 and L_2C_2 be the equilibrium points on each production function where the slopes $(dC/dL)_1$ and $(dC/dL)_2$, both equal $-w/g$. It is required to show that the change in C/L is a function of the elasticity of substitution of (1).

Consider the point L_3, C_3 on (1) where $C_3 = C_2$ and thus $L_2 = \lambda L_3$. Then

$$\frac{C_3}{L_3} = \lambda\frac{C_2}{L_2} \quad \text{and} \quad \left(\frac{dC}{dL}\right)_3 = \lambda\left(\frac{dC}{dL}\right)_2 = \lambda\left(\frac{dC}{dL}\right)_1.$$

The arc elasticity of substitution of (1) from L_1C_1 to L_3C_3 is defined as

$$\sigma_a = \frac{C_1/L_1 - C_3/L_3}{C_1/L_1} \bigg/ \frac{(dC/dL)_1 - (dC/dL)_3}{(dC/dL)_1}.$$

Substituting for C_3/L_3 and $(dC/dL)_3$

$$\sigma_a = \frac{C_1/L_1 - \lambda(C_2/L_2)}{C_1/L_1} \bigg/ 1 - \lambda,$$

$$\sigma_a = 1 - \lambda\frac{C_2/L_2}{C_1/L_1} \bigg/ 1 - \lambda.$$

Thus when $\qquad \sigma_a = 1 \quad \dfrac{C_2}{L_2} = \dfrac{C_1}{L_1},$

$$\sigma_a > 1 \quad \frac{C_2}{L_2} < \frac{C_1}{L_1},$$

$$\sigma_a < 1 \quad \frac{C_2}{L_2} > \frac{C_1}{L_1}.$$

CHAPTER IV

A MODEL OF THE DELAY IN THE UTILISATION OF NEW TECHNIQUES OF PRODUCTION

To date, productivity has been considered only within a world of plans and blue-prints. The previous chapters have examined the process whereby technical advances and changing relative prices result in a continuous stream of new best-practice techniques of production. Each year sees the emergence of a new technique of production with lower real costs and higher productivity for some or all factors of production. These new techniques, however, only provide a potential for increased productivity. In a world where adjustments take time, observed levels of productivity depend upon the extent to which the flow of new best-practice techniques are actually incorporated into production. This is our second problem—the problem of adjustment to continuous disturbance.

As a preliminary to the theoretical analysis, some additional empirical examples are useful to illustrate the magnitude of the phenomena we wish to consider. The original example drawn from the blast-furnace industry is set out in Table 5; it contains information concerning the rate at which two new techniques, mechanical charging and casting, were introduced into the industry. The three columns on the right

Table 5. *Methods in use in the U.S. blast-furnace industry, selected years, 1911–26*

Year	Gross tons of pig-iron produced per man-hour		Percentage of plants using the following methods		
	Best-practice plants	Industry average	Hand-charged and sand-cast (%)	Mixed types (%)	Machine charged and cast (%)
1911	0·313	0·140	50·0	22·7	27·3
1917	0·326	0·150	41·9	34·9	23·2
1919	0·328	0·140	42·0	28·0	30·0
1921	0·428	0·178	22·2	44·3	33·5
1923	0·462	0·213	20·7	39·7	39·6
1925	0·512	0·285	7·2	25·5	67·3
1926	0·573	0·296	6·1	24·5	69·4

Source: As for Table 1.

indicate that at least one important reason for the divergence between average and best-practice labour productivity lies in the failure of many plants to adopt these new methods as soon as they became available. More than two decades after their initial use in 1905, only

70 % of plants had adopted these techniques of mechanical charging and casting.

Another example of the wide divergences to be found between co-existing methods of production is the case of the United States cigar industry. Cigar-making machines were first introduced in 1919, yet, almost twenty years later, 25 % of medium-grade cigars were still hand-made. Table 6 sets out the labour requirements of methods in use in 1936. The best mechanical methods require only a third of the labour needed for hand manufacture.

Table 6. *Approximate labour requirements per thousand five-cent cigars for different manufacturing methods, United States, 1936*

Manufacturing methods in use in 1936	Man-hours per thousand cigars
Hand made	33·38
Machine bunched, hand rolled	27·38
Four-operator machine	15·96
Two-operator machine	11·94

Source: U.S. Bureau of Labor Statistics, *Mechanisation and Productivity of Labor in the Cigar Manufacturing Industry* (Bulletin no. 660, September 1938).

The case of the U.K. textile industry needs no emphasis for British readers. Automatic looms are not a new invention; their use dates back to the pre-1914 era. Yet in 1946 only 6 % of the looms in use were automatic types compared with 70 % in the United States.[1] A similar situation exists in the coke industry. Beehive coke ovens were first superseded by the by-product process, which uses half as much labour per ton, in the 1890's. In 1939 the beehive process still lingered on in the United States,[2] and even today produces a sizeable share of British coke output.

These examples should suffice to dispel any idea that only new techniques of production need be considered in the analysis of techno-logical change and its effects on productivity. Quite obviously this delay in the use of new methods is extremely important in productivity analysis; it cannot be neglected, or even relegated to a minor role. An understanding of productivity movements must include an analysis of the reasons for this delay in the utilisation of new techniques, and an appreciation of the forces which determine the rate at which new methods displace the old. Moreover, in relating productivity move-ments to changes in other economic quantities, this lag must be explicitly considered. Questions that immediately arise are whether prices are determined by best-practice costs, or the costs of other methods in use, what part do wages and investment play in determining this lag, what is the role of demand, and what are the economic conditions which reduce the lag to a minimum? At least some insight into these questions

[1] *Wool Working Party Report* (H.M.S.O., London 1946).
[2] Solomon Fabricant, *Employment in Manufacturing, 1899–1939* (National Bureau for Economic Research, 1942), p. 22.

is essential if we are to progress beyond a superficial appreciation of the significance of productivity movements.

This chapter sets up an extremely simplified model which isolates the strategic influences. The principles behind the model are then discussed. In the following two chapters the model is then put to work to answer some of the questions set out above.

I. ASSUMPTIONS AND DEFINITIONS

The first step is to specify the chief assumptions needed to set up the model. The first group of assumptions concerns the relationship between capital equipment and techniques of production. Capital equipment should be regarded as something more than the physical embodiment of 'free' capital; its physical form also reflects a specific embodied technique. For example, the 'free capital', measured say by initial cost, of five thousand shovels and one bulldozer may be identical, but this does not mean their effectiveness as instruments of production is the same or even comparable; built into the bulldozer is all the knowledge of modern science. Speaking loosely, the flow of capital services from a piece of equipment is a function not only of the amount of 'free' capital it represents, but also of the embodied technique. This characteristic of capital equipment implies that as new best-practice techniques of production become available, many cannot be effectively used without a new set of capital equipment—new machines are necessary. For this reason it is useful to divide the flow of new techniques into two categories: those which require specialised capital equipment, and those which do not. Most new techniques probably fall in the first category. To state the obvious, jet propulsion requires jet engines, mass production techniques need conveyor systems, and so on. Throughout this chapter we will assume that all new techniques coming forward are in the first category; they all need specialised capital equipment. This assumption serves to link the use of new techniques directly to investment; to use new techniques requires new capital equipment.[1]

A major complication for this type of analysis, and indeed for all production theory, arises out of the difference between production processes and the production of commodities. Techniques of production refer to processes, while to understand their economic implication we must think in terms of commodities to which prices, output, costs, and profit can be ascribed. The difficulty is that a plant producing a recognisable commodity very often carries out a large number of processes with semi-independent capital equipment for each process. For example, a plant producing shirts carries out the processes of cutting, sewing, pressing and packing, so that the overall 'technique' of the plant may change through piecemeal changes in these component processes. This very important problem will be considered in chapter VII;[2]

---

[1] This assumption is relaxed in chapter VII, p. 89.

[2] P. 83.

at the moment it is useful to push this whole complication to one side by regarding a plant as an indivisible unit. Of the factors of production that make up a plant, capital (apart from working capital) is assumed to be atrophied into an indivisible complex of equipment that reflects the embodied technique of production. A number of plants that produce the same or closely comparable commodities form an industry.

In order to focus attention on technological change alone, it is advisable to make another set of assumptions that temporarily exclude the effect of other sources of changes in productivity. Managerial efficiency is assumed constant in all plants, and labour is assumed homogeneous and of equal skill and personal efficiency.[1] These simplifying assumptions, in conjunction with those previously made, mean that once a plant is constructed, no changes occur in the input of factors of production required to produce the originally designed 'normal capacity output', apart from the extra labour and materials needed for repairs and maintenance as the plant physically deteriorates. To reduce the quantities of labour, materials and fuel needed to produce a given output requires a different technique, and this is only possible with a new outfit of capital equipment.

Yet another set of assumptions is needed to fix the character of our industry, and its relations with the rest of the economy. We assume throughout this chapter that the industry is competitive, particularly in the senses of freedom of entry, a common market, and that the actions of individual firms have a negligible effect on price.[2] This assumption does not debar a firm from controlling more than one plant; we are only interested in the distribution of the control of the output of the industry and assume this to be sufficiently diffused for competitive conditions to prevail. Similarly, we assume that all firms operate in factor markets that are approximately competitive, and particularly that all firms are on equal terms with regard to prices and supplies of factors of production and finance.

Since the analysis is only concerned with long-period problems (as defined), we assume all plants work at designed normal capacity.[3] And, for the sake of theoretical neatness, it is helpful (though not essential) to assume that all plants have short-period marginal cost curves that are constant or falling as far as designed normal capacity, and thereafter rise sharply. Because of these assumptions the output of the industry changes only when new plants are built and existing plants scrapped or replaced.

Finally, some definitions may aid clarity. It is useful to divide costs of production into two main categories corresponding to the long-period distinction between prime and supplementary costs. Current operating costs include all purchases from other trading enterprises on

---

[1] This complication is considered in chapter VII, p. 88.
[2] This assumption is relaxed in chapter VII, p. 90.
[3] This assumption is considered further in chapter VI, p. 78.

operating account—materials, fuel, etc.[1]—and expenditure for wages, salaries, and supplements. Included in this category are repairs and maintenance expenditures. On the other hand, supplementary costs and profit are grouped under the term surplus. This is approximately equivalent to the gross trading margin and includes allowances made for depreciation and obsolescence, rent, and profits (including any interest charges paid outside the enterprise). In general, operating costs refer to the costs of current factors of production, and surplus is the fund for the income of fixed factors.

2. THE ADJUSTMENT PROCESS AND THE CAPITAL STOCK

We may begin the construction of a model based on these assumptions by considering how a continuous flow of new and improved techniques of production reflects itself in the capital equipment in use. Plants built at different dates embody in the form of their capital equipment the best-practice technique of their construction date. Plants built this year embody this year's best-practice technique; plants built last year embody the technique that was best-practice last year but has since been outmoded by the improvements in knowledge and changes in factor prices between this year and last year; plants built even earlier embody even more outmoded techniques. Given a continuous stream of improvements in techniques of production, the plants in existence at any one time, are, in effect, a fossilised history of technology over the period spanned by their construction dates—the capital stock represents a petrified chronicle of the recent past. This time dimension of the capital stock is, however, of much more than historical interest for it is the means whereby outmoded methods of production continue into the present and determine the quantities of current factors of production required to produce present output. Only output from recently constructed plants meets current best-practice standards of labour, fuel, and materials per unit of output; plants of older vintage have their capital equipment in forms that embody superseded techniques of the past and are so unable to reach today's best-practice standards of efficiency in the use of labour, materials and fuel. Keynes has written that 'it is by reason of the existence of durable capital equipment that the economic future is linked to the present'.[2] Analogously, durable capital equipment links present production with past technology.

The relationship between the labour productivity of an industry and the range of techniques embodied in the capital stock at any one time, may be distinguished graphically. Fig. 5 is a highly stylised cross-section, or profile, of the capital stock of an industry.

The vertical axis measures man-hours per unit of output, the reciprocal of labour productivity. The horizontal axis measures output. O_n is the capacity output of plants built in period n, and L_n represents

---

[1] Henceforth the term materials will be taken to include all such purchases.
[2] *The General Theory of Employment, Interest and Money* (1st ed, London, 1936), p. 146.

their unit labour requirements. This corresponds to the unit labour requirements of the best-practice technique in period n. O_{n-1} represents the output of plants built in period $n-1$, and L_{n-1} measures their unit labour requirements, and so on. O_{n-t} is the capacity output of the oldest plants in use, and L_{n-t} represents the unit labour requirements of the outmoded equipment embodied in such plants. The height of each 'block' represents the unit labour requirements of each group of plants, and reflects the technique embodied in these plants, while the width of each block signifies the output they contribute to the total output of the industry. The difference in height reflects two influences: first, the

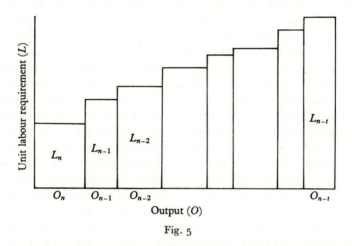

Fig. 5

extent to which period-to-period changes in best-practice techniques allow an absolute saving of labour; and secondly, the probably minor influence of the extra labour needed for repairs and maintenance and lower operating efficiency as plants physically deteriorate. The average unit labour requirements of the industry as a whole is a weighted average of these different blocks, approximately L_{n-3}.

It should be noted that there is no *a priori* reason why younger plants should have the lowest unit labour requirements. But there are two strong reasons why any other situation would be rare: first, few technical advances do not save labour absolutely and, secondly, the pressures for substitution generated by technical progress in the capital goods industries tend to encourage progressively greater savings of labour.

Looking at an industry in this way simply recognises that the output per man-hour of an industry is a statistical abstraction; it is a weighted average of a range of different values. And, like all weighted averages, it may change for a variety of reasons: by the addition of new plants with above-average output per man-hour; by closing down low output per man-hour plants; or by a general movement that affects all plants. In productivity analysis such a viewpoint is essential for, as our empirical examples have indicated, the range between the productivity of labour in different plants in the one industry can be very great; it is not unusual for productivity to be four or five times higher in modern plants than in some older plants.[1] This makes it quite inappropriate to discuss the productivity movements of an industry in terms of the productivity of a 'representative firm' or 'representative plant'—the dispersion around the average is so important that it must be explicitly introduced into the analysis.[2]

In this formulation of the problem, the age of each plant is identified with its standing in the range between the highest and lowest output per man-hour. This is simply an expositional device that by no means corresponds to reality for plants are not in fact indivisible.[3] It does, however, enable us to focus attention on the key points where technical change takes place. At the beginning of their life all plants are modern and their output per man-hour is high compared to the industry average; the rest of their life is spent in becoming progressively more outmoded as a continual flow of new techniques becomes available and are incorporated in the capital equipment of younger plants. A point is reached where their output per head is below average so that their existence tends to depress the industry-wide average. In the final stages of their degradation the best service they can render is to be scrapped and release their labour for service in more modern plants. Looking at the problem in this way immediately suggests that the rate at which new techniques are utilised and actually reflect themselves in industry-wide measures of output per man-hour is closely allied to investment. Given our assumptions two factors are involved: (i) the rate at which modern plants are built, including replacements that may have the same name and location as the plants they replace, and (ii) the rate at which out-moded plants are scrapped. We shall proceed by discussing the influences bearing upon these key factors, at first individually and then in relation to each other.

While the problem has been illustrated in terms of labour productivity, a parallel view is possible for materials, fuel, or any current factor of production:[4] a cross-section against a background of continually changing techniques of production implies plants at different stages in the inevitable progression from 'up-to-dateness' to obsolescence.[5]

---

[1] See the Appendix to chapter VII for examples of this.

[2] It is quite possible for output per man-hour to decrease in all plants yet rise for the industry as a whole through a redistribution of output between high and low output per man-hour plants. For an example of this in the short period see 'Technological Change and Labor Productivity in the Cement Industry 1919–38', *Monthly Lab. Rev.* Bureau of Labor Statistics (July 1940), pp. 47–50.

[3] It may help the reader to grasp this and following aspects of the model to think in terms of ships and aircraft where our simplifying assumptions are not unduly unrealistic.

[4] However, a cross-section where unit materials requirements are highest for the younger plants is likely to be less exceptional.

[5] The term obsolete will be reserved for plants which are sufficiently outmoded to be profitably replaced. Plants embodying techniques which are not up to current best-practice, but not yet obsolete, are termed 'out-moded'.

3. INVESTMENT, REPLACEMENT AND SCRAPPING

The criterion for investment in a competitive industry is the expectation of a flow of surpluses between revenue and current operating costs which, over the life of the investment, are sufficient to recover the principal of the investment and earn a normal rate of return. There are three elements in this calculation: the present and expected price of the product, the present and expected prices of factors of production, and the quantities of factors of production required to produce a unit of output. Technical change impinges directly on this last element; each period brings forth a new set of best-practice unit requirements for labour, investment and materials, which become data for investment decisions in that period. If the prices of the product and factors of production do not change, the improvement in best-practice techniques from one period to another allows a lower level of operating and capital costs and thus the possibility of super-normal profits.[1] These will induce entrepreneurs from either within or without the industry to build such technically superior plants.

The question that is relevant to the problem of utilisation is how many such plants are built in each period? The obvious answer is until output is expanded sufficiently in relation to demand conditions[2] to reduce price to a level where super-normal profits are eliminated—a fall in price equal to the reduction in total costs per unit of output resulting from period-to-period improvements in best-practice techniques. Thus in terms of Fig. 5 we can say that the capacity output represented by each block is that sufficient to replace the output from plants simultaneously scrapped and, over and above this, to cause a net expansion of output which in relation to demand conditions is just sufficient to lead to a price reduction which eliminates the possibility of super-normal profits.

There are innumerable complications that could be introduced: gestation periods, inertia, changes in confidence, and the supply of finance. But neglecting these complications and regarding the process as continuous we can say that the trend movement of output and price will be such as to abolish the possibility of super-normal profits by forcing selling prices to fall in relation to factor prices so that the use of best-practice techniques only yields normal profits.

We can now turn to existing plants and ask how they are faring while such modern plants are being built. Because of our assumptions these plants have their capital equipment in outmoded forms that make impossible the use of the new techniques. The problem is one of the appropriate criteria for scrapping and replacement decisions. The first

---

[1] Since profit is a small residual, even very small savings in the quantities of factors may have a large effect on profits; this is particularly true if the new techniques are of the type that save all factors of production simultaneously.

[2] At the moment, demand conditions should be interpreted broadly as all influences bearing upon the relation between changes in price and output. The whole question of demand is considered on p. 80.

step is to be clear concerning the relation between scrapping and replacement. These are often considered to be twin aspects of the same decision but, obviously, there is no necessary reason why this should be the case. It is quite possible for a firm to build modern plants and yet retain the old ones, or to scrap existing plants without replacing them. Indeed, this is a necessary accompaniment to the growth and decline of firms. Thus, one approach to the question would be to cast the analysis in 'gross' terms—to ask when existing plants are scrapped irrespective of whether they are to be replaced or not. This case will be considered first. Deliberate replacement decisions will then be introduced to see what difference, if any, they make to the analysis.

When we approach the question of scrapping in these gross terms, the appropriate question to ask is: here is a plant consisting of a given complex of capital equipment which determines the quantities of current factors required; when should it be abandoned? The obvious answer is when the plant fails to yield any surplus over operating costs; to abandon it earlier would be to forego any surpluses the plant could earn, while to abandon it later would be to make losses. This criterion recognises the well-established principle that outlays for specialised capital equipment are irrevocable. Once the investment has been made all that is possible is to make the best of it by extracting all possible surpluses over current operating costs. It is quite irrelevant whether the earned surplus is sufficient to cover depreciation allowances; in fact, the only sense in which depreciation is relevant is in the sense of physical deterioration and this is automatically included in the scrapping criterion since the additional outlays resulting from repairs and main-tenance and lower operating efficiency are reflected in operating costs. Similarly, the institutional arrangements for financing the investment are irrelevant. While rent and interest charges may appear as pressing as operating expenses to the individual firm, these charges are only contractual arrangements which represent a legal claim on the earnings of the plant. Even though they cannot be met, it will still pay someone to operate the plant—even the Receiver in Bankruptcy. Again from the point of the individual firm, an opportunity cost may appear in operating equipment which has a resale value. But to have a resale value (above pure scrap value) implies that the plant can still earn surpluses. The appropriate analogy is with motor-vehicles; no matter how many sales and resales take place, all continue in use until forced to the wrecking yard.

There are, however, three minor qualifications which should be made to the proposition that plants will remain in operation so long as revenue exceeds operating costs. These arise because some elements in the initial investment are not completely irrevocable. Site value, working capital, and scrap value are elements that can be withdrawn and employed in alternative uses. Thus, the more exact criterion is 'plants are scrapped when the earned surplus is just below that required to yield a normal rate of return on the present value of the site, working capital and scrap value'.[1] Since these qualifications are normally quantitatively insignificant, they will be neglected until chapter VII in which certain cases where they are important will be considered.

The second approach to scrapping is through deliberate replacement: by asking when will it be profitable to replace an existing plant by a new plant. The conventional criterion for replacement is whether or not the operating costs of an existing plant exceed the total of operating costs plus capital costs (including a normal return) of its best-practice alternative. This criterion may be put in another form which is analogous to the criterion for investment: that replacement will be profitable at the first date that the expected future surpluses over operating cost of the new plant exceed the expected future surpluses of the existing plant by a margin sufficient to repay the initial investment in the new plant, and earn a normal rate of return.[2]

If one approaches replacement in these terms it is quite obvious that, given our assumptions of indivisible plants and competition, the replacement criterion yields exactly the same results as the first case where an entrepreneur abandons his existing plant. Under competition, while the owner of an existing plant is deciding whether replacement is profitable, other entrepreneurs are taking advantage of the new methods by building best-practice plants which expand output and drive down price to a point where a new plant can *only* earn sufficient surpluses to recover the principal of the investment and earn a normal rate of return. The same set of data with respect to technique, factor prices, and product prices, enter into both new investment and replacement decisions and this is only consistent with competition if the surpluses of the existing plants are exhausted when replacement becomes profitable.[3] Thus, both approaches imply the same scrapping date for existing plants. Effectively a replacement decision is both a scrapping decision and an investment decision. Simply because they are carried out simultaneously does not alter their individual character; the businessman who decides to replace his plant is only scrapping the

---

[1] See H. Hotelling, 'A General Mathematical Theory of Depreciation', *J. Amer. Statist. Assoc.* vol. xx (1925), pp. 340–53; and F. and V. Lutz, *The Theory of Investment of the Firm* (Princeton, 1951), ch. VIII. In interpreting this treatment of replacement criteria it should be remembered that under competition (and imperfect competition for marginal investment or replacement) 'goodwill' is zero.

[2] This formulation of the conditions for replacement is strictly speaking inadequate, for while a necessary condition it is not a sufficient condition. In certain circumstances (say where a major improvement in technique is shortly expected) it may be more profitable to postpone replacement. But since such conditions apply to new investment as much as replacement investment, they do not affect the propositions of this section.

[3] In its simplest form this proposition may be set out as follows: a businessman will be indifferent between replacing and not replacing an existing plant when its operating costs equal total costs with a new plant. But under competition revenue equals total costs with a new plant. Therefore when the entrepreneur is indifferent between replacing and not replacing, the operating costs of an existing plant equal revenue. A more elaborate mathematical proof is set out below.

Let R_2 = revenue of the new plant, R_1 = revenue of the existing plant, V_2 = operating costs of the new plant, V_1 = operating costs of the old plant, I = initial cost of a new plant, S = site value plus working capital plus scrap value, r = normal rate of return, and n is in

plant he would be forced to abandon in any case, and in addition making an investment in a new plant. The only difference is that since he is already the possessor of a site, working capital, and scrap value, his initial investment is less than that of an entrepreneur starting afresh. This difference, however, is complementary to the exact criterion for abandonment: that the earned surplus equals a normal rate of return on site value, working capital and scrap value.

In the simple cases considered by this model, the identity of these two approaches is useful, for it shows there is no need to distinguish between scrapping for replacement and scrapping without replacement or, from another point of view, that there is no difference in principle between net investment decisions and replacement investment decisions. In more complex cases, such as the replacement of machines within a plant, this identity is more difficult to distinguish; but it is nevertheless important to illustrate the principles involved in the utilisation of new techniques of production.

4. A CONTINUOUS PROCESS

We are now in a position to examine the construction of modern plants and the scrapping of outmoded plants as simultaneous processes. A modification of the previous diagram is useful in this context. Instead of a cross-section in terms of labour requirement we can take a cross-section in terms of operating costs. This is equivalent to the addition of cross-sections in terms of labour and materials requirements multiplied by the ruling wage rate and current prices of materials respectively.

The previous discussion allows price and output to be introduced into this diagram. The current price is P_n composed of operating costs, AC, and capital costs (including normal profits), CD, of best-practice plants constructed in the current period. This price defines the oldest plants that can remain in operation, that is, the plants built in period $n-t$ whose operating costs, BF, are almost equal to price. At this instant, the industry is in a momentary equilibrium; no further new plants will be constructed, and at the current price none of the existing plants need be scrapped, nor will it be profitable to replace them by modern plants. The techniques of production in use range from the best-practice

---

each case the last prospective date where each plant is expected to earn a positive surplus, assuming revenue and operating costs rise or fall monotonically over time.

Then the entrepreneur will be indifferent between replacing and not replacing his existing plant when

$$\int_{t=0}^{t=n} (R_2 - V_2)\, e^{-rt} dt - \int_{t=0}^{t=n} (R_1 - V_1)\, e^{-rt} dt = I - S.$$

But under competition

$$\int_{t=0}^{t=n} (R_2 - V_2)\, e^{-rt} dt = I,$$

therefore

$$\int_{t=0}^{t=n} (R_1 - V_1)\, e^{-rt} dt = S,$$

that is, the existing plant can only anticipate sufficient surpluses to earn a normal rate of return on site value, etc., which is the exact condition for abandonment.

technique of period n, to the now outmoded technique of period $n-t$, and the productivity of labour of the whole industry is a weighted average of the productivity of labour in the plants comprising this range.

This equilibrium situation is neither long-term nor short-term in the usual sense. If there were no further changes in technical knowledge, factor prices and demand, the equilibrium would be long-term in the usual sense if capital equipment did not physically deteriorate. Then all operating costs would remain constant so that there would never be any incentive to replace or abandon outmoded plants. Where capital equipment deteriorates, these outmoded plants will be replaced as their

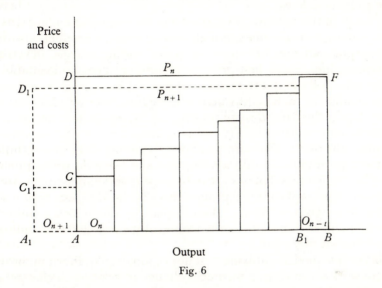

Fig. 6

operating costs rise above price, and finally the industry will approach a long-term equilibrium where all plants use the same technique and the only difference between plants is physical deterioration attributable to age.[1]

In fact, this long-term equilibrium is never reached, for as time progresses improving technical knowledge and changing factor prices bring forth a stream of new best-practice techniques. In period $n+1$, a new best-practice technique with operating costs $A_1 C_1$ and capital costs $C_1 D_1$ becomes available. Plants embodying this technique will be built until price falls to P_{n+1} where profits are normal. Simultaneously, some of the older plants will be scrapped, so that the output of the industry becomes $A_1 B_1$. This represents a net increase in output which is just sufficient in relation to demand conditions to reduce price by an amount equal to the total cost saving of the new best-practice technique. The industry is again in a position of momentary equilibrium where no further existing plants will be scrapped, or new plants constructed.

[1] The relationship between this equilibrium and short- and long-period equilibrium in the usual sense is considered further in chapter VI, p. 79.

When this process is regarded as continuous, it makes little difference whether the impetus comes from new investment decisions or replacement decisions. We may regard entrepreneurs as taking advantage of new methods by building new plants, which expand output, drive down price, and thus force some outmoded plants to be replaced. Alternatively one can regard the new techniques as making replacement more attractive to the owners of existing plants. When the plants with operating costs exceeding total best-practice costs have been replaced, there remains the incentive of super-normal profits to induce the construction of additional new plants which expand output and force down price to its new level.

In terms of this schema, if we trace the life-history of a plant it begins with modern best-practice methods, above average productivity, and a high surplus per unit of output, or gross trading margin. During its subsequent life, newer best-practice techniques become available and selling price follows the trend of total costs of best-practice techniques. Being unable to make equivalent cost reductions, the plant suffers a steady fall in the earned surplus as its capital equipment becomes progressively more outmoded. It will not, however, pay the entrepreneur to replace the plant; if he wishes to take advantage of the new techniques it is more profitable to build a new plant and leave his present plant in use. Only when its surpluses are exhausted does abandonment become necessary and replacement profitable. This is the last stage in the inevitable progression from a modern plant to obsolescence; only then does the plant become sufficiently technically outmoded to be no longer fit to economically exist.

This simple model, implying as it does a moving equilibrium, provides a framework for analysing technical change in relation to changes over time in productivity, prices, output and investment. Given the initial situation, the flow of new techniques of production, the movements of factor prices, and demand conditions, there is a series of momentary equilibrium points which trace out the path over time of output, price, productivity and gross investment. While short-term influences may cause aberrations around this path, the trend movements of these variables will correspond to their equilibrium values. Output will increase at a rate sufficient to allow price to follow best-practice total costs; gross investment in each period will equal the capacity output of new plants, including replacements, times the current best-practice unit investment requirements, while productivity may increase at a faster or slower rate than best-practice productivity, depending upon whether the range between best-practice and obsolete plants is increasing or decreasing.

Before examining these movements in detail, it is advisable to turn to a consideration of the principles which lie behind the continuous adjustment process.

5. THE PRINCIPLES BEHIND THE MODEL

The basic principle is a very old one. As Jevons first remarked, 'in commerce, bygones are forever bygones and we are always starting clear with a view to future utility'.[1] Although this principle is basic to all human action, economic or not, short-term or long-term, its application to questions of obsolescence and the life of capital goods has been honoured more in the breach than the observance.[2] An investment outlay in fixed capital equipment can only occur at one point of time. Once made, bygones are bygones, and the future life and earnings of the equipment depend solely on three factors: (i) the price of the product or products the equipment can produce, (ii) the quantities of current factors required to operate the equipment, and (iii) the prices of these current factors. This is true irrespective of whether the equipment is a marvel of technical efficiency or a museum piece; once in existence it is there to be used or not and the only criterion of its economic usefulness is the ability to earn a surplus over operating costs.

In this respect the stock of existing capital goods is comparable to land, and forms the rationale for Marshall's[3] dictum that the earnings of existing capital goods are quasi-rents, and the insistence of J. B. Clark[4] that such earnings are pure rents indistinguishable from those of land. In fact, when technology is continually improving, we can apply the concept of the Ricardian extensive margin to the existing capital stock with very few modifications. Capital goods in existence are equally as much a part of the economic environment as land or other natural resources. Both are gifts: natural resources are the gift of nature, capital goods are the gifts of the past.[5] The fertility of land corresponds to the level of technical knowledge embodied in capital equipment; modern capital equipment embodying recent best-practice techniques is analogous to the most fertile land, and older capital equipment embodying less advanced techniques corresponds to land of decreasing fertility as the margin of cultivation is approached. In exactly the same way as labour working with land of different fertility has differential products per worker, so also labour working with capital equipment embodying different levels of technical knowledge has differential products. And in both cases the margin of use is determined by the ability to show a surplus or rent; no-rent land corresponds to capital equipment that has just been abandoned.

[1] *Theory of Political Economy*, 4th ed. (1911), p. 164.
[2] For failing to recognise this principle, Pigou found occasion to reprimand Hobson (*Economics of Welfare* (1920), p. 164), Hayek to reprimand Plant ('The Trend of Economic Thinking', *Economica* (May 1932), p. 184), and in turn Robbins chided Pigou (*The Nature and Significance of Economic Science*, 2nd ed., p. 50).
[3] *Principles*, 9th ed., pp. 412 ff.
[4] *The Distribution of Wealth* (1899), p. 97.
[5] These points are well known but often neglected in any but short-period analysis. How often does one see the statement that an industry can produce cheaply because its capital equipment is fully depreciated!

From this viewpoint, the co-existence of plants with different techniques and costs is consistent with competition in exactly the same way as farms with different costs are consistent with competition in agriculture. Thus, the complaint that all firms do not adopt new techniques as soon as they become available is not necessarily inconsistent with competition or wasteful in any meaningful economic sense.[1] In the model, there is a delay in the utilisation of new techniques, despite the fact that each entrepreneur is looking for courses of action which will increase his profits. When new methods become available, the owner of existing plants as well as new entrants can build new plants which incorporate the new methods. If his existing plants are earning a surplus, then the new plants will be additions to his present output; if the surpluses of his existing plants are almost exhausted then the new plants will be replacements, and perhaps use the site and working capital of the plants they replace. When we step outside the assumptions of the model it is likely that the firms with the most vigorous management, or easy access to finance, or some such advantage will grow the fastest. But as long as the industry remains competitive this is of little significance for our purposes.

Even though such a delay in the use of new techniques is consistent with competition, this does not mean that old and new techniques do not actively compete. The reason why they can co-exist is that they compete upon unequal terms. Although production with modern techniques has an advantage in that lesser quantities of factors of production are required to produce a given output, to gain this advantage implies a cost—the cost of a new outfit of capital equipment. Such new plants will only be constructed when expected gross revenue is sufficient to cover the supply price of *all* factors of production: labour, materials, land and capital. On the other hand, in the plants which make up the capital stock in existence, capital is fixed equipment which is the result of a past outlay and, since bygones are bygones, no longer has a supply price. Thus, in such plants, production will continue so long as gross revenue is sufficient to meet the supply price of transferable factors: labour, materials, and that part of the initial investment which is transferable, such as the site and working capital. These unequal terms of competition give existing capital equipment a lease of life even when outmoded; the disadvantage of using current factors in excess of best-practice standards is more than balanced by the advantage that the capital equipment has no present cost. As the model indicates, competition on these terms is effective in two ways: first, by a direct comparison of operating and total costs in the case of deliberate replacement, and secondly by the price movements of the industry. These price movements are determined by total costs of best-practice plants and impose upon the industry the condition that the delay in the use of new techniques

---

[1] Hayek has pointed out that this complaint is inconsistent with the equally widely held idea that scrapping through obsolescence of equipment that is not 'worn out' is wasteful (*op. cit.* p. 132).

cannot exceed that which leads to operating costs per unit of output greater than price.

The fact that competition is conducted in these terms points up the necessity for distinguishing between *ex poste* and *ex ante* capital costs. Long-period economics has taught us to think of a stock or fund of capital which, although temporarily given physical forms, over time is capable of changing its physical form. However useful this concept may be for some purposes, it does not correspond to reality. For both long and short periods the capital stock is not a fund but actual capital goods in existence which cannot change their form. Effectively they are man-made resources which make our environment more favourable to production than that given to us by nature. Of the stream of output produced with the aid of this improved environment, some is devoted to additional capital goods, that is, gross investment. Only in this limited sense is capital ever free, and represents a fund with alternative uses. And only then does it have a cost—the expectation of rents sufficient to repay the initial outlay and earn profits. Capital costs are relevant solely for production decisions that involve this gross investment, such as the decision to build a new plant. In this *ex ante* sense alone are obsolescence, amortisation and profits, costs. Once gross investment becomes capital equipment in existence, these capital costs become rents, and, as rents, have no influence on output or investment decisions. True, businessmen regard capital costs as *ex poste* costs, but, in essence this reflects a division of the earned surplus into purely accounting categories. For example, a firm which suffers a reduction in gross revenue as the result of the introduction of a new technique in other firms may react by reducing the book value of its capital either by an obsolescence allowance or an admitted capital loss and still continue to earn normal profits on this smaller capital; or it may refuse to admit a capital loss and earn a sub-normal rate of profit. Which procedure is adopted is of no economic interest; output, the life of the plant and subsequent investment decisions will be unaffected.

A second feature of the model is the role of gross investment as the vehicle of technical change. When there is no technical change, investment is required only to make good the depletion of the existing capital stock through physical deterioration, and to add to this stock. But when technical change is taking place, gross investment has another extremely important role: that of providing the necessary specialised capital equipment required for new techniques, irrespective of whether or not they are more or less mechanised than their predecessors. Without gross investment, improving technology that requires new capital equipment simply represents a potential for higher productivity; to realise this potential requires gross investment. An economy with a low rate of gross investment is restricted in the rate at which new techniques can be brought into use; an economy with a high rate of gross investment can quickly bring new methods into use, and thus realise the benefits of improving technology. In this way, the rate of gross investment is a vital determinant of the extent to which observed productivity lags behind best-practice productivity.[1]

In fact, the pace of adjustment to all changes that require a different physical form of the capital stock depends upon the rate of gross investment; not only changes in techniques but changing patterns of demand and international trade. The physical form of the capital stock reflects not only the techniques in use but also the product structure of output. Any substantial changes in this structure requires gross investment and the rapidity of such changes depends upon the rate of gross investment. Thus, we may think of the physical form taken by each year's gross investment as reflecting current conditions in three ways. The physical form in each industry reflects current technical knowledge and relative factor prices, while the inter-industry distribution is a reflection of the current demand and total cost conditions for each commodity. In this sense the new capital goods resulting from each year's gross investment form the moving frontier to the capital stock; it is the only part in harmony with the present; the remainder has been outmoded by the march of events. Although outmoded, it cannot be immediately brought into harmony with the present, for gross investment is limited and the supply price of capital equipment is not zero. Only those parts of the existing capital stock that are so far out of harmony with present techniques and demand conditions that they cannot earn a surplus will be replaced. This forms the rearward frontier of the capital stock, the capital equipment which has become obsolescent. Over time both frontiers advance—best-practice techniques improve and the standards which define the permissible level of operating costs in outmoded plants becomes more exacting. In terms of the analogy with land, the flow of new best-practice techniques corresponds to the discovery of land of continually increasing fertility, while gross investment is equivalent to the opening up of such land. As newly discovered fertile land may draw inwards the margin of cultivation through its influence on wages and prices, so also gross investment forces the scrapping of the more outmoded portions of the capital stock. But, unlike land, the process does not end. The frontier of technical knowledge knows no limit so that the system is always expanding.

6. SUMMARY

1. In analysing the delay in the utilisation of new techniques and its relationship to movements of productivity, prices and costs, it is helpful to set up a highly simplified model based on the following principal assumptions: plants are indivisible complexes of capital equipment which embody the best-practice technique of their construction date and

---

[1] In analysis over time, the distinction between net and gross investment is very often quite meaningless. As D. H. Robertson has said '...if the capitalist is to be allowed time and facilities for turning his spades into a steam plough, it seems unreasonable not to allow him time and facilities to turn them into beer' (*Wage Grumbles, Economic Fragments*, reprinted in *Readings in the Theory of Income Distribution*, American Economic Association Series, p. 221).

cannot be adapted to any other technique; perfect competition is assumed; all plants work at 'designed normal capacity'; and labour and managerial efficiency are equal in all plants.

2. An industry may be viewed as a number of plants embodying techniques ranging between the most modern plant (or plants) embodying the current best-practice technique, and the oldest plant still in use which embodies the best-practice technique of an earlier date, and which is now outmoded.

3. The range of techniques in existence is defined by the condition that plants are not scrapped until their operating costs (labour plus materials, etc.) per unit of output equal price; or by the condition that replacement will not be profitable until their operating costs equal total costs (including amortisation and interest) of a new plant. It can be shown that these two conditions imply the same scrapping date. For the time being the complication caused by the fact that some elements in the original investment, site-value, working capital and scrap value, can be recovered if a plant is scrapped, is ignored.

4. The appearance of a new best-practice technique has the following effects: first, the output of the industry is expanded until price falls to equality with the total costs of plants employing the new technique; secondly, some of the older existing plants are scrapped or replaced until the operating costs of the oldest plant (or plants) equal the new level of price and best-practice total costs. A flow of new best-practice techniques leads to a series of such equilibria (which combine both short- and long-run elements) and so trace out the path over time of output, costs, prices and productivity.

5. This simple model, which provides a basic framework for the analysis of productivity movements, is based on two well-known principles. The first is that capital equipment in existence earns rents in a manner analogous to land. For this reason, the immediate general adoption of new techniques which require investment is uneconomic since new plants will only be constructed when receipts are sufficient to cover all outlays, while existing plants will remain in operation so long as they earn a positive rent, even though their productivity is lower and their operating costs higher than a modern plant. The second principle is that to employ all new techniques, irrespective of whether they are more or less mechanised than their predecessor, requires an investment outlay. Consequently, gross investment is the vehicle of new techniques, and the rate of such investment determines how rapidly new techniques are brought into general use and are effective in raising productivity.

CHAPTER V

FACTOR PRICES AND THE ADJUSTMENT PROCESS

THE model of the previous chapter implies a very considerable gap between potential technical progress, as reflected by best-practice techniques, and realised technical progress as reflected in the performance of the industry as a whole. In the model this inability to realise the full potential of technical progress arises out of the existence of fixed capital equipment which inhibits immediate adjustment to a flow of new techniques. This, of course, is not the only reason for the gap between potential and actual technical progress. The diffusion of knowledge is hampered by business secrecy, the patent system, and imperfect channels of communication; while the adoption of new methods, even when known, is restricted by the inertia of management and the fears of labour. This chapter, however, is concerned with the purely economic barriers to the utilisation of new methods rather than such semi-institutional barriers. It employs the simple model to show that the delay in the utilisation of new methods is a reflection of factor prices, and that the speed of the adjustment process may be regarded as a form of factor substitution.

1. THE RATE OF 'TURNOVER' OF THE CAPITAL STOCK

The previous chapter is based on the idea that gross investment is the vehicle of new techniques. From this simple idea it follows that an industry's average productivity is a function of the rate of replacement investment; a high rate of replacement investment leads to high productivity by enabling new methods to be rapidly brought into general use. To clarify the nature of this relationship consider two industries, or two economies, both with zero net investment and experiencing the same flow of best-practice techniques. The industry or economy with the greatest rate of replacement investment achieves the highest productivity for its capital stock is 'turned over' more rapidly, equipment has a shorter life and, on average, its outfit of equipment is more up-to-date than that of the industry or economy with a lower rate of replacement.

The rate of 'turnover' of the capital stock is reflected in the range between best-practice and obsolete techniques. Fig. 7 illustrates this by comparing the cross-section view of two industries or economies which have different rates of replacement investment. Both produce the same output, and best-practice labour requirements are, and have been in the past, identical.

Fig. 7 (a) portrays the case where the rate of replacement investment is low. Few modern plants have been built in each period and techniques in use range between the current best-practice technique with labour requirements of L_n and techniques on the margin of obsolescence with labour requirements of L_{n-t}. In Fig. 7 (*b*) the rate of replacement investment is much higher; each block is wider, since more modern plants have been constructed in each period, and unit labour requirements range between L_n and L_{n-s}. The result of this smaller range is a higher average level of labour productivity made possible by a more modern capital stock.[1]

It is important to realise that this relationship between investment and labour productivity is entirely different to that of the neo-classical schema. It does not depend upon positive 'net' investment nor upon techniques becoming more highly mechanised; it arises simply because the rate of replacement investment determines the speed at which the capital stock can be adjusted to the potentialities of technical change.

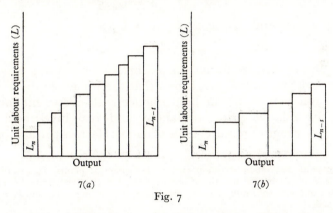

7(*a*)   7(*b*)

Fig. 7

With an infinitely high rate of replacement, adjustment would be instantaneous and average labour productivity would coincide with best-practice standards; with a very low rate of replacement the capital stock would stretch back into the distant past and a large proportion of the labour force would be forced to work with capital equipment embodying primitive levels of technique. Where the balance lies, between the advantages of a modern capital stock and the costs of devoting a high proportion of investment to replacement, depends upon relative supplies (or prices) of labour and gross investment. This question is considered below.

2. FACTOR PRICES

When the range between co-existing techniques is translated into costs and prices, it can easily be shown that its extent is a function of relative factor prices. Fig. 8 sets out the diagram of a momentary equilibrium where super-normal profits have been abolished and all obsolete plants have been replaced or abandoned. As a first step, consider the case

---

[1] For the purposes of this argument, it is immaterial whether output is measured before or after amortisation; although, of course, the differences in average productivity corresponding to differences in replacement investment will be much less if output is net of amortisation.

where all operating costs are labour costs, and surplus is composed entirely of capital costs, including normal profits.

The difference between the operating costs of the current best-practice plant $(L_n.w)$ and the operating costs of the plant on the margin of obsolescence $(L_{n-t}.w)$ is equal to BC, which in relation to best-practice plants is surplus per unit of output, or the gross trading margin (S).

Thus,

$$L_{n-t}.w - L_n.w = S,$$

that is, the difference in operating costs of co-existing plants equals the best-practice gross trading margin.

The gross trading margin may be divided into two components: C_n, real investment per unit of output, or the best-practice investment coefficient, and g, the 'price' of this real investment consisting of amortisation and normal profits.

Thus,

$$S = C_n.g$$

and

$$L_{n-t}.w - L_n.w = C_n.g$$

and

$$L_{n-t} - L_n = C_n.g/w.^1$$

This equation, derived from the equilibrium relationship between the costs of co-existing techniques, shows that the range of labour requirements is a function of: (i) the best-practice real investment coefficient, and (ii) the relative prices of labour and real investment. More generally, the range of requirements of current factors per unit of output

---

[1] A more precise formulation is as follows: Let R = revenue, V = operating costs, C_n and L_n = unit capital and labour requirements of best-practice plants, L_{n-t} = unit labour requirements of plants on the margin of obsolescence, l = the prospective life of the new plant, r = the interest/profit rate, w = the wage rate, P = selling price, and P_c = the price of capital goods.

The condition for investment, of amount I, is

$$\int_{t=0}^{t=l} (R-V)e^{-rt}dt = I.$$

Dividing each side by output and expressing operating costs as labour costs, this becomes

$$\int_{t=0}^{t=l} (P-L_n.w)e^{-rt}dt = C_n P_c.$$

But for plants on the margin of obsolescence

$$P = L_{n-t}.w.$$

Therefore

$$\int_{t=0}^{t=l} (L_{n-t}-L_n)w.e^{-rt}dt = C_n P_c.$$

Thus the range of labour requirements $L_{n-t}-L_n$ is determined by C_n and the factors which determine the relative costs of employing labour and capital equipment, w, r, P_c and l.

Similarly, if we begin from the condition for replacement,

$$\int_{t=0}^{t=l} (V_{n-t}-V_n)e^{-rt}dt = I,$$

this may be expressed in terms of unit labour and capital requirements

$$\int_{t=0}^{t=l} (L_{n-t}.w - L_n w)e^{-rt}dt = C_n P_c,$$

where again $L_{n-t}-L_n$ is determined by C_n, w, P_c, r and l.

is a function of best-practice standards of fixed factors per unit of output, and the relative prices of current and fixed factors.

The reason why relative factor prices influence the speed of the adjustment process is, of course, that the cost of new capital equipment is the barrier to the immediate general use of new techniques, and higher operating costs are the price paid for retaining outmoded methods. Both

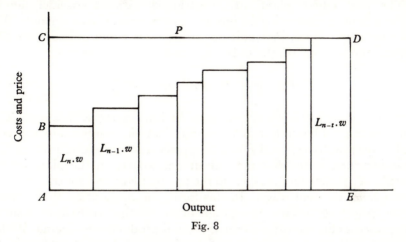

Fig. 8

the scrapping and replacement conditions reflect a balance between these opposing considerations. A change in relative factor prices upsets this balance and sets a new standard in the savings of current factors necessary for profitable replacement. Effectively, relative factor prices decide the degree of 'outmodedness' which is obsolete, and so the extent to which today's capital stock reflects past conditions. When real investment is cheap relative to labour, standards of obsolescence are high and the capital stock is up-to-date; when real investment is dear, rapid adjustment is uneconomic and the capital stock consists largely of outmoded equipment.

Factor prices operate through both voluntary replacement and scrapping decisions. In the first case, their role in determining standards of obsolescence may be seen directly from the condition for replacement, without recourse to the assumptions of the model. In its simplest form—which is applicable to plants and individual items of equipment—this condition requires that operating costs equal best-practice total costs. Both the prices of labour and real investment enter into this condition. A fall in either the interest rate or the price of capital goods lowers the capital cost component of best-practice total costs and so reduces the level of operating costs at which replacement first becomes profitable.[1] Conversely, a rise in the wage rate increases the operating costs of

---

[1] There are a number of complicated offsets to this relationship. As has been noted, increased standards of obsolescence reduce the prospective life of new equipment, and the consequent rise in capital costs per annum may partly offset the effects of a relative reduction in the price of capital goods in increasing standards of obsolescence. On the other hand, equipment with a shorter life may be less durable, thus tending to reduce capital costs per

outmoded plants and machines more than those of their best-practice counterparts and again induces earlier replacement. Thus, whether we think of the capital stock in terms of complete plants or individual items of equipment, it is still true that the standards of obsolescence which determine how far the past intrudes into the present are a function of relative factor prices.

The case where plants are abandoned without consideration of replacement is interesting in relation to the economy as a whole. The relevant condition is that unit operating costs equal selling price (P). When labour costs are the only operating costs we can write

$$L_{n-t}.w = P \quad \text{and} \quad \frac{1}{L_{n-t}} = \frac{w}{P}.$$

For an economy as a whole, this may be interpreted as follows: $1/L_{n-t}$ is net output per head (that is, free of duplication on account of materials and other purchases), and P is selling price also net of duplication. The equation then states that net output per worker in the plant on the margin of obsolescence is equal to the product wage or, for the economy as a whole, the real wage. In this form, the proposition that relative factor prices determine the range of co-existing techniques can be recognised as an extension of the marginal productivity schema. With a given capital stock, one means of employing additional workers is by not scrapping obsolete equipment; and, as we should expect under competition, the product of such marginal workers equals the real wage. Thus, we can say quite simply that the margin of obsolescence is determined by the level of real wages; when labour is an expensive factor of production, an economy must adjust rapidly to new methods which require less labour; when labour is cheap, this pressure is absent and outmoded methods of the past are retained in the capital stock. Again the parallel with land is relevant: as the level of real wages determines the fertility of marginal land, so also real wages determine the standards of past technology which are retained in today's capital stock.

3. THE ADJUSTMENT PROCESS AS A FORM OF FACTOR SUBSTITUTION

It is now clear that the lag in the utilisation of new techniques is primarily a reflection of an economy's supplies of investment relative to its labour force. In fact, the extent of this lag may be regarded as the manifestation of a form of factor substitution which is additional and complementary to the traditional form of substitution through the degree of mechanisation. Additional supplies of gross investment per worker may be employed to raise the productivity of labour in two ways: the first is to employ more mechanised techniques; the second is

---

annum and offsetting the effect of increased obsolescence. But since it is logically impossible for these complicated offsets to be more than partial, the net effect of a relative cheapening in the prices of capital goods must be higher standards of obsolescence.

to increase the volume of replacement expenditures and speed up the adjustment to new methods. Substitution via the degree of mechanisation raises labour productivity by providing each worker with a greater volume of capital equipment; substitution via the adjustment process gives each worker a more modern set of capital equipment. This additional dimension to the marginal productivity schema has its origin in the procedure of regarding the life of capital equipment and the rate of replacement investment as variables determined in a context of prices and costs. Thus undoubtedly the correct procedure for the working life of capital equipment is not a purely technical consideration, nor is replacement automatic; both are influenced by changes in product and factor prices. From this viewpoint the distinction between net and gross investment is largely artificial. It is not so much that net investment is of a different character to replacement investment, but that they represent alternative avenues by which gross investment may be applied to production; and, in a properly functioning economy, the marginal product of investment should be equal in both avenues.

These two forms of substitution are not independent. In the equation,

$$L_{n-t} - L_n = C_n \frac{g}{w},$$

the term C_n, the real investment coefficient, reflects the degree of mechanisation. It follows, therefore, that a wide range between the labour requirements of co-existing techniques is likely in highly mechanised industries. This is as we should expect; adjustment is most costly when highly mechanised techniques requiring large amounts of investment are involved. But to recognise this immediately raises the question of the complex interactions between the two forms of substitution. A fall in the prices of capital goods relative to wages (or a fall in the profit rate) has two effects: (i) standards of obsolescence become more ruthless, thus tending to decrease the range $L_n - L_{n-t}$; (ii) best-practice techniques become more mechanised and C_n increases, thus tending to increase the range $L_n - L_{n-t}$. Which effect predominates depends upon the elasticity of substitution; when this is greater than unity the use of more capital equipment outweighs the fall in its price and the best-practice gross trading margin increases, thus widening the range $L_n - L_{n-t}$; when the elasticity of substitution is less than unity the gross trading margin decreases, and the range narrows. But, while the range between co-existing techniques measured in terms of labour requirements may increase or decrease, the range measured as a degree of adjustment, or time-lag, always decreases as capital goods become cheaper relative to labour. The reason is that cheaper capital goods reduce best-practice total costs irrespective of the accompanying changes in the degree of mechanisation, so that L_{n-t} must decrease. Although this decrease may be offset or exceeded by the fall in L_n attributable to increased mechanisation so that the range $L_n - L_{n-t}$ may remain constant or increase, the number of years' lag represented by this range decreases—t becomes less. Relative to the year-to-year changes in techniques, the capital stock is more up-to-date even though it may contain a wider range of different techniques.

This way of looking at the whole question of the rate of utilisation of new techniques leads to three important implications. First, technical progress cannot be regarded as automatic and independent of accumulation. While for certain purposes it may be appropriate to regard the flow of new knowledge as exogenous to the economic system, the rate at which this knowledge is made effective in raising productivity is a function of the rate of gross saving, and this is mutually determined along with all the other elements of an inter-related economic system. The gap between potential and actual technical progress may be widening, constant, or narrowing, depending upon whether the marginal productivity of real investment allows an increasing or declining volume of replacement investment. Thus all investment, net investment and replacement investment, is important in economic growth. An increasing supply of real gross investment per worker allows progress on two frontiers: the mechanisation frontier as best-practice techniques become progressively more mechanised, and the obsolescence frontier as the gap between co-existing techniques is steadily narrowed.

Secondly, it is obviously impossible to regard obsolescence (as it so often is) as simply parallel to physical depreciation. Standards of obsolescence reflect basic characteristics of an economy and perform the important role of determining how far the past is allowed to intrude into the present. An economy in the process of change embodies its past in its capital stock. Standards of obsolescence determine how far it is economic to bring the capital stock into harmony with the present. An economy with meagre supplies of investment must accept low standards of obsolescence, and a slow adjustment to all changes involving new capital equipment; an economy with abundant investment can afford rigorous standards of obsolescence and a rapid adjustment process.

Finally, the implication has often been drawn from Working Party and Productivity Mission Reports[1] that the continued use of out-dated capital equipment is a sign of 'inefficiency'. If this ambiguous word means poor management or improper functioning of the economic system, then the implication is not necessarily correct; for the extent to which out-dated methods can survive is a reflection of factor supplies. Thus, the traditional willingness of American businessmen to abandon outmoded methods does not necessarily imply better management, but simply that they produce in an economic environment which makes necessary such ruthless 'creative destruction'. In fact, there is some evidence to suggest that one of the chief reasons for Anglo-American productivity differences lies in standards of obsolescence. It is a common theme in Productivity Mission Reports that the productivity of the best

[1] Anglo-American Council on Productivity, and U.K. Government Working Parties on Productivity.

plants in the United Kingdom is comparable with that of the best plants in the United States, and that the difference lies in a much higher proportion of plants employing outmoded methods in the United Kingdom—a much greater 'tail' of low-productivity plants. Such a situation is consistent with a higher standard of obsolescence in the United States which, as we have seen, follows from a higher level of real wages.

In conclusion, it should be noted that both substitution through the degree of mechanisation, and substitution through standards of obsolescence relate to capital equipment and labour. Consequently, technical progress in the manufacture of capital goods, which allows an increasing supply of capital goods per worker and a falling price relative to labour, is relevant in both cases. Even though the percentage of income devoted to investment may remain constant, technical progress alone will lead to both forms of substitution. In summary, we may think of technical progress as raising the productivity of labour in three distinct but interrelated steps: (i) the direct effect of technical advances, (ii) increased mechanisation induced by cheaper capital goods, and (iii) higher standards of obsolescence also induced by cheaper capital goods.

4. SUMMARY

1. If investment is required to utilise new methods of production, then the higher is the rate of replacement investment, the more rapidly are new techniques brought into general use.

2. The rate of replacement investment is a function of the relative prices of labour and real investment; or, from the point of view of the economy as a whole, relative supplies of labour and real investment. When real wages are high, standards of obsolescence are high, and a high level of replacement investment ensures rapid adjustment to new methods; conversely, when real wages are low, the capital stock is adjusted slowly to new methods and average productivity is lower.

3. This relationship may be regarded as an extension of the marginal productivity approach where not only the degree of mechanisation of best-practice techniques, but also the rapidity of adjustment to such techniques, depends upon the relative prices of labour and real investment.

4. The gap between actual and potential technical progress is not therefore a reflection of economic 'efficiency', but arises out of basic characteristics of an economy as reflected in standards of obsolescence. This finding is relevant to Anglo-American productivity differences.

CHAPTER VI

PRODUCTIVITY, PRICES AND COSTS

ALTHOUGH the previous chapter has been principally concerned with the application of the simple model to the problem of the utilisation of new techniques, the same framework is useful in analysing price and output movements over time. This question is particularly relevant to the interpretation of the empirical data of Part II. In the following, the problem is examined from a purely theoretical viewpoint. The model is employed to relate long- and short-period conventional marginal criteria, so providing a means of escape from the limitations of purely short-period analysis which assumes zero investment and given techniques, and the limitations of conventional long-period analysis which assumes instantaneous adjustment of the capital stock. By combining both forms of analysis, the movements over time of costs, prices, productivity and output in industries experiencing technical change may be examined. The analysis proceeds in three stages: first, the marginal relationships implicit in the approach of chapter IV are derived; second, these relationships are employed to link conventional long- and short-period analysis; and third, propositions are set out concerning long-run price and output movements.

I. THE MARGINAL RELATIONSHIPS

The first step in considering price and output movements is to derive the formal relationship between prices and costs, which defines the series of temporary equilibria reached after each round of improvement in best-practice techniques. The plant, or plants, with the highest unit operating costs (*BF* in Fig. 6, p. 59) are on the margin of obsolescence, and their output may be regarded as marginal to that of the industry. But, from another point of view, the newly constructed plant, the output of which just proved sufficient to remove the possibility of super-normal profits, is also a marginal plant (that is, the plant with unit total costs of *AD* in Fig. 6). In this sense there are two long-run margins of output of an industry: the margin at the front of the capital stock and the margin at the rear. These dual margins arise because the output of the industry may change either through adding new best-practice capacity, or by scrapping (or not scrapping) existing capacity. The important difference, however, between these two margins is the relevant cost concepts; for the forward margin total costs are relevant, while for the rearward margin only operating costs are significant. Thus the formal condition for such an equilibrium is:

Price = best-practice unit total costs = unit operating costs of plants on the margin of obsolescence,

or, more generally,

price = total costs of marginal new capacity = operating costs of marginal existing capacity.[1]

This condition, which is fundamental to the analysis, provides a link between conventional long- and short-period analysis. The first part of the condition expresses the condition for long-period equilibrium, marginal total costs equal price. But since only newly constructed plants and not the industry as a whole is in long-period equilibrium, to this must be added the short-term condition, marginal operating costs equal price. These two conditions are related by the condition for replacement: that unit total costs of marginal new plants equal unit operating costs of marginal existing plants. This condition provides the link between the past and the present—between the inherited capital stock where short-term analysis is relevant, and marginal additions or replacements to the capital stock where long-period analysis is appropriate.

This formal statement requires qualification for both very young and very old industries. An industry may be so recently established that it has no capacity which is sufficiently outmoded for operating costs to equal price; in such cases only the first part of the condition is relevant. At the other extreme, an industry may have so much excess capacity that replacement of existing plants is not profitable and, in this case, only the condition that unit operating costs of marginal existing capacity are equal to price is relevant.

These marginal relationships can be expressed in terms of demand and supply curves. A rather clumsy construction is necessitated by the restriction of two dimensions but, even so, the diagram is useful to illustrate the interaction between conventional long- and short-period supply curves. Fig. 9 is built up by considering the supply curve of an industry with respect to both expansion and contraction of output. DD' is the demand curve for the product of the industry; this is assumed to remain constant. We begin from an equilibrium at the price P_1 and output OA which has followed the previous period's improvement in

---

[1] It is at this point that the ambiguities associated with alternative depreciation methods and the concept of total costs are important. For the sense in which total costs of a new plant are relevant to price determination is that of operating costs plus the surplus (or gross trading margin) required in the first years of its operation. This in turn depends upon the expected future behaviour of costs and prices; for if price is expected to fall relative to operating costs as the plant becomes outmoded, it is appropriate to require a large gross trading margin in the first years of operation in order to offset the subsequent lower gross trading margin. More precisely, the total gross trading margin in the first year of the new plant's operation (S_n) may be defined as that which satisfies the condition for investment, that is, S_n is defined by the condition

$$\int_{t=n}^{t=n+l} Se^{-rt}dt = I,$$

where n to $n+l$ is the expected future life of the plant, G present and expected future gross margin having regard to expected cost and price movements, $r =$ the interest/profit rate, and $I =$ the investment outlay. If s_n is defined as the gross margin (or capital costs) per unit of output 'required' in the first year of operation, and v_n as the operating costs in the first year of operation, then total costs per unit of the new plant is $s_n + v_n$ which, in equilibrium, is the price plus the operating costs of the marginal existing plant. All references to new plants earning 'normal profits' must be understood in this sense.

best-practice methods. New best-practice plants have been constructed until there are no super-normal profits and existing plants whose operating costs exceed price have been abandoned or replaced. To draw the supply curve one must ask how output would change if price were lower or higher. If price were lower, the output from existing plants would be less. Neglecting stocks and remembering the simplifying assumption that plants have L-shaped cost curves, this reduction in output would be achieved by closing down existing plants. The first plant to be closed down would be the one with the highest operating costs;

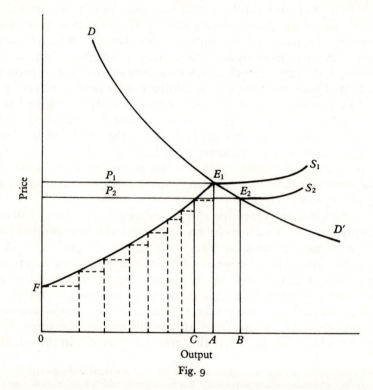

Fig. 9

if price were still lower, the plant with the next highest operating costs would close down; and so on until we come to the modern plants that have just been built. In other words, the supply curve to the left of the present output, that is, FE_1, is determined solely by operating costs. Its shape corresponds to that of our block diagram and is determined by past events—past rates of year-to-year savings in operating costs of new best-practice techniques, and the past rates of construction of modern plants. Fluctuations in past gross investment are embedded in this part of the supply curve; for example, in most industries the curve appropriate to 1929 would have a very different shape to that of 1939.

To draw the supply curve beyond E_1, one must ask how output would respond if price were to rise fractionally. Since to expand output, given the past, is only possible by building new modern plants, price must be sufficient to cover not only operating costs but total costs, and thus the shape of the curve $E_1 S_1$ reflects current best-practice total costs. In terms of our partial assumptions there is no reason why this curve should either rise or fall; but if, for example, the supply of factors is not elastic, or there are external dis-economies of scale to the industry, the curve would tend to rise. This part of the supply curve bears no direct relation to the past and, in fact, approximates a portion of the conventional long-period supply curve.[1] The reason for this change in the nature of a supply curve at present capacity output is that, wherever fixed capital equipment is involved, the technical conditions and costs relevant to an expansion of output are of a quite different character to those relevant to a contraction of output.

This supply curve applies to only one time period. In the next time period a new best-practice technique becomes available and initially reflects itself in a new supply curve for additional capacity, S_2, which by virtue of the savings in total costs lies below S_1. We can now trace the series of reactions to this new supply curve. Output will be expanded to OB and price will fall to P_2; this is necessary to ensure that the new best-practice plants earn only normal profits.[2] Simultaneously, some of the more outmoded existing plants are rendered obsolete and are either voluntarily replaced because their operating costs exceed the new best-practice total costs, or are forced into disuse by the lower selling price. The total amount of best-practice capacity constructed is CB, of which AC effectively replaces the capacity rendered obsolete, and AB is a net addition to the output of the industry. To prepare for the next round of improvements in best-practice techniques the part of the old supply curve under OC must be moved so that it is adjacent to the demand curve at the point where S_2 intersects, while the operating costs of the newly constructed modern plants form the lowest part of the new supply curve. Then, with another improvement in technique the process is ready to begin all over again. If we think of this process as continuous, each improvement in best-practice techniques will lead to a series of points E_1, E_2, E_3, ..., etc., each of which is an equilibrium in the sense that best-practice total costs equal price, and the replacement conditions are satisfied. These points trace out the time-path of output and price, and so enable both short- and long-period supply conditions to be related to the movements of price and output. Before making this step, it is advisable to indicate the way in which the additional complications that arise out of variations in capacity working may be introduced into the analysis.

---

[1] For the purpose of the diagram one must assume that the act of building new plants is timeless, that is, a zero gestation period. For, if we allow time to creep in here, both best-practice techniques and the supply curve to the left of E_1 will change.

[2] In the sense defined in the footnote on p. 75.

2. VARIATIONS IN CAPACITY WORKING

In order to introduce this complication, one should first consider its relationship to the condition for scrapping a plant. The key consideration is whether or not minimum average operating costs lie at normal capacity. If so, the condition that plants are scrapped when price equals unit operating costs needs no modification. In other cases, however, it may be possible to extend the life of a plant by working below capacity where average operating costs are less. To include such cases one must recast the condition for abandoning a plant. Following Pigou,[1] a more general condition may be set out as follows: price = marginal operating costs = average operating costs. This condition ensures that average operating costs are at a minimum so that no matter whether output is increased or decreased the plant is incapable of earning a surplus. The

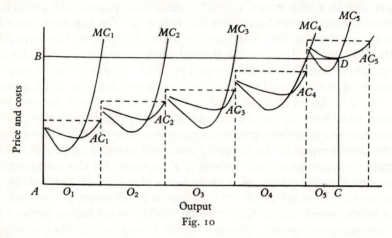

Fig. 10

increased generality of this condition, together with the fact that plants within the margin of obsolescence may depart from their normal capacity output, introduces a number of additional complications into the simplified block diagram. Fig. 10 illustrates these complications by superimposing average (AC) and marginal (MC) curves of short-period operating costs upon each block of output.

Plants in groups one to four are within the margin of obsolescence and operate at points where their marginal operating costs equal price. Plants in group one are best-practice plants where total costs, AB, equal price in the long-period sense. Plants in group five have just reached the stage where, even after reducing output below normal capacity, they cannot earn a surplus. Here price equals both average and marginal operating costs, and thus such plants are at the margin of obsolescence.

This diagram is, of course, similar to that employed to relate the supply curve of an industry to the cost curves of individual firms which earn rents.[2] In this context, however, the rents are not permanent rents

---

[1] *Economics of Welfare*, 1st ed. (London, 1920), p. 165.
[2] For example, by Boulding, *Economic Analysis* (revised edition), p. 480.

but quasi-rents arising out of the various stages in the progression towards obsolescence. Our previous analysis enables the level of these cost curves to be related to past events—past rates of improvement in best-practice techniques and past rates of gross investment.

The parallel modification to the supply and demand diagram (Fig. 11) is to draw the supply curve to the left of the demand curve, the range E_1F, as a true short-period industry supply curve which reflects not only the closing down of existing plants but also variations in capacity working. Then the equilibrium point E_1 will have the characteristic that in all senses marginal costs equal price: price = marginal total costs of new capacity = marginal operating costs of all existing plants = average operating costs of marginal existing plants. This is an equilibrium in the sense that the industry is adjusted to present demand conditions, present best-practice techniques, and the present stock of capital equipment which it has inherited from the past. Best-practice plants can only earn normal profits, all existing plants operate at the most advantageous points on their short-period cost curves, and the replacement and abandonment conditions are satisfied.

3. PRICE MOVEMENTS

Continuous change in best-practice techniques leads to a series of such equilibrium points. Since these points represent equilibria with respect to both present and inherited conditions, they trace out the time-path of output and price. In determining the trend of price movements it is best-practice costs which are important. So long as there are entre-preneurs able and willing to build new best-practice plants, selling prices must move *pari passu* with best-practice costs—apart from short-term aberrations due to gestation periods, expectations and inertia. Operating costs of existing plants are much less important; rather than determining price they are largely price-determined (at least for partial analysis). In this context, the analogy with land is misleading. Because it is possible, in effect, to add to the most fertile land—the equivalent of plants embodying best-practice techniques—the cost of doing so (best-practice capital costs) and the costs of farming this land (best-practice operating costs), determine price and thus the margin of cultivation, rather than price and the margin of cultivation being mutually determining as they must be when the quantity of land is fixed. The closest analogy is the development of agriculture in the United States where the price of corn was determined by the costs of opening up and farming the fertile lands of the Middle West, rather than by the costs of production on the marginal infertile land of New England. In this sense the operating costs of existing plants play a passive role in determining price movements.

This is an interesting result for it indicates that the time-path of price and output can be approximated by a series of long-period equilibrium points of comparative statics, *despite* the fact that the industry is never in long-period equilibrium. The reason for this apparent paradox is, of course, that the marginal new plants at the forward margin of the industry's capital stock are in long-period equilibrium, and since it is their costs which determine price, it does not matter that the remaining part of the industry's output is produced by plants which are not in long-period equilibrium. Even if these plants were transformed into best-practice plants with the same capacity-output, so that the whole industry was in long-term equilibrium, the selling price and output of the industry would be unchanged. It is this paradox which makes it possible to say, quite simply, that price movements in a competitive industry are determined by changes in best-practice costs. These, in turn, depend upon: (i) movements of factor prices, and (ii) rates of technical advance—our measure T of chapter III. In a broadly competitive economy, where factor prices tend to equality in all industries, it will, accordingly, be relative rates of technical advance which dominate changes in relative prices. Industries close to the most rapidly expanding areas of technical knowledge—such as chemicals, artificial fibres, electricity and aircraft—will have rapidly falling relative best-practice costs, and thus rapidly falling relative prices. On the other hand, less fortunate industries where the pace of technical advance is much slower —coal, textiles, leather goods, shipbuilding, etc.—have few opportunities for reducing best-practice costs and thus their relative prices tend to rise. The importance of such inter-industry differences in the pace of technical advance on the structure of relative prices will become apparent when we come to examine empirical data in Part II.[1]

4. OUTPUT MOVEMENTS

Although price movements are closely linked with rates of improvement in best-practice techniques, output movements reflect in addition the influence of demand. This is illustrated by Fig. 11 where the effect on output of a new best-practice technique (represented by the movement from S_1 to S_2) is compared for three cases: (i) a high price elasticity, (ii) a low price elasticity, and (iii) a shift in demand.

It can readily be seen that the greater is the price elasticity, the greater is the net expansion of output in each period before an equilibrium is achieved. Demand elasticity has no effect on the amount of new capacity devoted to replacement; in all cases BA remains constant. Rather it is the capacity devoted to expanding output which is sensitive to demand. Where the demand curve shifts because of increases in real income, population increase, other prices, etc., expansion of output is similarly favoured. Taking all these considerations together, we may simply speak of demand conditions favourable to expansion of output. Then, if we compare two industries both experiencing the same rate of improvement in best-practice techniques, even though their price movements may be similar, the industry with the most favourable demand conditions will experience the most rapid rate of increase in

---

[1] Chapter x and chapter xi.

output. Thus, the changing pattern of relative prices, which arises out of inter-industry differences in rates of improvement in best-practice techniques, may lead to quite a different pattern of output movements. How far this possibility is realised is a question that will be examined in Part II.[1]

Such differences in the rate of expansion of output lead to an interesting side relation with productivity movements. We have seen that the average output per head of the industry as a whole is a weighted average, in which the weights are the output represented by each period's best-practice plants. By definition, an expanding industry is

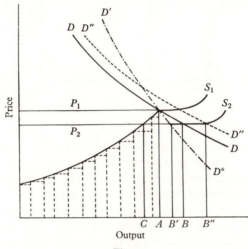

Fig. 11

constructing new modern capacity at a faster rate than existing capacity is being replaced. This leads to a concentration of the total output of the industry into relatively modern plants, and increases the weight given to such plants in assessing the average output per head of the industry as a whole. Conversely, a declining industry has a high proportion of its output concentrated in older plants, and average output per head is lower. Fig. 12 illustrates this effect by comparing the cross-section curves of an expanding and declining industry. Both have the same range between the unit labour content of best-practice and obsolete plants, but the position of average unit labour content is influenced by the distribution of output.

This distributive effect does not influence either the best-practice margin or the margin of obsolescence, and thus has no direct effect on price and output. Moreover, except where industries are declining absolutely, substantial variations in the rate of growth of output are required to induce small differences in industry-wide output per head. The reason is that this effect is dependent solely on the relative weighting of different age-groups of plants and, as with all such weighted averages, the average is relatively insensitive to changes in the weights alone.

[1] Chapter x, p. 122.

In summary, industries with rapid rates of improvement in best-practice techniques may be expected to record high rates of increase in labour productivity for two reasons: (i) the direct effect of a rapid succession of new techniques which save labour, and (ii) the less important distribution effect which follows upon expanding output induced by rapidly declining relative best-practice costs.

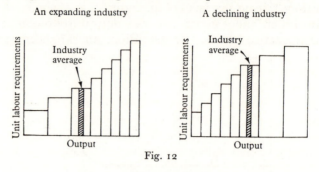

Fig. 12

5. SUMMARY

1. An industry may change its output both by constructing new modern capacity, and by scrapping existing capacity. Price forms the link between these two margins, and the basic relationship is:

Price = total costs of expansion by means of marginal new capacity = operating costs of marginal existing capacity.

This relationship combines conventional long- and short-run equilibrium conditions, linked together by the conditions for replacement and scrapping. 'Total costs' for new capacity must be understood to include the high rate of gross profit expected from a modern plant in its early years of operation.

2. Variations in capacity working may be easily introduced into the model. Their most important effect is to add to the scrapping criterion the condition that short-run marginal costs equal average operating costs in the plant, thereby ensuring that plants are scrapped when they cannot earn a surplus at any level of capacity.

3. New best-practice techniques impinge upon the total costs of marginal new capacity, and lead to an expansion of output, a fall in price, and scrapping or replacement of existing plants. Since it is the total costs of best-practice plants (which approximate the normal concept of long-run costs) the paradox emerges that price and output movements resulting from technical change may be approximated by a series of conventional long-run equilibria even though the industry as a whole is never in long-run equilibrium.

4. Since the average productivity of an industry is a weighted average of the productivity of its component plants, a rapid rate of increase of output tends to raise average productivity through a concentration of output in relatively modern plants; conversely, a contraction of output tends to lower average productivity because of a high proportion of older plants.

CHAPTER VII

A MORE COMPLEX VIEW

THE discussion of the three preceding chapters has been insulated from the complexities of reality by a set of quite restrictive assumptions. This chapter carries out the tedious but necessary task of relaxing the main assumptions. Five problems which have been assumed away in the simple model are considered: the complications which arise out of semi-independent machines within a plant, resale value, technical advances leading to improved products, the influence of non-technical factors on productivity, and the additional problems which arise out of non-competitive market structures. An Appendix to this chapter sets out a number of empirical examples which help to establish the relevance of the theoretical approach and give some idea of the magnitudes involved.

I. MACHINES AND PLANTS

One of the most restrictive assumptions of the simple model is that of indivisible plants. Rarely do we find that scrapping and replacement decisions refer to whole plants; rather, the majority of such decisions deal with individual machines within plants. Because of the possibility of such piecemeal changes, the assumption of an inflexible technique embodied in an indivisible plant bears very little relation to reality except in a small number of special cases. The most useful starting point for a more detailed examination is to consider the additional problems thrown up by the existence of semi-independent machines. Even a very simple plant carries out a number of different processes and operations, and, since techniques of production essentially refer to such processes, the rate of improvement of best-practice techniques may be uneven over the whole range of processes carried on within the plant. For example, in the United States cotton textile industry, the increases in best-practice output per man-hour shown in Table 7 took place between 1910 and 1936 in each of the main processes of the industry.

Table 7 highlights the diversity in rates of improvement in best-practice methods which can occur even within the one industry. Quite apart from changes in the relative prices of different types of machinery, it would clearly be profitable to replace spooling and warping equipment much earlier than spinning machinery. Such possibilities lead to two important problems which have not been considered in the simple model.

The first is the impossibility of determining whether or not an individual machine is obsolete simply by the condition that it earns zero surplus above operating costs. Individual machines (a conveyor belt, for example) do not produce a 'product' which has a price, and

Table 7. *Percentage increases in best-practice output per man-hour by processing departments of the cotton textile industry, United States, 1910–36*

Department	Percentage increase in output per man-hour
Carding	85·1
Spinning	32·2
Spooling and warping	150·0
Slashing and drawing	50·0
Weaving	48·4
Cloth room	11·8

Note: Data refer to the production of carded broadcloth and are based upon engineering studies.

Source: 'Mechanical Changes in the Cotton Textile Industry from 1910 to 1936', by Boris Stern, *Monthly Lab. Rev.* (August 1937), p. 316.

consequently their earnings cannot be calculated, nor the total earnings of the plant allocated to its component machines.[1] This means that the whole question of obsolescence of machines must be approached entirely through the replacement condition: machines are obsolete when the future savings in operating costs which can be achieved by installing a new machine are just sufficient to cover installation cost and earn a normal rate of return. By simply applying this replacement condition, three of the propositions of the previous chapter may be substantiated.

(i) The range of techniques embodied in co-existing equipment carrying out the same process will be such that the difference in unit operating costs of best-practice and obsolete equipment equals the unit capital costs of best-practice equipment. This follows directly from the principle that existing machines are gifts from the past, whereas to employ new methods which require new machines implies a present cost.

(ii) As has been shown, the substitution of labour and capital through the obsolescence of the capital stock is still operative in such circumstances, for the relative prices of labour and capital enter into the replacement condition.

(iii) By the same type of argument, the delay in the use of new techniques is likely to be greatest where the new machinery is highly mechanised.

One mechanism that requires re-examination is the role of price movements in forcing the abandonment of obsolete equipment. In the case of complete plants, we have seen that the entrepreneur who disregards his self-interest and does not replace his plant at the appropriate date is forced to do so by the lower prices which result from the actions of his competitors. This mechanism is not operative in the case of individual machines. Even though it may be in the entrepreneur's best

---

[1] One cannot calculate the surplus of a machine by asking how much would the surplus of the plant be reduced if the machine were abandoned, for in many cases where the machine carries out a key process, the surplus of the plant would be zero.

interest to replace obsolete machinery,[1] if he does not choose to do so because of ignorance, inertia, or lack of finance, then there is no external pressure to abandon the machinery so long as the plant as a whole is earning a surplus. As a result, price movements cannot be regarded as directly forcing the abandonment of obsolete items of equipment. They only have a long-run disciplinary effect; the entrepreneur who for one reason or another neglects to replace obsolete equipment runs the danger of being forced to abandon his whole plant.

The second problem caused by the existence of semi-independent machines is the fact of complementarity between different items of equipment, or to use Professor Frankel's term 'inter-relatedness'.[2] This arises out of the difficulties which are inherent in attempting to introduce modern equipment into a plant composed of older complementary equipment. For example, modernisation in the United Kingdom cotton industry has been hampered by the 'unsuitability of many sheds for highly mechanised equipment, particularly with respect to pillar-spacing, layout of departments and interior shed conditions such as lighting, driving floors, etc.'.[3] Such inadequacy of existing buildings for modern methods is a simple but extremely common form of technical complementarity.[4] The extent and importance of complementarity probably varies widely between one industry and another. In the light metal-fabricating trades much equipment is relatively independent; there are few difficulties in replacing one lathe with another. Where equipment is of the more structural type, as in the steel, coke and chemical industries, the degree of complementarity is probably much greater, and consequently the problem of achieving an harmonious balance between equipment embodying different levels of technique is more acute.[5]

The importance of such complementarity lies in the fact that a modern machine may have higher operating costs or a greater installation cost when installed in an older plant than the same machine in a completely modern plant. For example, higher operating costs per unit may result if the new machine is forced to operate at a slower speed than necessary because of the existence of older complementary equipment.

[1] It could be argued that consideration of such cases is redundant, since they imply that entrepreneurs act against their best interests. Two very practical considerations, however, give such cases relevance: first, the sheer difficulty of obtaining the data to make correct replacement decisions and, secondly, the uncertainties involved. As a result correct replacement decisions are very difficult. In practice, replacement is based upon rule of thumb criteria, such as a 'four-year write-off period' or, even worse, nothing more substantial than hunches. For a discussion of replacement decisions in practice see the excellent volume by George Terborough, *Dynamic Equipment Policy* (New York, 1949).

[2] Marvin Frankel, 'Obsolescence and Technological Change', *Amer. Econ. Rev.* vol. XLV, no. 3 (June 1955), p. 296.

[3] *Report of the Cotton Textile Mission to the U.S.A.* (H.M.S.O., London, 1944), p. 33. See also the *Jute Working Party Report* (H.M.S.O., London, 1948), p. 40.

[4] This is a common theme in many of the United Kingdom Working Party reports.

[5] The numerical examples of Professor Frankel illustrate how important such complementarity may be, especially when the number of complementary components is large (*op. cit.* p. 299).

Or, a high installation cost may be necessary if new buildings or strengthened floors are required, as in the cotton industry. In general, since complementarity leads to smaller savings in operating costs and greater installation cost, replacement is discouraged and the rate of introduction of new techniques is retarded.

To allow for these very important considerations, the replacement criterion must be further modified. Instead of comparing machines on their individual merits, the comparison must be made in terms of the plant as a whole. The relevant comparison is between the future operating costs of the whole plant if the existing machine were retained, and the future operating costs if the new machine were installed. For replacement to be profitable, the present value of this cost saving must exceed not only the purchase price of the new machine but, in addition, any other special investment outlays associated with installing the new machine. This procedure automatically allows for complementarity; the cost savings are only those which the new machine can achieve in the old plant after allowing for complementarity, and the investment outlay is the total amount required to make the change-over.[1] While the nature of the replacement criterion is unchanged by complementarity, its existence leads to a more stringent test and so increases the difficulties of older plants in keeping abreast of new techniques. In effect, technical complementarity is the bridge between the plant as a whole and its component equipment. Throughout the life of the plant many new techniques may be introduced by replacing existing equipment. But in nearly all cases they will be less effective and more expensive to install than in a completely modern plant. In the extreme case it may be absolutely impossible to use new techniques in conjunction with older equipment; for example, the important case where the superiority of new techniques arises out of newly discovered economies of plant scale. In such circumstances, the analysis in terms of complete plants is applicable. At the other extreme, where there is no complementarity, analysis in terms of machines is adequate, for then a machine has the properties of a plant. In intermediate cases, one must consider both machines and plants; complementarity makes it increasingly difficult to use new equipment in conjunction with older equipment, so that eventually the whole plant must be abandoned or rebuilt.

Because these complications do not affect the principles behind obsolescence, few modifications of substance to the simple model are required. The procedure of placing overmuch significance on the construction date of a plant must be abandoned. Even so, there will still be differences in the operating costs and productivity of plants within the one industry. Completely modern plants employ all new techniques

---

[1] This procedure has one further advantage. It may happen that, by comparing machines individually, replacement is found to be profitable even though the whole plant is likely to be scrapped or replaced shortly. However, if the comparison is made in terms of the effect on the operating costs of the whole plant over its remaining life, this further complication is avoided, for unless the new machine can 'pay for itself' before the plant is scrapped, it will not be installed. In such cases, however, resale value becomes important.

and complementary equipment is in balance. Older plants have higher operating costs and lower productivity both because some of the new methods are not sufficiently improved to displace existing methods, and because complementarity acts to further delay the introduction of new methods. The cross-section diagrams can then be interpreted as an arrangement of plants in rising order of unit operating costs, or unit labour content, whichever is relevant to the problem in hand. Whatever the reasons for such differences, one can still say that the lower limit to costs is set by modern best-practice plants, and the upper limit by price. Between these two extremes all plants range themselves according to what may loosely be called their average degree of outmodedness.

2. SCRAP VALUE AND RESALE VALUE

In the simple model, interest on resale and scrap value in the replacement and scrapping criteria have been neglected as quantitatively unimportant. However, in certain cases they may be significant and it is, therefore, advisable to re-examine this complication.

An important distinction is the value of equipment within an industry, and the value outside the industry. Internal resale value is irrelevant to the analysis, for this reflects future quasi-rents within the industry and has no bearing upon the period the equipment remains in service to influence costs, prices and productivity. What is relevant, however, is external resale value, for this does affect the date when equipment is withdrawn from service. Normally, all equipment has some external resale value—even if only as a source of raw materials (pure scrap value). But equipment which is not specific to particular products may have a resale value considerably above scrap value; for the value of such equipment is determined by the future quasi-rents which can be earned in any avenue of employment in the whole economy. Perhaps the most important case is that of buildings which are frequently not at all specific, and where interest on resale value may be considerable. Also, equipment may have value for purposes quite different to those for which it was originally designed. Terborough has termed such changes in function 'functional degradation'[1]—a progressive decline in the quality of the function performed; for example, the use of factory buildings for storage, the use of obsolete main-line locomotives for shunting; and, outside the industrial field, the degradation of city mansions to tenements.

Quite obviously, such considerations do not affect the principles underlying the model. But they do imply a distinction between obsolescence in particular industries, and obsolescence in the economy as a whole. Equipment is obsolete in a particular industry (or function) when its operating costs plus interest on external resale value exceeds its earnings; but it is only obsolete in the economy as a whole when its operating costs plus interest on pure scrap value exceed its earnings in

[1] *Dynamic Equipment Policy*, chapter II.

any use whatsoever. Frequently the difference is not significant, but the less specific capital equipment is to particular industries, the greater is the likelihood of such a divergence.

3. QUALITY CHANGES AND NEW PRODUCTS

By assuming that technical change may be regarded as lower costs for existing products, the simple model avoids all reference to one of the most important features of new technology: the emergence of new products and improvements to existing ones. In principle, these may be introduced into the model for the distinction between price and output (which forces us to define products) is not fundamental to its operation. Thus, if a new technique produces a superior product (in the eyes of the consumer) with unchanged total costs, new plants will be constructed to produce the product, the gross trading margin of existing plants will fall, and some will be replaced or abandoned. Similarly, the propositions regarding the nature of obsolescence and the role of relative factor prices in the adjustment process are not dependent upon a clear-cut distinction between price and output; for we may state the scrapping criteria in terms of the value of trading receipts and the value of operating costs. But the important consequence of quality changes and new products is that they make difficult a precise definition of terms such as productivity, relative prices, and costs: all become ambiguous since the comparison of different situations must involve a direct appeal to consumers' preferences. This means that it is difficult to state the operation of the model in easily identifiable terms, even though its basic mechanisms are unchanged.

4. NON-TECHNICAL INFLUENCES ON PRODUCTIVITY

The discussion to date has considered only purely technical reasons for inter-plant differences in operating costs and productivity. In practice, of course, a number of other influences are relevant. Differences in the personal skill, effort, intelligence and co-operation of labour may alone lead to substantial inter-plant variations in productivity.[1] Equally, if not more, important are variations in the efficiency of management which are not reflected in the managers' salaries; an efficiently managed firm employing outmoded capital equipment may achieve lower operating costs than a poorly managed firm using modern equipment. Other special advantages, such as a favourable location, access to ancillary services, trade goodwill, etc., may also contribute to inter-plant differences in operating costs and productivity. Barriers to the diffusion of knowledge, especially the patent system, are also relevant in this context. Some plants may employ outmoded methods, not

---

[1] It is probable that worker efficiency is higher in modern plants; workers are more likely to put effect and intelligence into their work in a clean, modern and efficient factory than those employed in older obsolete plants. See Duane Evans, 'Productivity and Human Relations', *Amer. Econ. Rev.* vol. xxxviii, suppl. (May 1947), p. 412.

because replacement is unprofitable, but simply because patent restrictions prevent the use of the best methods. Other restrictions, such as imperfect channels for the diffusion of technical knowledge, ignorance and inertia, may have the same effect.

These qualifications are also relevant to new technical knowledge which does not require specialised capital equipment. If there were no barriers to the diffusion and use of such new techniques, they could be introduced in all plants without delay; an immediate industry-wide reduction in costs and an increase in productivity would result. Price would fall and output would expand; but there would not be any scrapping and replacement which could be attributed to the new knowledge. However, it is extremely unlikely in practice that such new methods would be introduced immediately, and to the extent they are not, inter-plant differences in costs and productivity will result.

All these additional influences on costs and productivity constitute another layer of complication that has to be superimposed upon the simple model. Their most significant effect is to introduce an element of ambiguity into the idea of best-practice costs. These may have to be thought of as the costs of a modern plant exclusive of special advantages which are not available to all firms in the industry—costs after allowance has been made for rents attributable to patent rights, superior management, location, etc. But, irrespective of the definition of best-practice costs at any one time, the essential point is that improving technology leads to a continually improving standard of best-practice costs. Trailing behind this standard is another standard—the minimum degree of efficiency in the use of current factors of production. Price is the link between these two standards; it is determined by best-practice total costs and sets the upper limit for operating costs. Plants whose operating costs rise above this standard must be abandoned, modernised (either wholly or partly), or take steps to improve the efficiency of management and labour.

Moreover, we cannot expect price to be adjusted to best-practice total costs with the speed and precision implied by the simple model. Management is rarely so quick to seize the opportunities of new techniques as the model suggests, so that price may lag behind movements of best-practice costs. In any case, gestation periods and the uncertainties involved in investment and the use of new methods inhibit rapid adjustment. This is particularly the case when the optimum size of plant is large; then, adjustment is likely to proceed by a series of discreet jumps rather than the smooth process implied by the model. Such considerations mean that the analysis has little bearing on short-period movements of costs, prices and productivity, but is more relevant to trend movements where such short-run aberrations decline in importance.

5. NON-COMPETITIVE MARKET SITUATIONS

The final assumption of the simple model which stands in need of re-examination is the assumption of virtually perfect competition. It is also the most difficult to relax. The analysis of the previous chapters raises a host of very difficult questions on the production side of imperfect competition. No attempt is made in this section to present a complete analysis of these problems; the aim is simply to throw out some leading ideas concerning some of the many complications which could arise.

In terms of the simple model, the competitive structure of an industry refers to the distribution of ownership and control. To date, we have assumed that control is sufficiently widespread for the actions of each firm to have a negligible effect on price. The other extreme is where control is centralised, either directly, through subsidiaries, or some form of close association. This is effectively a monopoly situation. Consider how such a monopolist will behave with respect to replacement decisions. If replacement is simply a question of replacing one machine or plant with another so that output is unchanged, the monopolist will employ the same criterion as a producer in a competitive industry: will the flow of savings in operating costs repay the installation cost and earn a normal rate of return?[1] However, when investment and replacement decisions involve changes in output, it is obvious that the monopolist will act differently to the producer under competition. His range of vision includes the industry as a whole, and he knows that to expand output and lower price will reduce the surpluses earned by the existing plants under his control. Consider how a monopolist who maximises profits will behave in such circumstances. As we should expect, the formal relationship between prices and costs in a momentary equilibrium is that unit total costs of the marginal best-practice plant equals marginal revenue which in turn equals the unit operating costs of the marginal existing plant. This may be illustrated by Fig. 13.

As in the case of competition, the diagram portrays a situation where the previous period's round of adjustments has been completed. For outputs less than present output OA, the supply curve, or in the case of monopoly the cost curve, is determined by operating costs; it ranges between the costs of the most modern and the highest cost plant in use. Beyond present output the relevant cost curve relates to total costs of expansion with new capacity. Unlike the competitive case, this change in the nature of the 'supply' curve takes place at the intersection with the marginal revenue curve. Expansion beyond OA would involve a

---

[1] Mrs Robinson (*The Accumulation of Capital*, p. 407) objects to this argument on the grounds that the monopolist may have more profitable investments. But, if the monopolist is a true monopolist and has maximised his profits, at the margin all his investments only earn the competitive rate of return so that the marginal opportunity cost of devoting investment to replacement is equal to the competitive rate of return. Mrs Robinson's argument is only relevant in the case where the monopolist does not fully exploit his monopoly position; this is considered on p. 92.

greater increase in total costs than marginal revenue, while to reduce output by abandoning the highest cost existing plant would reduce costs less than the reduction in revenue. Also, to replace this highest-cost plant with a modern plant would not be justified since its operating costs are less than total best-practice costs. With respect to both output and replacement decisions, this is an equilibrium position for the monopolist.

When new techniques with total costs of C_2 become available the monopolist will increase output to OD by building new capacity of output AD, and will replace the plants producing output AE. Compare

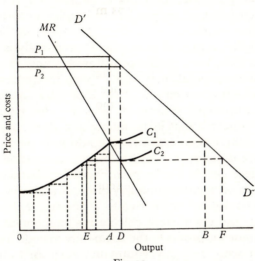

Fig. 13

this with a competitive industry. Output is less and price higher, and a smaller expansion of output with modern capacity takes place. A competitive industry would have increased output by the distance BF; this distance must be greater than AD since the demand curve has a lesser slope than the marginal revenue curve. Only in the extreme case where the elasticity of demand is infinite would the two reactions be identical. Additionally, the monopolist will probably scrap fewer plants, but this is only because in the past he has constructed less of this now obsolete capacity than would have been the case if the industry were competitive. It is important to note that the range of co-existing techniques is no greater under monopoly than competition; in both cases the difference between operating costs of best-practice and obsolete plants is equal to unit capital cost of best-practice techniques.[1] This will be the same in both cases, for, if the monopolist is maximising his profits, the rate of profit on a marginal new plant will be the normal rate of return, rather than the higher average rate of return he achieves from

[1] In the context of monopoly where a small number of plants is probable, indivisibilities are much more likely, so that there may be no plant which is truly on the margin, and adjustment is therefore much more likely to proceed as a series of discreet jumps.

all his operations. In this respect formal analysis reveals no difference in the rate of utilisation of new techniques, nor any reason why a monopolist should scrap outmoded techniques any less rapidly than a producer in a competitive industry. Equally as much as under competition, it is irrational to retain a plant the output of which can be produced at a lower total cost than the operating cost at present being incurred. It is not so much that new techniques are unused, or that obsolete methods remain in use, but rather that the new techniques are employed to produce a smaller output at a higher price than would be the case under competition. New methods that reduce cost make a smaller impact on the price and output structure under monopoly simply because a given reduction in best-practice cost results in a smaller increase in output and a lesser reduction in price.

However, in the context of monopoly formal analysis which assumes profit maximisation may easily prove misleading. There are many reasons why a monopolist may not exploit his position to the full: a desire not to attract attention, a sense of duty (or fear), or simply inertia.[1] The important difference between the monopolist and a competitive producer is that if the monopolist does not wish to replace obsolete plants, there is no external compulsion to do so. The producer in a competitive industry is forced to carry out a rational replacement policy; if he does not do so the plant must be abandoned. A monopolist, because of his higher monopoly price, is under no such pressure; his self-interest is the only incentive to a rational replacement policy.[2] In this respect, the completely calculating monopolist who is determined to maximise his profits to the last penny may do less damage than the monopolist who is simply content to earn an 'adequate' profit. Such a monopolist may plead that he does not abuse his position and point to a 'normal rate of return' on capital as proof. But, his rate of return *may* be 'normal' for the wrong reason. It may be normal, not because output cost and price are as they would be under competition, but because output is less and price higher and, since he is able to employ obsolete methods, costs are also higher. The implication is that rates of return can prove a treacherous guide to whether or not a monopoly position is being exploited. This may even be true of a statutory monopoly—including one which makes losses. The losses may

---

[1] Of course, one of the aims of the monopolist is to perpetuate his monopoly and patents provide one well-known means of achieving this aim. If he can ensure that the best methods available to outsiders are such that they cannot yield normal profits even at the monopoly price, he is completely safe, and the closer he can approach this ideal, the less is the risk of new entrants. For example, in 1938 the Bell Telephone Company held 44% of all long-distance telephone patents. The Commissioner in charge of an inquiry concluded that these were acquired 'not with the intention of use, but to foster a monopoly'. Quoted, along with other examples, in: *Industrial Research and Changing Technology*, National Research Project, *W.P.A.* (Philadelphia, 1940). See also F. L. Vaughan, *The United States Patent System* (Univ. of Oklahoma Press, 1956), chapter VIII.

[2] This situation is analogous to the producer under competition who fails to carry out a rational replacement programme with respect to machines within his plant. The difference lies in the fact that eventually competition penalises the producer by forcing him to abandon his plant whereas the monopolist has much more leeway.

be caused by the use of obsolete equipment that would not be tolerated in a competitive situation.[1]

This argument can be extended to the field of imperfect competition. The devices of imperfect competition—product differentiation, advertising and the emphasis on quality rather than price—may be regarded as attempts to make the fixed capital equipment of the firm mobile, an attempt to produce in a market where competition is less intense. A firm owning only obsolete equipment may endeavour to move away from the undifferentiated market where it cannot earn surpluses, by producing say 'quality' products buttressed with appeals to prestige and the age of the firm.[2] It is not so much that the market imperfections which make this possible lead to high profits, but rather that they allow some profit to be earned rather than none at all. Something of this nature may account for the common case where a number of low-cost large firms compete vigorously on the basis of price for the mass-production market, while a fringe of small high-cost firms employing obsolete methods survive by producing specialities and using anything but price as selling points for their products.

Finally, a brief comment on oligopolistic market structures. The previous discussion suggests a possible reason for the stability of such situations. Like the monopolist, the oligopolist knows that expansion with new capacity will tend to reduce the surpluses of his existing capacity; but, in contrast to the monopolist, some of the burden of lower prices will fall on the existing capacity of his competitors; how much depends upon his share of the market. He also knows that if he expands aggressively with the aim of driving his competitors out of the market, they will continue operations so long as price exceeds operating costs. But to expand output and lower price to this extent may well mean that his new capacity could not earn even normal profits and the surpluses from his own existing capacity would be drastically reduced. In such circumstances, the oligopolist may decide that the cost of gaining control by direct aggression is too great; rather he will attempt to grow relative to his competitors by capturing any increase in the market. This places a premium on being one jump ahead with respect to new techniques, so as to ensure the expansion of output which these allow is achieved by his new capacity rather than that of his competitors.

[1] To take a balanced view of monopoly in relation to new techniques we should consider the view expressed by Schumpeter that monopolistic concerns are at the forefront of industrial research, and that many of the most technically progressive industries have a monopolistic structure. Here it is difficult to distinguish cause from effect. Does industrial research foster monopoly, or does monopoly foster industrial research? I would prefer to leave this as an open question. We can never be sure that such industries would not be even more progressive if they were competitive. For a very useful empirical discussion of this problem see W. Rupert Maclaurin, 'Technological Progress in Some American Industries', Amer. Econ. Rev. suppl. vol. XLIV, no. 2 (May 1954), p. 178.

[2] Schumpeter describes such firms as 'living on the name, connections, quasi-rents and reserves acquired in their youth, decorously dropping into the background, lingering in the fatally deepening dusk of respectable decay' (Business Cycles, vol. I, p. 94).

6. SUMMARY

1. A plant normally carries out a number of processes, each involving semi-independent capital equipment. The possibility of unequal rates of technical advance in individual processes raises two problems. The first is that much greater reliance must be placed on the replacement criterion, since the condition for scrapping—operating costs equal to revenue—is not applicable to individual items of equipment. However, it can be shown that the analysis of obsolescence derived from the simple model is unaffected by such cases. The second problem is that of complementarity, or 'inter-relatedness', between items of equipment. This forms the link between individual machines and the plant as a whole and, because of the difficulty of introducing modern equipment into older plants, restricts the rate of utilisation of new techniques.

2. The exact criterion for scrapping and replacement includes interest on resale value. This must be interpreted as resale value external to the industry (which may be only pure scrap value) since internal resale value does not determine the date at which equipment will cease to operate in the industry. External resale value is important in the cases where capital equipment is versatile (such as buildings) and may imply a distinction between obsolescence in a particular industry (or function) and obsolescence in the economy as a whole.

3. Inter-plant variations in costs and productivity may arise for many reasons apart from those considered in the model: variations in the ability of management and the personal efficiency of labour, barriers to the diffusion of technical knowledge (including the patent system), geographical location, ancillary services, etc. Such considerations must be superimposed upon the model, and they imply that best-practice costs may have to be regarded as costs in a modern plant which does not enjoy special advantages. Moreover, inertia, gestation periods and uncertainties inhibit the exact and precise adjustment to new best-practice techniques pre-supposed by the model. For this reason the analysis is most relevant to trend movements, and not year-to-year movements.

4. Formal analysis of monopolistic markets yields the relationship: marginal revenue = total costs of marginal new capacity = operating costs of marginal existing capacity. This relationship, based on profit-maximisation, reveals no reason for a greater delay in the introduction of new techniques in monopolistic industry compared to competitive industry. However, the important difference is that the monopolist is under no external pressure (that is, other than his own self-interest), to scrap obsolete equipment; while the producer in a competitive industry is forced to do so by the price changes resulting from the actions of his competitors. A corollary to this argument is that the rate of return on capital does not necessarily indicate whether or not a monopoly exists; for a monopolist is free to employ obsolete high-cost methods which would not be tolerated under competition.

APPENDIX TO CHAPTER VII

EVIDENCE RELATING TO THE DELAY IN THE UTILISATION OF NEW TECHNIQUES

Since there is no organised body of data concerning the rate of introduction of new techniques, evidence is necessarily in the form of individual instances from a variety of sources, and so is inadequate to provide a fully representative picture. Even so, the available evidence is striking.

Where labour productivity studies have been carried out by means of direct reporting from individual plants rather than census-type data, the inter-plant variation in output per man-hour can be established. Some of the available evidence from such sources is summarised in Table 8.

Table 8. *Variation in labour content per unit of output in selected industries*

			Man-hours per unit of output			Ratio of range to mean	
Industry, time and place	No. of plants	Unit of output	Mean	Range of all plants	Range of middle 50% of plants	All plants	Middle 50%
Bricks, U.K. 1947	17	1000 bricks	1·36	2·12–0·54	1·75–0·93	1·16	0·61
Houses, U.K. 1948	160	Standard house	3080	4300–2150	3530–2630	0·66	0·29
Men's shoes, U.K. 1949	12	Dozen pairs	9·70	12·34–7·30	11·02–8·53	0·53	0·26
Cement, U.S. 1935	60	100 barrels	46·7	86·0–25·3	57·9–39·3	1·30	0·40
Beet sugar, U.S. 1935	59	Ton of beet sliced	1·46	2·81–0·88	1·98–1·20	1·32	0·53
Sole leather, U.S. 1949	8	1000 lb.	48	—	61–39	—	0·47

Sources: (1) Bricks: *Brickmaking, Labour Requirements*, National Brick Advisory Council (H.M.S.O., 1947).

(2) Houses: *Productivity in Housebuilding*, National Building Studies, Special Report, no. 18 (H.M.S.O., 1950).

(3) Shoes: *The Productivity of Making, Finishing, and Shoe Rooms of Twelve Goodyear Welted Shoe Factories*, A. R. J. Cooper and C. J. Martin, Research Report RR. 106 British Boot, Shoe and Allied Trades Research Association (London, 1948).

(4) Cement: *Mechanisation in the Cement Industry*, Works Progress Administration, National Research Project (Philadelphia, 1939, M-3).

(5) Beet sugar: *Works Progress Administration and NBER* (Philadelphia, 1938, N-1).

(6) Leather: *Bureau of Labor Statistics Productivity Report, Selected Types of Leather 1948–50* (October 1951, Washington).

These figures indicate large variations in the output per man-hour of different plants in the one industry.[1] The differential between the highest and lowest is striking: for bricks the differential is equal to a factor of almost 4, for houses 2, cement 3·5, beet sugar 3, and shoes 1·7. As the model would lead us to expect, this differential is least in the two most labour-intensive industries, shoes and houses.[2]

While such evidence is suggestive, it does not directly support the idea that such differences can be traced to the co-existing techniques in use. More direct evidence for two industries is set out in Table 9.

Table 9. *Age of plant and unit labour requirements*

Beet sugar industry, United States, 1933–5

Construction date	Man-hours per ton
1890–9	2·08
1900–09	1·74
1910–19	1·42
1920–9	1·26

Cement industry, United States, 1935

Construction date	Man-hours per hundred barrels	
	Wet process	Dry process
Before 1906	55·1	54·3
1906–15	44·7	55·4
1916–25	42·5	42·9
1926–30	40·9	33·4

Sources: As for Table 8.

In these two cases variation in age accounts for a considerable part of the overall variation revealed in Table 8. In terms of our schema we would expect this relationship between unit labour requirements and age for two reasons: the plants built in the 1920–9 period would embody almost all new techniques, while older plants would embody only those with savings in operating costs sufficient to meet the replacement criteria and, secondly, technological complimentarity provides greater barriers for the use of new methods in older plants. While these figures refer to only two industries, there are some grounds for regarding them as illustrative of a widespread phenomenon. A spokesman for the Bureau of Labor Statistics writes:

Typically there are wide disparities in productive efficiency among different plants, because of differences in equipment and methods as well as the quality of management, worker efficiency, and other features. Mechanical equip-

---

[1] It is unlikely that much of the variation can be ascribed to quality differences. For houses the unit is a standard council house of defined specifications built under standard conditions, for shoes the survey included adjustments for quality differences, the bricks are wire-cut plastic types, while for beet sugar, cement and leather significant quality differences are unlikely.   [2] Chapter V, p. 71.

ment, especially, varies widely, reflecting differences in the scale of operation, the date of plant construction, and management policy with respect to modernisation.[1]

While this evidence is an opinion, it is an opinion that deserves respect. It is based upon scores of careful investigations and the analysis of confidential reports collected in over half a century of interest in productivity.

A similar suggestion that such differences arise out of the co-existence of techniques of different vintages is to be found in a report on the United Kingdom cement industry.

...and any given works is at any one time part-way through the cycle from up-to-dateness to obsolescence. Hence any investigation at any one time would be bound to reveal differences between the efficiency of one works and another.[2]

In addition to the example of the blast-furnace industry, the magnitude of the differences between best and average practice output per man-hour can be gauged by figures relating to the cotton textile industry that have been prepared for input-output studies. Table 10 compares these two measures for 1946.

Table 10. *Cotton processed per man-hour for best- and average-practice methods in the United States cotton yarn and cloth industry, 1946*

Process	Best-practice (lb.)	Average practice (lb.)	Average as a percentage of best-practice (%)
Picking	985	575	58
Card tending	296	272	98
Drawing frame	493	461	94
Spinning	86	53	61
Doffing	141	115	81
Slashing	979	545	56
Weaving	89	56	63
Loom fixing	151	143	95

Source: Anne P. Grosse, 'The Technological Structure of the Cotton Industry', *Studies in the Structure of the American Economy*, W. W. Leontief and others, p. 140.

As in the case of the blast furnaces, significant differences between average- and best-practice productivities are revealed. In some cases, however, the difference is almost negligible; this could be either because few technical advances had taken place in these processes, or that such operations are predominantly labour-intensive.

Direct evidence of the role of gross investment as the vehicle of new methods of production is provided by Table 11. The figures have been collated from the productivity studies of the Bureau of Labor Statistics.

[1] 'Productivity Changes since 1939', *Monthly Lab. Rev.* (December 1946), p. 2.
[2] *Cement Costs, Report to the Minister of Works* (H.M.S.O., 1947), p. 17.

Table 11. *Increases in output per man-hour by plants classified according to the extent of changes in equipment, methods and plant layout, United States, 1939–48*

(1939 = 100)

Industry	Plants with significant improvements	Plants with no significant changes
Metal-forming machinery	115	94
Mining machinery	111	97
General industrial equipment*	122	90
Selected types of leather	112	102
Household electrical equipment	131	114
Construction machinery†	115	100

Notes: * Covers 1939–47 only.   † Refers to 1945–48 (1945 = 100).

Sources: Derived from reports on man-hours expended per unit of output for the above industries, Bureau of Labor Statistics.

It is significant that where little new equipment was installed output per man-hour rose very little or even fell. This supports the idea that changes in techniques of production are the major determinant of productivity movements. How far such increases in output per man-hour are due to more mechanised methods, the use of more modern techniques, or economies of scale, it is impossible to tell. But, whatever the reason, the installation of new equipment is a necessary condition to bring observed output per man-hour up to best-practice standards.

Evidence relating to the time-lag in the general use of new techniques of production is widespread; two examples are set out below:

1. Despite very considerable advantages of the newer types of jute-processing machinery, new and old types co-exist as the following table indicates:

Table 12. *Types of plant in use in the jute industry, United Kingdom, 1946*

	Number of plants	Number of spindles
New types	9	30,789
Mixed types	19	118,058
Old types	10	36,912

Source: Jute Industry Working Party Report (H.M.S.O., 1948), p. 74.

2. In the United States copper mines, electric locomotives allow a cost saving of 67 %, yet, although first used in the mid-twenties, by 1940 less than a third of the locomotives in use were electric.[1]

Such examples could be multiplied almost indefinitely. H. Jerome's *Mechanisation in Industry* contains a long appendix giving lists of new techniques and the lag in their general use. The Bureau of Labor Statistics sums up its experience in the following words:

The advance in output per man-hour has its origin in technical innovations, but it continues for many years after the new methods are first introduced.

[1] *Technology, Employment, and Output per Man in Copper Mining.* National Research Project, W.P.A. E-12 (Philadelphia, 1940), p. 53.

Since most industrial equipment has a long life and is not scrapped until significant economies can be gained, new methods are not adopted throughout industry as they are introduced, but find acceptance only after a period of years. Thus output per man-hour continues to rise even where there are no new technological developments, as additional plants adopt the most efficient methods.[1]

Finally, two examples of the role played by expansion or contraction of output in the utilisation of new techniques are set out below:

1. The National Research Project study of the United States cement industry summarises the relationship between output per man-hour and output in the following words:

The greatest decline in unit labor requirements occurred during the period 1919–29, which was characterised by a tremendous expansion of the industry's productive capacity. The fifty-one new plants constructed during the period 1919–29, utilising the most advanced techniques and the best equipment available on the market, raised the productive performance of the cement industry.... During the period of expansion more advanced techniques were also frequently adopted by the older plants, especially when they required overhauling and modernisation.[2]

2. On the other hand, the Wool Working Party Report claims: 'The mere fact that the total amount of equipment in use was shrinking rather than expanding tended to limit the pace at which advantage could be taken of technique.'[3]

---

[1] 'Productivity Changes since 1939', *Monthly Lab. Rev.* (December 1946), p. 2.
[2] *Mechanisation in the Cement Industry,* p. 72.
[3] *Wool, Working Party Report* (H.M.S.O., 1948), p. 77.

PART II

CHAPTER VIII

AN INTER-INDUSTRY SURVEY

In this and the following chapters the formal precision of theory is abandoned in favour of the much rougher but equally useful empirical approach. The factual raw material is provided by a statistical investigation into the behaviour of labour productivity, costs, prices, output, wages and employment, in a number of British and American industries. One purpose of these chapters is simply to present the results of this investigation. The second, more ambitious purpose, is an attempt to interpret the results by probing behind them to distinguish the pattern of cause and effect of which they are the product. This involves carrying over as much of the theoretical framework as seems relevant to suggest reasons for the statistical results and to draw out their implications.

For a number of reasons this interpretation can only hope to be suggestive. The most important is the lack of information concerning some of the factors which the theoretical analysis has shown to be important: the rate of technical change, relative factor prices, best-practice productivity, and the competitive structure of various industries. These gaps make interpretation a hazardous procedure so that any implications drawn from the data must be regarded as highly tentative until we have more insight and more information. This is not simply the formal caveat which is relevant to all applied economics but, in my opinion, is the appropriate status of the explanations and implications of the following chapters.

The present chapter briefly indicates the methods and main results of the British survey. To aid the reader who is not interested in statistical technicalities, detailed treatment of methods, sources, sampling questions and error problems has been relegated to appendices.

I. THE UNITED KINGDOM SURVEY

The empirical approach to an understanding of productivity movements is to ask what relationships can in fact be observed between changes in productivity and other economic quantities—to ask questions such as: whether there is any association between changes in productivity and relative prices; what are the empirical relationships between wages and productivity; are changes in capital productivity associated with changes in labour productivity; and so on? An inter-industry survey attempts to gain some insight into these and similar questions by comparing the experience of a number of industries over a given period, in this case the years 1924–50 for the United Kingdom survey, and 1923–50 for the United States. Data for the changes in output per head in each industry can be compared with the movements of other relevant variables, such as prices, wages, costs, output and employment. In this way it is possible to build up a picture of the behaviour of prices, wages, costs, etc., in industries where productivity is increasing rapidly compared to their behaviour in industries where few productivity gains occur.

Such a statistical analysis, based upon Census of Production Reports has been carried out for the following British industries. (Full titles of the trades under each heading are set out in Appendix A.)

coal-mining	cotton (spinning and doubling)
brick and fireclay	jute
glass	hosiery and other knitted goods
cement	leather
coke ovens	boots and shoes
chemicals	cocoa and confectionery
paint and varnish	brewing
matches	spirit distilling
blast furnaces	paper and board
iron and steel	wallpaper
tinplate	rubber manufactures
steel tubes	linoleum
cutlery	brushes and brooms
wire and wire working	electricity generation

These industries do not comprise a randomly selected sample; the choice of industries has been governed solely by the quality of the data available. As will become apparent later in this chapter, there is little point in such a survey if the statistical material is riddled with errors, particularly errors in the estimation of changes in output and output per head. Only those industries qualified for inclusion in the sample where such estimates appeared likely to yield valid results.[1] The sample is admittedly small; but it could only be increased at the risk of greater inaccuracies in the estimates. A sample of twenty-eight is an attempt to strike a balance between the dangers of too small a sample and in-

Table 13. *Coverage of the sample in relation to total of manufacturing, mining and public utilities sectors*

	1924 (%)	1950 (%)
Net output	37·6	32·5
Employment	37·5	29·8

[1] The quality of the volume of output measures was the main deciding factor. Volume measures (at 1935 prices) are published in the 1935 Census report for the years 1924–35. These have been linked with estimates of similar definition for the years 1935–48 prepared by Mr B. C. Brown of the Board of Trade and later published in the *Bulletin of the London and Cambridge Economic Service* (December 1954). Relative freedom from immeasurable quality changes, detailed product classification, and a high degree of coverage have been the main criteria. Other reasons for exclusion are changes in classification, and discrepancies through inconsistent treatment of Northern Ireland in the different censuses. Only industries where Northern Ireland's production is insignificant have been included in the sample.

accurate measures. Even so, as Table 13 indicates, the sample covers approximately 30 % of the industrial sector.

For each of the sample industries estimates have been prepared of the movements between the years 1924, 1930, 1935, 1948 and 1950, of the following quantities:[1]

volume of output	unit labour cost
employment	unit wage cost
output per head	unit materials cost
output per operative	unit gross margin cost
operative earnings	
gross prices	
net prices	

Some explanation of the precise meanings of these measures may be desirable. Volume of output refers to the changes in gross output valued at 1935 prices, that is, a fixed weight volume index.[2] Employment includes both operative and salaried workers. Output per head is the volume of gross output per person employed, including both operatives and salaried staff, while output per operative excludes salaried staff. Although output per man-hour estimates would be preferable, the quality of information on hours of work precludes any such adjustment. However, an examination of the available data suggests that the reduction in hours worked between 1924 and 1950 has been small, and spread evenly over the industrial sector. For the purposes of inter-industry comparisons it is likely that such an omission is not at all serious. Similarly with changes in the age and sex composition; these have been small and would have little effect on the figures. The figure for earnings refers to all wage payments including overtime per operative worker. The estimates of gross price changes refer to prices in the usual sense. They are the implied current weighted indexes of average values obtained by dividing output at current prices by output at 1935 prices. Net price refers to value added per unit of output or, precisely, the value of net output at current prices per unit of volume of output. This is a useful measure of the charges made by an industry for its services in transforming materials to finished goods, or an additional stage in processing. It is effectively selling price less materials costs and is made up of wage, salary and gross margin costs. In this study its measurement is principally of value in relation to certain problems of aggregation,[3] for this is the price that is implicit in aggregate volume of output and output per head measures.

The remaining items refer to the costs making up selling price: unit labour costs are wage and salary payments per unit of output. This has been divided into two components, unit wage cost and unit salary cost.

---

[1] Estimates have also been prepared for the years 1933, 1934, 1937 and 1949. These are less accurate than estimates for other years and have not been used in the following analysis. They are included in the detailed tables in Appendix A.

[2] Details of coverage, etc., of these indices are set out in Appendix A.

[3] See chapter XI, p. 152.

Unit materials cost refers to the outlay on materials and other purchases per unit of output. It includes actual materials for processing, fuels and, for post-war years at least, parts, etc., for repairs and maintenance. Unit gross margin cost is the residual element in price after outlay on materials, wages and salaries have been deducted; it approximates the gross trading profit, or surplus element in price, and includes depreciation allowances, direct taxation, rent, interest, profits, as well as some minor cost items that should properly be included with materials cost.

Although the choice of industries has been governed by the need to ensure some degree of accuracy for these estimates, there is nevertheless the possibility of serious errors. The output series in particular are subject to all the hazards encountered in the measurement of long-period production movements. Index-number biases and quality changes are inescapable sources of serious errors. Moreover, the presence of errors in the output series influences the accuracy of other estimates derived from these figures: output per head (and per operative), unit labour cost, unit materials cost, unit gross margin cost, and the price estimates. Errors of this nature play an important part in subsequent analysis. For these reasons, it is appropriate to regard the estimates simply as indications of the order of magnitude of the changes that have taken place.

2. THE BASIC DATA

Table 14 sets out the most interesting aspect of these estimates, the long-term changes since 1924. The figures are relatives of the movements over the period 1924–50 and, although the weight base is 1935, the comparison is in terms of 1924 = 100 in order to facilitate comparisons with that year. Figures for the quartiles are included to aid inter-industry comparisons.

One feature of Table 14 which may usefully be examined at this stage is the wide diversity in the experience of different industries. This is illustrated by Table 15 which sets out the frequency distributions, standard deviations, and coefficients of variation (standard deviation as a percentage of the mean). Output movements show the greatest diversity: five industries have more than quadrupled output—electricity, rubber, chemicals, cutlery and steel tubes—and six industries have recorded absolute declines—brewing, tinplate, cotton, coal-mining, wallpaper and jute. Employment movements show much less variation. Large increases are rare, and only two industries, electricity and chemicals, have more than doubled their work-forces; the inter-quartile range is 86–143 (1924 = 100). The very considerable variation in movements of output per head, and output per operative, is extremely important; for, as we shall see, this variation is reflected in relative prices. Six industries have more than doubled output per head and five industries have recorded increases less than 25 %. In contrast to movements of output per head and output per operative, earnings

Table 14. *Changes over the period 1924–50 for selected United Kingdom industries*

1924 = 100

Industry ranked according to increases in output	Gross output (1935 prices)	Total employ-ment	Output per head	Output per operative	Earnings per operative	Unit wage cost	Unit salary cost	Unit wage and salary cost	Unit gross margin cost	Unit material cost	Net price	Gross price
1. Electricity generation	1094	351	311	372	170	46	91	56	70	66	64	67
2. Rubber manufactures	568	193	294	302	277	91	286	90	84	151	87	120
3. Chemicals	528	272	194	236	257	109	286	142	143	141	143	142
4. Cutlery	434	140	312	324	237	73	95	77	373	80	147	99
5. Steel tubes	402	167	240	259	282	106	128	110	187	172	136	153
6. Glass (containers and other)	369	174	211	226	259	115	177	123	135	148	128	136
7. Cement	276	116	239	251	266	102	200	120	143	206	150	158
8. Wire and wire working	254	143	178	194	255	131	213	143	170	199	155	184
9. Paper and board	239	138	173	184	269	146	313	162	229	183	196	187
10. Paint and varnish	227	178	128	124	203	141	246	184	184	141	206	207
11. Spirit distilling	201	106	191	205	209	102	188	104	122	175	120	155
12. Iron and steel	198	142	140	152	275	181	289	193	482	199	261	220
13. Brushes and brooms	197	131	151	160	233	145	196	154	291	257	198	228
14. Hosiery and knitted goods	183	119	153	159	255	160	242	172	324	202	230	212
15. Linoleum	176	114	154	184	238	129	381	159	92	218	118	171
16. Cocoa and confectionery	171	86	199	211	250	120	150	128	146	217	136	182
17. Brick and fireclay	158	111	142	147	270	185	265	193	162	244	182	201
18. Coke ovens	137	100	137	165	223	147	426	167	164	274	165	244
19. Blast furnaces	127	104	122	132	260	197	391	213	648	229	307	240
20. Leather	125	112	111	115	231	200	360	225	393	261	304	273
21. Matches	124	79	156	169	217	128	272	150	87	171	107	218
22. Boots and shoes	112	90	125	129	218	181	224	188	313	276	222	253
23. Brewing	97	108	91	93	198	214	346	247	151	254	173	280
24. Tinplate	86	60	144	152	229	150	409	158	362	214	215	214
25. Cotton (spinning and doubling)	83	64	129	133	278	209	437	224	227	324	225	204
26. Coal-mining	73	61	120	124	302	243	399	250	245	280	248	253
27. Wallpaper	72	86	84	82	229	261	418	298	246	254	264	259
28. Jute	65	49	134	140	262	186	478	205	368	324	254	303
Median	175	112	151	160	250	145	265	162	184	206	173	204
Upper quartile	276	143	194	211	266	185	381	193	313	257	225	240
Lower quartile	112	86	128	132	223	109	188	128	143	171	136	155

Sources: Based principally on Census of Production Reports, with additional data from B. C. Brown, 'Industrial Production in 1935 and 1948', *London and Cambridge Economic Bulletin* (December 1954). For details see Appendix A.

Table 15. *Frequency distributions of changes in output, employment, output per head, wages, prices and costs, in twenty-eight United Kingdom industries, 1924–50*

1950 relative to 1924 (1924 = 100)

Number of industries	Output	Output per head	Employ-ment	Earnings per operative	Unit wage cost	Unit salary cost	Unit labour cost	Unit materials cost	Unit gross margin cost	Gross price
Over 550	2	—	—	—	—	—	—	—	1	—
500–549	1	—	—	—	—	—	—	—	—	—
450–499	—	—	—	—	—	1	—	—	1	—
400–449	2	—	1	—	—	—	—	—	—	—
350–399	1	—	—	—	—	4	—	—	4	1
300–349	—	2	1	1	1	4	—	2	2	5
250–299	2	1	—	14	4	2	2	7	1	10
200–249	3	3	—	11	7	4	5	7	4	7
150–199	6	9	4	2	13	5	12	3	6	3
100–149	5	11	14	—	2	4	6	2	5	2
50–99	6	2	7	—	1	1	3	—	4	—
Less than 50	—	—	—	—	—	3	—	—	—	—
Mean	242	170	128	245	150	275	165	202	234	199
Standard deviation	211	61	64	27	52	113	57	40	137	58
Coefficient of variation (%)	87·2	35·7	50·1	10·9	34·7	41·2	34·6	29·5	58·2	29·1

Source: As for Table 14.

movements show a relatively small dispersion; the coefficient of variation is only 10·9 %. Although the absolute dispersion may be important in some contexts, it is important to note that all industries have had much the same experience in respect to earnings movements, despite the very great diversity of experience in all other respects. One consequence of the small dispersion of earnings movements is that inter-industry variations in movements of output per operative have been reflected in movements of unit wage cost. Movements of unit wage cost are the net results of earnings and output per operative movements; and, if the inter-industry variation in earnings movements is small, the inter-variation in movements of output per operative must therefore be reflected in movements of unit wage cost. The very great variations in unit salary cost are largely due to considerable increases in the number of salaried employees in some industries; but, since such employees are normally only a small fraction of the total, this has little effect on unit labour (wage and salary) costs which show almost the same variation as unit wage cost. Movements of unit gross margins also show considerable diversity; but it is possible that the hazardous nature of these estimates (unit gross margins are residual items) may tend to amplify the true diversity. The final point of importance to emerge from Table 15 is that price movements are much less diverse than output movements.

3. THE INTER-INDUSTRY CORRELATION ANALYSIS

Examination of the estimates of Table 14 reveals a common pattern in the experience of different industries. Large increases in output per head are associated with large increases in output, substantial declines in relative costs, and falling prices. This pattern can be made explicit and summarised by the use of correlation analysis. Each industry is treated as an observation, and the movements of the variables correlated with each other—an inter-industry cross-section analysis.[1] A summary of the results is set out in Table 16. In this context, correlation coefficients serve simply as a numerical measure of association.

Table 16 reveals a number of quite sizeable correlation coefficients. The question which must precede any attempt to read economic significance into these results, is whether or not they are statistical freaks of one sort or another. Four possibilities deserve consideration: (i) skewed distributions of the observations which could make the results depend unduly upon extreme cases, (ii) deficiencies in the extent to which the sample is representative, (iii) the ratio form of the correlations, and (iv) errors of measurement which, in the present context, could lead to unduly high coefficients. These questions are considered in detail in Appendices B and C; only a brief summary is set out below (and even this may be omitted by the non-statistical reader).

---

[1] A similar approach has been employed by Solomon Fabricant in his *Employment in Manufacturing* (N.B.E.R., 1940). The results are broadly similar but cover the period 1899–1937, and a larger number of industries.

Table 16. *Product-moment coefficients of correlation with respect to changes in output per head and related quantities: selected United Kingdom industries, 1924–50*

	Volume of output	Output per head	Output per operative	Earnings per operative	Unit wage cost	Unit wage and salary cost	Unit gross margin cost	Unit material cost	Gross price	Net price	Total employment
Volume of output	—	+0·81	+0·86	—	—	—	—	—	−0·84	−0·63	+0·93
Output per head	+0·81	—	—	—	—	−0·91	−0·37	−0·79	−0·88	−0·73	+0·61
Output per operative	+0·86	—	—	−0·09	−0·89	—	−0·37	—	−0·89	−0·75	—
Earnings per operative	—	—	−0·09	—	+0·27	—	—	—	—	+0·80	—
Unit wage cost	—	—	−0·89	+0·27	—	—	+0·78	+0·86	+0·86	—	—
Unit wage and salary cost	—	−0·91	—	—	—	—	+0·39	+0·74	—	—	—
Unit gross margin cost	—	−0·37	−0·37	—	+0·78	+0·39	—	+0·10	+0·45	+0·83	—
Unit material cost	—	−0·79	—	—	+0·86	+0·74	+0·10	—	+0·90	+0·63	—
Gross price	−0·84	−0·88	−0·89	—	+0·86	—	+0·45	+0·90	—	+0·76	—
Net price	−0·63	−0·73	−0·75	+0·80	—	—	+0·83	+0·63	+0·76	—	—
Total employment	+0·93	+0·61	—	—	—	—	—	—	—	—	—

Source: Data from Table 14.

(i) *Skewed distributions.* A glance at Table 15 and the scatter diagrams in the following chapter is sufficient to show that no serious element of skewness is present. Moreover, rank correlation coefficients which are free from this danger yield similar results. Table 16 recalculated in terms of rank coefficients is set out in Appendix A, Table A (5).[1]

(ii) *The sampling problem.* Since the sample is not randomly selected the usual tests are inapplicable, and *ad hoc* methods must be employed. Appendix B compares the characteristics of the sample and the population (the United Kingdom industrial sector) in three respects: employment movements by industries between 1924 and 1950, output movements by industries between 1935 and 1948, and output per head movements by industries between 1935 and 1948. These tests reveal no evidence to suggest that the sample is significantly unrepresentative. There are two additional reasons for confidence in the sample: first, similar results are yielded by a sample of American industries (chapter XIII); and secondly, Fabricant's study of a much wider range of American industries over the years 1899–1937 also reveals a similar pattern of associations. While these tests are reassuring they do not completely dispose of the risk that the statistical results are the product of sampling deficiencies, so that all generalisations based on the sample must be tentative.

(iii) *Correlation of ratios.* Correlation between quantities such as output and output per head involves a ratio form, that is,

x/y correlated with x where x = change in output,
                                             y = change in employment.

Similarly, the correlation between changes in output per head and price is effectively of the form

x/y correlated with z/x where z = the gross value
                                               of output at current prices.

Correlations between such ratios might be 'spurious', in the sense that since x is present in both variables, independently distributed values of x, y and z will tend to produce some degree of correlation[2] (approximately $r = 0.50$). However, in the present context such correlations are not spurious in any economic sense. Consider the simple case of output and output per head. While independently distributed movements of output and output per head would tend to produce some degree of correlation, this is not spurious for the simple reason that output and employment movements are not quantities which would be expected to be independent of each other. The observation that employment and output movements are independently distributed would be an interesting and unexpected observation which has exactly the same significance as the statement that there is some degree of correlation between movements of output and output per head. The

---

[1] P. 184.
[2] See G. U. Yule and M. G. Kendall, *An Introduction to the Theory of Statistics*, 19th ed., p. 330.

same argument applies to the other cases. Independently distributed values of changes in output, employment, and the gross value of output are not to be expected and, if so, this can be expressed by the statement that movements of output per head are correlated with changes in prices. Moreover, in this case the ratio form derives entirely from the methods of estimation. If price movements were derived directly (as with the United States data), rather than by dividing changes in the gross value of output by changes in output, there would be no question of a ratio form. From this discussion it is apparent that the ratio form is irrelevant to the significance of the correlation coefficients of Table 16. We are dealing with quantities where independently distributed values are not to be expected, and correlations which arise in this way are equally as significant as those derived in other ways.[1]

(iv) *Errors of observation.* Normally errors of observation tend to reduce correlation coefficients, but in the present context this is not necessarily so. Almost all the figures in Table 14 are processed figures that have been derived with the aid of the volume of output series. Errors in this series cause complementary errors in other series, and in this way may lead to some degree of spurious correlation. For example, in correlating output with output per head, an upward error in the output series causes an upward error in the output per head series, so that errors alone could cause some degree of spurious correlation. Almost all the coefficients of Table 16 are open to this danger and it is conceivable that the whole table is the result of errors of observation.

This possibility has caused a good deal of concern; index-number ambiguities, quality changes, and changes in classification are virtually inescapable sources of serious errors. The vital question is how large are the errors required to cause a significant degree of spurious correlation? This question is largely unexplored in mathematical statistics and no tests are readily available. However, a mathematical analysis of this type of problem in so far as it concerns the calculations made in the present chapter is given in Appendix C. The treatment is based on a more general study undertaken by Mr F. E. A. Briggs, who has kindly made his results available to the author. For convenience, the results of tests designed in this appendix are set in Table 17. They indicate the manner in which errors of observation affect the more important coefficients.

A comparison between the observed and the 'true' correlation coefficients, for various degrees of error, indicates that the errors need to be extremely large before a significant degree of spuriousness is involved. In fact, for some of the most important correlations in the subsequent interpretation, errors of any magnitude leave the coefficient relatively high. This is even more marked when logarithmic coefficients are employed as a measure of association, for errors of up to 100 % do not cause any significant degree of spuriousness in the more important results.

[1] This point is discussed further in Appendix C, p. 191.

Table 17. *Results of tests to determine the effect of random errors in the estimates of changes in output on selected correlation coefficients*

Variables	Observed correlation coefficient	Estimates of 'true' correlation coefficients when errors range between		
		± 10 %	± 20 %	± 30 %
Output per head and				
(i) Unit wage and salary cost	−0·91	−0·91	−0·92	−0·94
(ii) Gross price	−0·88	−0·88	−0·89	−0·33
(iii) Unit gross margin cost	−0·37	−0·36	−0·33	−0·27
(iv) Unit material cost	−0·79	−0·79	−0·78	−0·77
(v) Output	+0·81	+0·81	+0·82	+0·83
Unit wage and salary cost and				
(i) Gross price	+0·86	+0·84	+0·78	+0·56
(ii) Unit material cost	+0·74	+0·71	+0·61	+0·32
(iii) Unit gross margin cost	+0·39	+0·34	+0·17	−0·38

Apart from these tests, there are two other reasons for believing the degree of spuriousness to be small. First, as the following chapter shows, it is possible to derive the main results independently of correlation analysis by examining the percentage components of each industry's gross value of output in 1924 and 1950. Secondly, the American survey which records similar results has been designed to avoid the worst dangers of spurious coefficients.

4. SUMMARY

1. The empirical analysis is based on a comparison of the experiences of twenty-eight industries. Movements of output, employment, output per head, prices, costs and earnings are compared over the period 1924–50. The interpretive conclusions derived from the analysis should be regarded as highly tentative.

2. The basic data are derived from Census of Production sources. Industries have been chosen on the basis of the reliability of the output measures. The sample of twenty-eight is a compromise between the danger of a small sample, and the danger of inaccurate measures. However, inescapable sources of error (such as quality changes) make it necessary to regard some of the figures simply as indications of the order of magnitude of the changes which have taken place.

3. When expressed as relative movements since 1924, the figures reveal a very great diversity in the experiences of different industries. Output and output per head movements are particularly diverse; so also are cost and price movements. Earnings movements, however, show a relatively small dispersion compared to cost, prices and productivity movements.

4. Cross-section correlation analysis where each industry is treated as an observation reveals sizeable associations between movements of many of the variables. These coefficients appear to reflect underlying real associations even when allowance has been made for the statistical problems of skewed observations, errors of observation and deficiencies in the sample.

CHAPTER IX

CHAPTER IX

THE PATTERN OF INTER-INDUSTRY EXPERIENCE

HAVING examined the purely statistical problems associated with the inter-industry survey, we are now entitled to read some economic significance into the results. The first step, which occupies the major part of this chapter, is to gain an overall impression of the pattern in cost, price and productivity movements which is implied by the coefficients of Table 16. At this stage no attempt is made to go beyond simply reporting the results; the task of explaining and interpreting them is reserved for the following three chapters.

I. WAGES, PRODUCTIVITY AND LABOUR COSTS

Although the correlation coefficients of Table 16 are so highly inter-related that they should properly be treated as a whole, a useful first step is to examine each of the more important associations individually. First, consider the very low correlation between movements of earnings per operative and output per operative.[1] Fig. 14 compares the changes over the years 1924–50; each point on the scatter diagram is one industry.

There is no tendency for greater than average increases in earnings to be associated with greater than average increases in output per operative. In fact, increases in earnings vary relatively little between industries irrespective of the behaviour of output per operative. The average movement (1924 = 100) is 245 and the inter-quartile range is from 229 to 259. This variation is small compared to that of output per operative and implies that increases in earnings have been of a similar order of magnitude in industries which have trebled output per operative—electricity, rubber and cutlery—and industries where output per operative has increased only slightly, or even declined—jute, coal-mining and brewing.

It is important to realise the limited nature of the deductions which may legitimately be drawn from this finding (and from the more positive results reported later in this chapter). The technique of inter-industry cross-section analysis does not enable us to say anything about the relationship between wages in general and labour productivity in general—to claim, for example, that movements in wages are not correlated with movements of output per operative. The average movement of earnings is 245 and the average movement of output per operative is

---

[1] United States data (chapter XIII) yield a correlation coefficient of $+0.22$. Other American investigations are considered on p. 167.

183; and there is nothing in this finding to indicate whether greater or smaller increases in average output per operative would be accompanied by greater or smaller increases in average earnings. Cross-section correlation analysis deals entirely with variations in the experiences of different industries around the mean experience, and all our results refer to such variation. For example, it is conceivable that industries which exceeded the average increase in output per operative would also exceed the average increase in earnings, and vice versa. If this were the case, a positive correlation would be recorded. In fact, the recorded correlation coefficient is near zero, indicating that there is no such

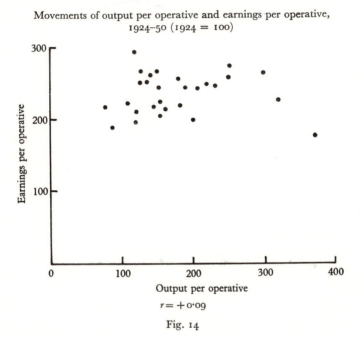

Movements of output per operative and earnings per operative, 1924–50 (1924 = 100)

$r = +0.09$

Fig. 14

systematic relationship between variations of wage and productivity movements around their respective means.

We shall return to this result in later chapters. At the moment it need only be noted that, viewed in the light of the above discussion, the finding that inter-industry movements of earnings and output per operative are uncorrelated is not at all surprising. The market for labour is common to all industries and, over the long run, the movement of wages in each industry is primarily determined by the movements of wages in the economy as a whole. This is supported by the relatively small dispersion of earnings movements.[1] In any case, productivity movements are only one of a number of factors determining the demand for labour in individual industries; output movements are equally important. Moreover,

[1] The coefficient of variation in earnings movements is 10·97 % compared to 37·97 % for output per operative, 29·1 % for prices, 50·1 % for employment and 87·2 % for output movements.

in view of the extreme unevenness of productivity movements, any direct link between wages and productivity in individual industries would soon lead to a hopelessly distorted wage structure. The only circumstances in which there is any reason to expect such a direct relationship is when the increases in labour productivity are directly attributable to characteristics of the labour itself—such as greater skill or effort—or where strong trade unions are successful in capturing a direct share in the 'gains' of higher productivity. Such cases are considered subsequently.[1]

One consequence of the low correlation between movements of earnings and labour productivity is to ensure that the inter-industry variation in productivity movements is reflected in movements of labour costs. Fig. 15 sets out the observed relationship, first, between move-

Movements of output per operative and unit wage cost, 1924–50 (1924 = 100)   Movements of output per head and unit labour cost, 1924–50 (1924 = 100)

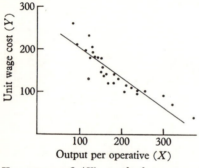

$Y_c = 272\cdot4 - 0\cdot67(X)$; standard error $= 22\cdot2$, $r = -0\cdot89$

$Y_c = 305\cdot3 - 0\cdot82(X)$; standard error $= 23\cdot0$, $r = -0\cdot91$

Fig. 15

ments of output per operative and unit wage cost and, second, between movements of output per head and unit labour cost (unit wage and salary cost).

Between 1924 and 1950, unit wage and labour costs have risen considerably, as a result of the rise in money wages and salaries. The average indices, with 1924 = 100, are 150 and 167 respectively. How far this general increase has been reflected in the wage and labour costs of individual industries has depended on their success in saving labour. Industries which have achieved large increases in output per operative and output per head have been able to offset the increased wages and salaries and so minimise the effects on wage and labour costs. Three industries, electricity, rubber and cutlery, have even achieved absolute reductions in labour costs. Industries with small increases in output per head and output per operative have been forced to accept increases in wage and labour costs which are almost equivalent to the rise in money wages and salaries. The net result has been that inter-industry variations

[1] Chapter xi, p. 153 and chapter xii, pp. 157–9.

in movements of labour productivity have led to a parallel but inverse variation in the inter-industry structure of labour costs.[1]

In summary, these two results suggest that no special advantages have accrued to employees in industries where increases in labour productivity have been the greatest. The initial impact of inter-industry variations in productivity movements has been on labour costs rather than earnings. Whether these cost savings have led to reductions in relative prices, or have been offset by increases in other costs or profits, is a question which the remainder of this chapter attempts to answer. The first step is to examine the relationship between movements of output per head and other costs.

2. LABOUR PRODUCTIVITY AND NON-LABOUR COSTS

Fig. 16 sets out the observed relationship between movements of output per head and unit gross margin cost, and movements of unit labour cost and unit gross margin cost.

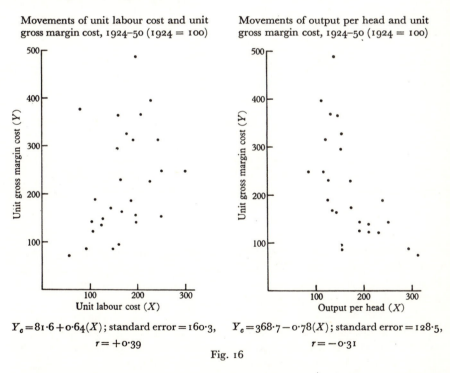

Movements of unit labour cost and unit gross margin cost, 1924–50 (1924 = 100)

Movements of output per head and unit gross margin cost, 1924–50 (1924 = 100)

$Y_e = 81 \cdot 6 + 0 \cdot 64(X)$; standard error $= 160 \cdot 3$,
$r = +0 \cdot 39$

$Y_e = 368 \cdot 7 - 0 \cdot 78(X)$; standard error $= 128 \cdot 5$,
$r = -0 \cdot 31$

Fig. 16

These associations are not high and statistical tests suggest that there is a possibility that they could arise by chance in a sample of industries, even if there were no association over industry as a whole. Even so they are extremely interesting for they suggest that differential savings in

---

[1] Fabricant's results show a rank correlation coefficient of 0·87 between changes in unit man-hour requirements and unit wage cost over the period 1899–1937 (*Employment in Manufacturing*, p. 105).

labour costs resulting from unequal increases in labour productivity have not been offset by increased gross margins. Rather, the tendency is for the differential savings in labour costs to be augmented by differential savings in unit gross margin costs. Those industries with the greatest increases in output per head and the smallest increases in labour costs have tended to increase unit gross margins the least; while industries which have been unsuccessful in saving labour and reducing labour costs have recorded the largest increases in unit gross margins. Why this should be so will be considered in the next chapter. At the moment we need only note that the slight tendency for differential increases in unit gross margin costs to be associated with differential increases in labour costs reinforces the impact of uneven increases in labour productivity upon the inter-industry cost structure.

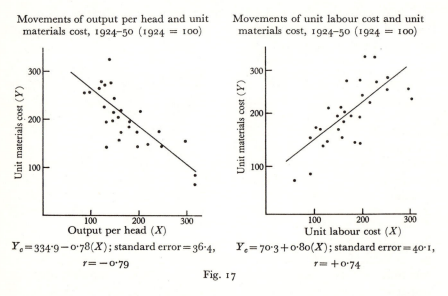

Movements of output per head and unit materials cost, 1924–50 (1924 = 100)

Movements of unit labour cost and unit materials cost, 1924–50 (1924 = 100)

$Y_c = 334 \cdot 9 - 0 \cdot 78(X)$; standard error $= 36 \cdot 4$,
$r = -0 \cdot 79$

$Y_c = 70 \cdot 3 + 0 \cdot 80(X)$; standard error $= 40 \cdot 1$,
$r = +0 \cdot 74$

Fig. 17

A similar pattern is to be observed in the movements of unit materials costs. Fig. 17 illustrates the relationship between changes in output per head and unit materials cost, and the relationship between changes in unit labour cost and unit materials cost.

This result repeats, in a more clear-cut form, the tendency apparent in movements of unit gross margin cost. Differential increases in unit materials cost are directly associated with differential increases in unit labour costs, and inversely associated with differential movements of output per head. Again there is no question of differential savings in labour cost being offset by above-average increases in materials costs; in fact they have been augmented. Industries such as electricity, rubber, chemicals and cutlery have achieved large differential reductions in both unit labour and materials costs—indeed in some cases these have been reduced in money terms, despite the general rise in prices and wages; while less fortunate industries such as cotton, coal, wallpaper and jute have recorded increases in both types of cost approaching two hundred per cent.

Leaving aside the reasons for this association, it is clear that there exists a marked pattern in the behaviour of all costs. In general, the largest increases in labour productivity have accompanied the smallest increases in all costs—not only labour costs but also materials and gross margin costs—while the smallest increases in labour productivity have been associated with the largest increases in all types of cost. It appears, therefore, that unequal movements of labour productivity are closely associated with changes in the inter-industry structure of total costs. Why this should be so is something of a problem. But, whatever the reason, this cost behaviour leads to two further important associations: the correlation between movements of labour productivity and relative prices, and the correlation between changes in labour productivity and output.

3. LABOUR PRODUCTIVITY AND RELATIVE PRICES

Since the sum of labour, materials and gross margin costs is selling price, and all are correlated with movements of labour productivity, price movements must also be correlated with movements of labour productivity. Fig. 18 sets out the actual relationship.

Viewed by itself, this result is quite remarkable for a correlation coefficient of -0.88 suggests that approximately 77 % of changes in relative prices can be explained (in a purely statistical sense) by differential movements of labour productivity.[1] The analysis of costs suggests that this result is largely a reflection of the phenomenon whereby all costs tend to decline as labour productivity increases. Because industries such as electricity, rubber and chemicals have been able to achieve considerable reductions in unit labour, materials and gross margin costs, their relative prices have fallen at the same time as their relative labour productivity has increased. Industries with much smaller increases in labour productivity, such as cotton, coal and wall-paper, have recorded relatively large increases in all costs, and consequently their relative prices have risen.

This result, which is one of the most significant to emerge from the survey, leads to the paradoxical situation where changes in relative prices accompanying increases in labour productivity are much greater than those made possible simply by saving labour. If labour alone were saved the maximum reduction in relative prices would be equal to the saving in labour costs. However, the regression coefficient approaches unity (-0.84); this implies that, on average, a differential increase in labour productivity of 10 % leads to an 8 or 9 % reduction in relative prices. This is simply not possible if labour alone were saved; for labour

---

[1] The American data (chapter XIII, p. 168) yield a correlation coefficient of -0.76 between changes in output per man-hour and wholesale prices. This result is free from any dangers of spurious correlation.

costs are only a fraction of price—at best we could expect a reduction of 3 or 4 %. Moreover, since labour costs are a widely varying fraction of price, a given differential increase in labour productivity allows very different proportionate price reductions in different industries; for example, a 10 % saving in labour costs makes possible a much greater price reduction in the coal industry, where labour costs exceed 60 % of price, than in the coke industry, where labour costs comprise only 10 % of price. For this reason the high correlation coefficient, as well as the regression coefficient, cannot be explained by savings in labour alone. The formal explanation of this apparent paradox is, of course,

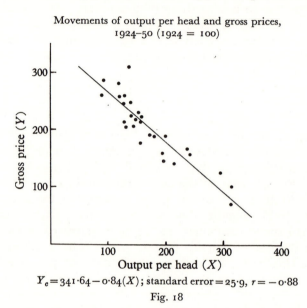

Movements of output per head and gross prices, 1924–50 (1924 = 100)

$Y_c = 341.64 - 0.84(X)$; standard error $= 25.9$, $r = -0.88$

Fig. 18

the behaviour of non-labour costs: differential reductions in unit materials and unit gross margin cost have accompanied differential increases in labour productivity and made possible the high inverse correlation between movements of prices and labour productivity.

A second means of considering this relationship is through the relative shares of the gross value of output. Table 18 sets out the percentage break-up of the gross value of output in 1924 and 1950 for each of the twenty-eight industries. These percentages apply equally to the components of selling price, that is, gross value per unit of output.

These percentages do not vary greatly considering the extremely uneven increases in labour productivity which have taken place. Moreover, there is no evidence of any systematic relationship between changes in shares and movements of labour productivity; the correlation coefficient between changes in shares of wages and movements of output per head is only -0.11. Since each type of cost has maintained a broadly constant relationship with price, it follows that their movements between 1924 and 1950 have been of a similar magnitude; dispropor-

Table 18. *Percentage components of gross value of output 1924 and 1950. Selected United Kingdom industries*

Industry		Materials (%)	Wages and salaries (%)	Gross margins (%)	Industry		Materials (%)	Wages and salaries (%)	Gross margins (%)
Coal-mining	1950	18·3	65·5	16·2	Cotton, etc.	1950	73·5	13·1	13·4
	1924	16·5	66·7	16·8		1924	76·0	11·9	12·1
Brick and fireclay	1950	37·5	42·3	20·2	Jute	1950	73·6	14·2	12·2
	1924	31·0	44·2	24·8		1924	69·2	21·2	9·6
Glass	1950	40·7	34·2	25·1	Hosiery and	1950	57·8	18·2	24·0
	1924	38·3	38·2	23·5	knitted goods	1924	64·2	21·3	14·5
Cement	1950	55·5	14·6	29·9	Leather	1950	70·8	11·5	17·7
	1924	42·6	26·2	31·2		1924	73·7	13·9	12·4
Coke ovens	1950	81·0	10·3	8·7	Boots and shoes	1950	61·8	23·5	14·7
	1924	72·0	12·8	15·2		1924	56·5	31·6	11·9
Chemicals	1950	58·3	19·3	22·4	Cocoa, con-	1950	68·4	15·1	16·5
	1924	59·3	18·6	22·1	fectionery	1924	58·3	18·7	23·0
Paint and	1950	62·0	15·9	22·1	Brewing	1950	22·7	60·6	16·7*
varnish	1924	56·7	16·9	26·4		1924	23·1	69·2	7·7
Matches	1950	16·3	8·5	75·2*	Spirit distilling	1950	71·1	7·6	21·3
	1924	20·8	12·3	66·9		1924	63·0	10·1	26·9
Blast furnaces	1950	81·5	10·5	8·0	Paper and	1950	63·1	15·4	21·5
	1924	85·6	10·9	3·5	board	1924	64·9	17·7	17·4
Iron and steel	1950	68·6	17·6	13·8	Wallpaper	1950	47·4	21·4	31·2
	1924	73·2	20·3	6·5		1924	45·0	19·6	35·4
Tinplate	1950	71·6	16·5	11·9	Rubber manu-	1950	64·0	19·5	16·5
	1924	71·7	19·7	8·6	factures	1924	50·9	26·2	22·9
Steel tubes	1950	65·5	18·8	15·7	Linoleum	1950	68·7	15·1	16·2
	1924	61·0	25·5	13·5		1924	53·7	16·1	30·0
Cutlery	1950	31·6	26·8	41·6	Brushes and	1950	56·8	23·2	20·0
	1924	40·5	34·5	25·0	brooms	1924	50·6	30·8	18·6
Wire, etc.	1950	70·5	15·8	13·7	Electricity	1950	41·7	23·7	34·5
	1924	65·0	20·3	14·7	generation	1924	40·8	27·0	32·2

* Includes Excise.

Sources: Census of Production Reports, 1924 and 1950.

tionate movements would lead to substantially changed percentages. Thus the broad tendency for non-labour costs and price to move parallel with labour costs is simply a reflection of the approximate stability of shares. In fact, the whole pattern of results may be viewed as the product of three tendencies, each of which is well known but together lead to these paradoxical results: (i) the marked differences between industries in productivity movements, (ii) the broad tendency for earnings to increase by the same proportion in all industries, and (iii) the approximate stability of shares in the gross value of output. The first two tendencies ensure that uneven movements of labour productivity are reflected in movements of labour costs, while the stability of shares leads to movements of materials costs, gross margin costs and selling price, which are parallel to movements of labour costs.[1] It is clear that any attempt to explain these results must centre around the puzzling problem of why relative shares should change so little in spite of very large increases in labour productivity.

[1] This approach has the advantage that it enables the main results to be substantiated independently of correlation analysis.

4. LABOUR PRODUCTIVITY AND THE STRUCTURE OF
OUTPUT AND EMPLOYMENT

The immediate effect of the changes in relative costs and prices is to induce substantial alterations in the inter-industry output structure. Fig. 19 sets out the relationship between price and output movements; the broken line excludes the extreme observation for the electricity industry, which would otherwise have an excessive influence on the placing of the line.

The relationship, as might be expected, is clearly inverse. Industries with the smallest increases in selling prices have recorded the largest increases in output; and industries with the largest increases in prices

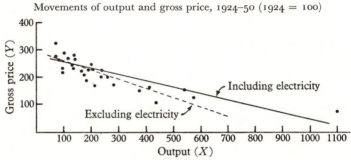

Movements of output and gross price, 1924–50 (1924 = 100)

Including electricity $Y_c = 251 \cdot 1 - 0 \cdot 22(X)$; standard error $= 34 \cdot 7$, $r = -0 \cdot 84$
Excluding electricity $Y_c = 269 \cdot 5 - 0 \cdot 31(X)$; standard error $= 31 \cdot 2$, $r = -0 \cdot 81$

Fig. 19

have recorded the smallest increases in output. As the previous chapter has pointed out, the variation in price movements is substantially less than the variation in output movements.[1] This fact, combined with the low regression coefficient, suggests that, on average, a comparatively small change in relative prices has been accompanied by a significantly greater differential increase in output. One consequence of these disproportionate movements, is that unequal increases in labour productivity have been associated with even greater differences in output movements. This can be seen directly from Fig. 20 which compares the movements of output and output per head. The broken line again excludes the extreme observation for the electricity industry.

Although some industries have achieved small increases in output per head while output has remained stationary, or even declined, the significant increases in output per head have invariably accompanied large increases in output. All industries which have more than doubled output per head have at least doubled output. In general, the relationship is that a 2–3% differential increase in output per head has accompanied a 10% differential increase in output. This much greater variation in output movements is almost certainly due in part to the savings in total

[1] The coefficient of variations for output movements is 87·2% compared to 29·1% for price movements.

·costs which have accompanied increases in labour productivity. They have made possible much greater changes in selling prices than would have occurred if labour costs alone were affected, and consequently have led to considerable changes in output.

Accompanying changes in the structure of output have been parallel changes in the inter-industry employment structure.[1] Fig. 21 relates movements in output per head to changes in employment.

The correlation coefficient is not high so that this result deserves to be treated with some caution.[2] However, it is interesting in relation to discussions of technological unemployment. Whether increased labour productivity in an individual industry tends in itself to expand or contract employment in that industry relative to the average movement

Movements of output and output per head, 1924–50 (1924 = 100)

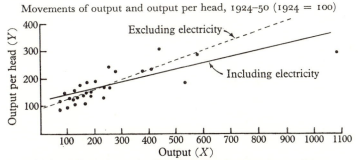

Including electricity $Y_c = 113.3 + 0.23(X)$; standard error $= 35.6$, $r = +0.81$
Excluding electricity $Y_c = 94.4 + 0.34(X)$; standard error $= 31.4$, $r = +0.82$

Fig. 20

depends upon, first, the direct effect of the possibility of producing the same output with less labour and, second, the indirect expansive effect arising out of lower costs. This result suggests that the expansive effect has predominated in the majority of cases: of the ten industries with above-average increases in output per head, above-average increases in employment were recorded in eight; and, of the eighteen industries with below-average increases in output per head, below-average increases in employment were recorded in fifteen. Although there are many exceptions, the general pattern is that a 10 % differential increase in output per head has normally been accompanied by a 6–7 % differential increase in employment. The previous results suggest two reasons for this predominance of the expansive effect: the first is the reductions in total cost which have accompanied increases in labour productivity, and the second is the relatively large differential

[1] The analysis of relationships between movements of output, employment, and output per head, may be summarised by directly correlating output and employment movements. If X = output movement, and Y = employment movement, the regression equation is $Y_c = 61.14 + 0.28 (X)$ $(r = +0.93, \sigma_{ys} = 23.45)$. The form of this regression implies an association between movements of output (X) and output per head (X/Y); and an association between movements of employment (Y) and output per head (X/Y). This approach is free of any danger of spurious correlation arising out of errors.

[2] This association is not duplicated in the American data. The coefficient between increases in output per man-hour and man-hours is only $+0.05$. See p. 169.

output movements which have been associated with changes in relative prices.

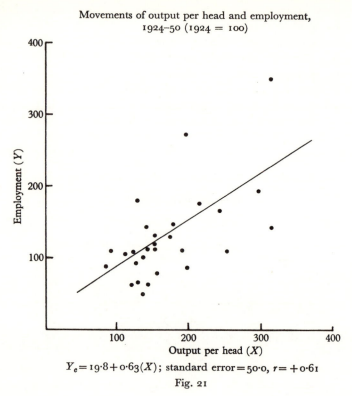

Movements of output per head and employment,
1924–50 (1924 = 100)

$Y_e = 19.8 + 0.63(X)$; standard error $= 50.0$, $r = +0.61$

Fig. 21

5. THE OVERALL PATTERN

This empirical analysis suggests that uneven rates of productivity growth are closely associated with the main features of the inter-industry pattern of growth. Industries which have achieved substantial increases in output per head have, in general, been successful in other respects: their costs have risen the least, the relative prices of their products has fallen, output has expanded greatly, and in most cases employment has increased by more than the average. On the other hand, industries with small increases in output per head are generally declining industries— at least in relative terms. Their costs and selling prices have risen the most, output has increased much less than average (or even fallen), and increases in employment are below average. These general tendencies are illustrated by Fig. 22 which reproduces the data of Table 14 in diagrammatic form. The diagram brings out the parallel variation in many of these variables, and shows that most of the important changes in industrial structure—as far as they are revealed by this sample—are associated with differential movements of labour productivity.

While the pattern of associations is most marked over the whole period 1924–50, the same relationships are present in shorter periods.

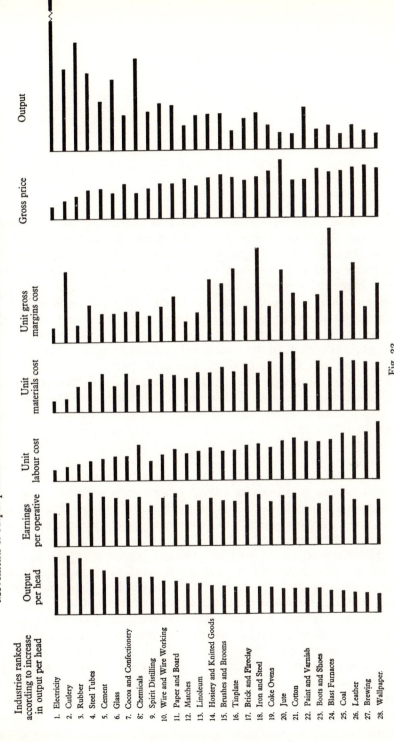

Movements of output per head and related variables. Twenty-eight United Kingdom industries, 1924–50

Fig. 22

Table 19 sets out the more important correlation coefficients for four sub-periods and for 1924–50.[1]

Table 19. *Coefficients of correlation between changes in selected variables within the following periods*

Period	Earnings and output per operative	Output per operative and unit wage cost	Price and output per head	Output and output per head
1924–30	+0·18	−0·80	−0·50	+0·77
1930–35	−0·08	−0·71	−0·75	+0·72
1924–35	+0·04	−0·83	−0·68	+0·67
1935–48	−0·18	−0·71	−0·79	+0·66
1924–50	−0·09	−0·89	−0·88	+0·81

The first two lines refer to short periods of five and six years' duration. Despite the distortions of the depression years, the pattern is similar to that for the whole period 1924–50: movements of output per operative are uncorrelated with earnings movements, but negatively correlated with changes in unit wage cost; movements of output per head are negatively correlated with price movements (but the coefficient is not so high as for the years 1924–50) and positively correlated with output movements. The third and fourth lines set out the coefficients for two longer periods which, in their terminal years at least, avoid some of the distortions of war and depression. The same pattern of associations is again evident, although the coefficients are generally lower than for the whole period 1924–50. This suggests that the forces responsible for these associations, while still effective, are distorted by short-term influences.

6. SUMMARY

1. The inter-industry correlation analysis reveals that unequal increases in labour productivity have not been accompanied by unequal increases in earnings. As a result, their initial impact has been on labour costs, the movements of which are inversely correlated with movements of output per head ($r = -0·91$).

2. There is evidence of a slight tendency ($r = -0·37$) for industries with the greatest increases in output per head to record the smallest increases in unit gross margin cost. This implies that the unequal savings in labour costs referred to above have not been offset by increased gross margins. In fact they have been augmented. Movements of unit material cost show a similar tendency; industries with the largest increases in output per head have recorded the smallest increases in unit material cost, and vice versa ($r = -0·79$). These two results imply that above-average increases in output per head are associated with below-average increases in all costs, not only labour costs but also materials and gross margin costs.

[1] The choice of periods is determined by Census of Production years, 1924, 1930, 1935, 1948.

3. Movements of relative prices and output per head are highly correlated ($r = -0.88$). This is a consequence of the association between movements of output per head and all costs. The nature of the relationship is such that the savings in costs and reductions in relative prices which have accompanied increases in labour productivity are much greater than those directly made possible by saving labour. An alternative means of approach is through the approximate stability in each industry of the shares of labour, gross margins and materials outlays in the gross value of output. Such stability implies equal movements of price and unit labour, materials and gross margin costs; and if movement of unit labour cost are inversely correlated with movements of output per head, then each type of cost and selling price must also be inversely correlated.

4. Industries with the smallest increases in selling prices have recorded the greatest increases in output. Since price and output per head movements are inversely correlated, industries with the greatest increases in output have also recorded the greatest increases in output per head ($r = +0.81$). Also industries with above-average increases in output per head have also normally recorded above-average increases in employment, and vice versa.

5. These results suggest that a large part of the changes in the inter-industry structure of prices, costs, output and employment which have taken place since 1924 have been associated with unequal rates of productivity increase. An examination of shorter periods reveals a similar pattern of results, although the coefficients are rather lower than for the whole period 1924–50.

CHAPTER X

AN EXPLANATORY HYPOTHESIS

THE question which arises naturally from the previous chapter is why such a marked pattern should emerge from the statistical analysis? Quite obviously, powerful mechanisms must be at work to produce a consistent pattern of experience in industries with such diverse technical, economic and institutional backgrounds. This chapter attempts to derive an explanation. It begins from the premise that, because the observed pattern of cost, price and output movements are closely associated with changes in labour productivity, the most appropriate means of seeking for a satisfactory explanatory hypothesis is to consider possible causes of changes in labour productivity. The rationale of this approach is that we should expect costs and prices to behave in different ways depending on the reasons for changes in productivity. For example, if factor substitution were the main cause, we should expect some costs to rise and others to fall; if increased labour efficiency were the dominant influence we should expect only labour costs to be affected, while if improving technology were the major influence a completely different pattern of cost behaviour would be likely. In searching for a satisfactory explanation we can proceed by setting up a number of alternative hypotheses as to the reasons for these changes in labour productivity and then consider how successfully each hypothesis can be matched against the data. This procedure has the advantage that it kills two birds with the one stone: not only can we search for an explanation in this way but, at the same time, extract from the data all information relating to the causes of increased labour productivity. This is an area where our knowledge is so deficient that it is well worth taking some trouble to extract all information which has some bearing on the question, tentative though it may be.

1. THE PERSONAL EFFICIENCY OF LABOUR

Of the many possible causes of increased labour productivity, the simplest and most direct is improved personal efficiency of labour. In the present context the relevant question is how far the pattern of results may be explained simply by attributing the observed increases in labour productivity to more skill, more effort, and more intelligence on the part of labour? At this stage only the immediate and direct effects of increased labour efficiency are under consideration; the role of labour efficiency in making effective increases in productivity directly attributable to other causes is considered in the latter part of this chapter.

An explanation based upon labour efficiency alone meets three difficulties. The first is the very considerable variation between industries in movements of labour productivity. Some industries have trebled their output per head while others have recorded an absolute decline. The hypothesis would explain these differences by uneven improvements in the personal efficiency of labour; labour trebles its input of skill, effort and intelligence in some industries and decreases it in others. While such differences are not inconceivable, one would expect increases in labour efficiency to be spread much more evenly—a general improvement throughout all industries rather than such marked differences.

The second difficulty has been touched upon in the previous chapter, where it was pointed out that there is no reason to expect any correlation between movements of output per head and earnings in individual industries. The one exception is the very special case of this hypothesis which identifies increased output per head with increased labour efficiency. In such circumstances, an association between output per head and earnings would be expected; for, if each worker contributes more 'efficiency units' to production, earnings per worker should rise even though the wage rate per efficiency unit remains unchanged between industries. The simplest case is where labour works longer hours at the same hourly wage rate. However, there is no evidence of any such association at industry level. This can only be reconciled with the hypothesis by assuming the existence of large and systematic imperfections in the labour market. While it is possible that such imperfections do exist, the relatively small dispersion of earnings movements does not support this idea and, in fact, suggests the existence of a semi-unified market for labour.

Finally, this hypothesis cannot explain the phenomenon of simultaneous relative reductions in both labour and non-labour costs in those industries with the greatest increases in labour productivity. Even if one were prepared to allow increased labour efficiency to affect labour costs, there is no reason of substance[1] to expect materials and gross margin costs to be also affected. By the same reasoning, increases in labour efficiency are powerless to explain the association between changes in relative prices and labour productivity. Even if all increases in efficiency were reflected in labour costs, this would be insufficient to explain the equal but inverse movements of relative prices and labour productivity, for labour costs are only a fraction of price.

In summary, we find that the data do not match the hypothesis in three respects: the wide dispersion of labour productivity movements, the lack of any association with earnings and the behaviour of costs— not only labour costs but all costs. These are by no means sufficient grounds for a flat rejection of the hypothesis. It is possible to imagine circumstances where the data and the hypothesis could be reconciled. All that can really be said is that there is nothing in the data to support

---

[1] It could be argued that more efficient labour would lead to economies in the use of materials and better utilisation of capital equipment. However, such savings would be unlikely to be of sufficient magnitude to account for the large savings in materials and gross margin costs.

the view that increased personal efficiency of labour is a dominant immediate cause of increases in labour productivity. And, following on from this, one must draw the conclusion that this hypothesis does not provide a promising basis for an explanation of the data.

2. FACTOR SUBSTITUTION

The classical prescription for increased labour productivity is the substitution of capital for labour. The first step in determining whether such substitution is capable of explaining the data is to formulate the hypothesis with some care. A simplistic form of the hypothesis would be that increases in wages relative to the interest rate and the price of capital goods have induced a transition to more mechanised methods which were already known in 1924. This form of the hypothesis is hardly worth considering. We know that many of the methods in use today were completely unknown in 1924. A form of the hypothesis which deserves much more serious consideration can be derived from the analysis of chapter II.[1] There a distinction was drawn between techniques developed in detail and techniques which could be developed from existing technical knowledge if the necessary economic pressures were present. Thinking in these terms it could be argued that our fundamental technical knowledge has changed very little (the fundamental production function of each industry is substantially unchanged), but that the majority of new methods are simply new designs within the fold of existing knowledge. Pressed by changing relative prices engineers have simply rearranged knowledge into designs which save labour. This hypothesis would imply that much of what we call technical progress is really a sham—a disguised form of factor substitution.

Over the economy as a whole, substitution of this nature, or substitution of a simple form, implies an increase in aggregate labour productivity and a decline in aggregate capital productivity. However, the question which is relevant to an explanation of the data is that of inter-industry difference in productivity movements, and these turn largely on inter-industry variations in the elasticity of substitution. Since the change in relative factor prices which initiates such substitution is general for all industries, the inter-industry variations in productivity movements must arise because of variations in the ease by which capital can be substituted for labour. Consequently, industries with high elasticities would record the largest increases in labour productivity, and industries with low elasticities the smallest increases. Thus the hypothesis would explain the very large variations in movements of labour productivity by differences between industries in the elasticity of substitution.

However, when we attempt to align this explanation with the behaviour of costs certain difficulties arise. Industries with a high elasticity, and thus the largest increases in labour productivity, would on this

---

[1] Pp. 13–16.

hypothesis require the most additional capital and thus their unit capital costs should rise relative to those with low elasticities and small increases in labour productivity. Accordingly, the hypothesis would lead us to expect that the largest increases in labour productivity would be accompanied by the largest increases in capital costs, and vice versa. Similarly, industries with high elasticities which are most successful in substituting capital for labour should record the smallest increases in labour costs and the largest increases in capital costs; and conversely for industries with low elasticities. This implies an inverse association between inter-industry movements of labour and capital costs.

In testing the hypothesis that factor substitution is the dominant element in these movements of labour productivity, the empirical question is then whether or not labour and capital costs do behave in this manner? Unfortunately our statistical data are rather crude for answering this question. They have two main shortcomings. First, factor substitution of this type is largely confined to the moving frontier of each industry's capital stock, and the relevant cost data is consequently that of best-practice plants. The statistical data are an imperfect guide to the movements of best-practice costs for they refer to industry-wide averages which will only record the same movements as best-practice costs if the 'tail' of outmoded plants remains constant relative to best-practice techniques. This requires that there are no significant changes in the working life of equipment over the period or, if so, they are of the same relative proportions in all industries so that the comparative movements of costs in different industries are not affected. Secondly, the statistical measure of unit gross margin cost is a poor approximation to unit capital costs; besides amortisation and interest (or profit), unit gross margins include monopoly profits, taxation,[1] rent, and a number of minor operating costs. However, amortisation and interest are such a sizeable fraction of the total that at least some sympathetic movement between unit capital costs and unit gross margin costs may be expected. These shortcomings make the process of matching theoretical expectations against the statistical data a rather hazardous procedure.

Despite the crudities of the data such a comparison is suggestive, for the observed results are the reverse of those implied by the hypothesis. Those industries with the largest increases in labour productivity have recorded the smallest increases in gross margin costs ($r = -0.37$); not the largest as suggested by the hypothesis. Similarly, instead of a negative correlation between inter-industry movements of labour costs and gross margin costs, the data reveal a tendency towards positive correlation ($r = +0.39$). Even after making all allowances for the

---

[1] Company taxation poses rather a serious problem in this context for it may imply a quite substantial divergence between unit capital costs and unit gross margin costs. However, in the case where the incidence of such taxation is on profits, unit gross margin costs correspond to unit capital costs and the analysis is unaffected; while, if company tax is reflected in prices, the ability of industries to achieve relative reductions in both labour and gross margin costs is even more remarkable.

shortcomings of the figures, this cost behaviour is extremely difficult to reconcile with substitution on a scale sufficient to account for increases in labour productivity of the observed magnitude. How is it possible for industries such as electricity, rubber and cement, to achieve such large differential increases in labour productivity by replacing labour with capital, and at the same time achieve such large differential—and in some cases absolute—reductions in unit gross margin costs?

The behaviour of relative prices presents a similar difficulty for this hypothesis. Essentially, factor substitution involves substituting one type of outlay for another. The net reduction in costs is always much less than the change in either labour costs or capital costs. Thus, we cannot expect large reductions in total costs to accompany increases in labour productivity caused by substitution. But, in fact, very large differential cost reductions have accompanied differential increases in labour productivity; they have even been sufficient to allow relative prices to show an almost parallel variation to inter-industry movements in labour productivity. This makes it impossible to explain by factor substitution not only the behaviour of costs but also the behaviour of prices.

A similar picture emerges when we consider substitution between labour and materials. Instead of finding labour and materials costs moving in opposite directions, there is a marked tendency towards similar movements ($r = +0.78$). And, as before, such substitution cannot account for the large changes in relative prices which have been associated with movements of labour productivity.

In general, it appears that the statistical results give little support to the idea that increases in labour productivity are largely attributable to factor substitution. While this finding must be highly tentative because of the crudities of the data, it does appear certain that any attempt to explain the pattern of results primarily by means of factor substitution would run into many difficulties. It is important, however, to place these doubts in perspective. The analysis only asks the question whether these labour productivity movements can be largely explained by substitution, either of a simple form, or one that involves new designs but little new knowledge. It is quite possible, and indeed likely, that substitution can play a very significant role when coupled with other factors, for example, as a complementary process to improving technical knowledge. Subsequently, it will be shown that our results are quite consistent with a considerable amount of factor substitution taking place simultaneously with improved technology, in the manner indicated in chapter III.

3. TECHNICAL CHANGE

From the progress of the inquiry it is apparent that neither labour efficiency nor factor substitution are likely to provide promising lines of explanation. Both these hypotheses have foundered on the behaviour of costs. Speaking loosely, the increases in labour productivity appear to have been costless; they have not been achieved by bribing labour to greater effort, nor by saving labour at the expense of using more of other factors. This suggests that any satisfactory explanation must be one where savings in labour and labour costs are part of a wider process that extends to all factors of production. Two causes of increased productivity meet this requirement: economies of scale and improved techniques arising out of increasing knowledge.[1] These two sources of increased productivity are difficult to separate for newly discovered economies of scale are a very important aspect of improving technology. In this section all new technical knowledge, including that which leads to scale economies, will be considered. The problem is then to gauge to what extent such new knowledge can provide an adequate explanation of the data.

The hypothesis of improving technology would explain the very great differences in productivity movements between industries by uneven rates of improvement in technical knowledge. Although satisfactory empirical evidence is impossible to obtain, such unevenness does appear to be a characteristic of technical progress; it is implicit in the distinction between technically progressive and stagnant industries. One of the most important reasons for such differences is the uneven impact of the growth of science. Some industries owe their origin to relatively recent scientific advances, and have been subsequently stimulated by the rapid growth of their parent sciences—industries such as chemicals, plastics, artificial fibres and aircraft. At the other extreme are industries whose basic processes relate to fields of scientific advance where progress is much less spectacular—industries such as textiles, leather and coal-mining. This is not to say they are untouched by scientific advance; many advances, such as progress in engineering techniques, apply universally. Even so, such industries are at a disadvantage compared to industries in the centre of scientific progress; here innovations that double productivity are almost a commonplace; in less fortunate industries they are an event.

Related to the character of scientific advance is the question of the age of an industry. An industry may be born around some new scientific principles—steam-power in the eighteenth century and electricity at the end of the nineteenth century, for example. Even though methods and techniques may be very crude it is often economic to begin production almost immediately, because a high price can be charged. Subsequently, there is a great potential for improvements around the same basic principle. A new specialised technology arises and, for a period at least, brings forth a continuous flow of significant improvements and modifications. Something of this sort is going on with respect to nuclear-power generation at this very moment. At any one time, some industries are in this stage of rapid improvement, while others,

---

[1] Increases in the efficiency of management also come into this category, but since one of the main avenues of such improved efficiency is the use of more efficient methods of production, the immediate cause can most usefully be regarded as part of improved technique.

more mature, find significant advances less frequent and less rewarding. For example, between 1850 and 1950 fuel consumption per draw-bar-horsepower of steam locomotives remained constant (although there have been other improvements); while in the more youthful field of electricity generation coal consumption per kilowatt-hour has been reduced from 3·47 lb. in 1908 to 0·09 lb. in 1950.[1] New knowledge of economies of plant scale are important in this context. Young industries have only just begun to explore the possibilities of scale; for a period each new plant is bigger than its predecessors, very often with important economies. In the electricity industry this probing for the limits of scale-economies has extended over half a century and is still not completed: the first turbo-generators had a capacity of a thousand kilowatts; scale progressively increased until units of two hundred thousand kilowatts are in use.[2] Taking all these factors together, it is not unreasonable to expect substantial differences in the impact of improving technology on different industries.

The much more puzzling feature of the results is the tendency for all costs in each industry to record similar movements despite the inter-industry variation in movements of labour costs and labour productivity. This is the central problem facing interpretation and, to be satisfactory, the hypothesis of improving technology must be able to account for this phenomenon.

As a first step, consider the case where improving technology is the only force leading to changed techniques of production. This case is quite unrealistic for, as chapter III has shown, improving technology generates its own pressures for substitution by cheapening capital goods. As a first step, however, it is convenient to exclude temporarily this indirect effect and think only of the direct effects of technical advances within each industry.

In chapter III[3] it has been argued that new technical knowledge by itself tends to save all factors of production. If these arguments are accepted, then the tendency for all costs to fall together can be explained by new techniques which save labour, capital and materials. For example, the substantial differential reductions in labour, materials and gross margin cost of the electricity industry could be explained by new techniques such as faster and larger turbines, economies in steam generation, improved design and layout of power-stations, the use of automatic controls, the reduction in waste power and greater continuity of operation. These advances tend to save *all* factors and so lead to a general reduction in costs. Similarly with other industries; depending upon the rate at which new methods and improvements to existing methods have come forward, economies have been achieved in the use of labour, capital and materials. There is no need to assume that technical advances are invariably of this character for the associations are only broad tendencies. All that is necessary to explain the data is

[1] *A Century of Technology*, ed. by P. Dunsheath (London, 1951), pp. 243 and 125.
[2] *Ibid.* p. 123.   [3] P. 33.

that absolute factor saving should be more important than biases towards uneven factor saving—that the general effect of technical advance (as measured by our measure T) should be more important than the bias effect (D).

While such an explanation is consistent with the data it is logically unacceptable, for it is impossible to conceive of technical advance without factor substitution (except in the unreal case where there are no advances in the capital-goods industries). The observed changes in costs are the net result of both technical advances within each industry and economy-wide substitution; so that, even if the technical advances are largely unbiased, this is inadequate to explain the data. Consequently, the hypothesis must be revised to include uneven rates of technical advance and, superimposed upon this, economy-wide factor substitution. As we have seen in chapter III, the effects of such substitution is to add to the savings in labour realised by technical advance alone, and detract from the savings in capital. But, because this substitution is reflected in the pattern of costs, the question which must now be considered is how far the cost data are consistent with the revised hypothesis.

4. FACTOR SUBSTITUTION: A RECONSIDERATION

Although our initial examination of factor substitution suggested that it is impossible to explain the inter-industry variation in productivity movements solely by substitution, there is nothing in this argument which conflicts with the possibility of substitution having taken place alongside (uneven) technical advance. For example, the finding that industries with the greatest differential reductions in labour costs have also tended to record above-average reductions in gross margin costs is inconsistent with an explanation of increased productivity based solely on factor substitution. But it is quite consistent with factor substitution having taken place. Thus, to take a simple example, there might have been substitution of capital for labour in every industry, on a scale which, taken by itself, would have produced a roughly equal rise in output per head in each industry; and this might have been accompanied by uneven technical progress, which explained the *differential* increases in productivity. So far as costs are concerned, the effect of such factor substitution would be, in each industry, to add to the reduction in labour cost obtained through technical advance and to detract from the saving in gross margin cost so obtained.[1] In such circumstances the industries with the biggest falls in labour cost would, if anything, tend to have also the biggest falls in gross margin cost: at any rate there would be no reason to expect an inverse association between inter-industry movements of labour and gross margin costs, such as one would get if the sole reason for increased labour productivity were factor substitution, operating very unevenly as between industries.

[1] See chapter III, p. 40.

However, the important feature of this cost behaviour which is relevant to our revised hypothesis is that substitution might be expected to lead to unequal cost movements *within each industry*; or, from another viewpoint, to changes in the relative shares of different costs in an industry's total costs. At first sight this appears to imply a contradiction between the data and the hypothesis. For as we have seen, labour, materials and gross margin costs have tended to record similar movements. But it is important to note that this tendency is only a broad one. This is reflected in relative shares. While this stability is quite remarkable in view of the large changes in productivity which have taken place, there are nevertheless quite significant variations. In some industries shares have changed by as much as 12 %, and the average change is of the order of 5 %. In assessing whether the revised hypothesis is consistent with the data, the vital question is therefore whether these changes in share are sufficient to be consistent with a considerable amount of substitution having taken place.

This is an extremely difficult question, and it is only possible to derive some insight into the likely magnitudes by employing a very indirect approach. The extent of changes in shares caused by factor substitution depend upon (i) the magnitude of the change in relative factor prices, and (ii) the elasticity of substitution. The latter is relevant because the change in shares is the product of two opposing influences: as labour becomes dearer relative to capital, labour costs tend to rise relative to capital costs; but when as a result capital is substituted for the dearer labour, the initial change in shares may be either under or over-compensated. When the elasticity of substitution is unity, the two opposing influences exactly counter-balance and shares are unchanged; when the elasticity is less than unity labour costs rise relative to capital costs; and when the elasticity is greater than unity labour costs fall relative to capital costs. Since changes in shares are determined by these two factors—the change in relative factor prices and the elasticity of substitution—by making assumptions about their magnitude we can calculate the resulting change in shares, and in this way gain some insight into the extent of changes in shares likely to be caused by factor substitution. While it is impossible to measure the change in the relative prices of labour and capital between 1924 and 1950 in the United Kingdom, the United States figures suggest that an increase in the costs of employing labour relative to capital of between 50 and 100 % can plausibly be inferred.[1] Taking these two figures we can then calculate the change in shares which would result if elasticities of substitution range between certain values, say zero and 2·0. Table 20 sets out these calculations.[2]

[1] The U.S. figures (chapter III, p. 37) range between an increase of 62 and 128 %. Since productivity appears to increase much less rapidly in the United Kingdom, the range 50–100 % would appear to be the extreme likely figures for the United Kingdom.

[2] These calculations are based on the formula $d\alpha = \alpha\beta(\sigma-1)\,dr/r$, where α and β are relative shares, σ is the elasticity of substitution, and dr/r is the relative change in factor prices. This formula is derived from the definition of σ. See Appendix A, p. 185.

Table 20. *The magnitude of changes in shares in net output caused by factor substitution*

Initial share of capital (%)	50% change in relative factor prices. Elasticity of substitution					100% change in relative factor prices. Elasticity of substitution				
	0	0·25	1·0	1·5	2·0	0	0·25	1·0	1·5	2·0
	% change in share of capital					% change in share of capital				
10	−2·9	−2·2	—	+1·5	+2·9	− 4·5	−3·3	—	+2·2	+ 4·5
20	−5·3	−3·9	—	+2·7	+5·3	− 8·0	−6·0	—	+4·0	+ 8·0
30	−6·9	−5·2	—	+3·5	+6·9	−10·5	−7·9	—	+5·2	+10·5
40	−7·9	−5·9	—	+4·0	+7·9	−12·0	−9·0	—	+6·0	+12·0
50	−8·3	−6·2	—	+4·1	+8·3	−12·5	−9·4	—	+6·2	+12·5

The important point which emerges from this table is that relative shares are remarkably insensitive to factor substitution. For example, if the share of capital costs is 30% and relative factor prices change by 50%, the share increases to 36·9% if the elasticity is 2·0 and falls to 24·8% if the elasticity is 0·25.[1] When wages double relative to the cost of employing capital, the share of capital costs increases from 30 to 35·2% if the elasticity is 1·5 and falls to 22·1% if it is 0·25. The economic reason for this insensitivity is, of course, that changes in shares are the result of two forces pulling in opposite directions: the relative cheapening of one factor, and the tendency to use more of this factor. Consequently, large changes in relative factor prices, or large differences in the strength of the opposing forces (as measured by the elasticity of substitution) are necessary to induce moderate changes in shares. Moreover, these illustrative calculations refer to only two factors; where there are more than two factors the change in relative shares is likely to be even less.

It is interesting to compare the magnitude of these calculated shares with those actually observed. Table 21 sets out the frequency distribution of the observed change in shares.

It is apparent, from a comparison of Tables 20 and 21, that the changes in shares which have taken place *are* sufficiently large to be consistent with a considerable amount of substitution having taken place, even if the elasticity of substitution in some industries is markedly different from unity. This exercise does not justify the assumption that such substitution has actually taken place, for the observed changes in shares may be caused by other factors; but it does nothing to upset our logical presumption that some substitution will have taken place as a result of labour becoming relatively dearer.

A second statistical exercise of an even more hazardous nature is useful to supplement this finding.[2] We may begin, as before, from the theoretical proposition that the extent of changes in shares induced by substitution depends upon both the change in relative factor prices and

[1] In interpreting Table 20 it is significant that in the absence of any special knowledge it is equally likely that an elasticity will fall between 0·01 and 1·0 as that it will fall between 1·0 and 100. Because of the logarithmic nature of the elasticity of substitution the range 0–2·0 covers a wide range of possible elasticities.

[2] The formula employed is (6) in the Appendix to chapter III.

Table 21. *Frequency distribution of observed changes in shares, twenty-eight industries, United Kingdom, 1924–50*

Observed change in percentage shares (+ or −)	Materials cost (No. of industries)	Labour cost (No. of industries)	Gross margins (No. of industries)
0–0·99	3	2	2
1–1·99	3	6	5
2–2·99	4	5	3
3–3·99	0	4	2
4–4·99	5	3	5
5–5·99	3	0	2
6–6·99	3	1	3
7–7·99	0	4	1
8–8·99	2	2	1
9–9·99	1	0	2
10–10·99	1	0	0
Over 11·00	3	1	2
Average change (%)	5·5	4·1	5·0
Range (%)	0·4–14·9	0·4–12·6	0·3–16·6
Inter-quartile range (%)	2·0–6·99	2·0–6·99	2·0–6·99

Source: Table 14.

the elasticity of substitution. Hence, given the observed changes in shares and the assumed changes in relative factor prices of 50 and 100 %, it is possible to calculate the increases in labour productivity which would be caused by such substitution. Ideally, one requires data relating to shares of best-practice plants at the beginning and end of the period; to use industry shares implies the assumption that industry shares have changed similarly to best-practice shares. Also the calculation assumes that elasticities of substitution are constant in each industry, both over time and for different labour/capital ratios. Both these assumptions are unlikely to be realised, but if one regards these calculations as simply an illustrative statistical exercise rather than telling us something definite about the extent of substitution, then these difficulties may be overlooked.

Table 22 sets out these calculations. Column (1) is the observed change in the share of labour in net output (net output because this calculation does not consider substitution between materials and labour). To illustrate the method the calculation is set out as two steps. Columns (2) and (3) are the values of elasticities of substitution which, together with the assumed changes in relative factor price of 50 and 100 %, would lead eventually to changes in shares of the observed magnitude. Having derived these elasticities, we can now calculate the increases in labour productivity which are implied by such elasticities and the assumed changes in relative factor prices. This yields columns (4) and (5). Column (6) sets out the actually observed changes in labour productivity for comparison with columns (4) and (5). Such a comparison indicates the part of the observed increase in labour pro-

Table 22. *The extent of increases in labour productivity attributable to factor substitution and consistent with observed changes in relative shares*

	Observed change in share of wages in net output, 1924–50 (%) (1)	Values of elasticities of substitution consistent with these changes when the change in relative factor prices is		Percentage increases in labour productivity implied by these elasticities when the change in relative factor prices is		Observed increase in labour pro-ductivity, 1924–50 (%) (6)
Industry		50% (2)	100% (3)	50% (4)	100% (5)	
Electricity	− 4·7	3·74	2·49	39	60	211
Cutlery	−18·8	4·84	3·23	90	115	212
Rubber	− 0·1	4·33	2·89	18	29	194
Steel tubes	−11·5	5·14	3·43	40	52	140
Cement	−13·7	3·26	2·17	90	128	139
Glass	− 4·2	4·14	2·76	24	35	111
Confectionery	+ 3·0	2·70	1·80	13	26	99
Chemicals	+ 0·6	2·68	1·79	20	34	94
Spirits	− 0·9	1·96	1·31	38	61	91
Wire	− 4·4	3·13	2·08	27	40	78
Paper	− 8·7	2·55	1·70	51	72·	73
Linoleum	+13·3	1·62	1·08	(−14)	(−5)	56
Hosiery	−16·4	2·57	1·71	69	91	54
Brushes	− 8·6	2·69	1·79	36	48	53
Tinplate	−12·5	3·12	2·08	38	48	51
Bricks	+ 3·7	2·47	1·64	6	14	44
Iron and steel	−19·0	3·46	2·30	51	60	42
Coke	+ 8·5	1·49	0·99	(−1)	9	40
Jute	−15·0	2·44	1·63	47	60	37
Cotton	− 0·2	1·34	0·89	21	34	34
Paint	+ 2·8	1·08	0·72	15	30	29
Boots and shoes	−11·2	2·19	1·46	32	41	28
Blast furnaces	−19·0	2·36	1·57	50	60	25
Coal	+ 0·3	2·48	1·65	7	11	22
Leather	−13·4	0·64	4·24	70	96	20
1. Weighted average increase				24	39	97
2. As percentage of total observed increase				26·2%	40·2%	100%

Notes: (i) Brewing and match industries excluded because change in shares includes excise, and wallpaper excluded because labour productivity declined.

(ii) Figures in parentheses are impossible negative values.

ductivity which could be attributed to substitution and be consistent with the observed changes in shares. In general, the values of columns (4) and (5) are significantly less than those of column (6). This supports our previous finding that it is impossible to explain the observed increases in labour productivity solely by substitution. In some cases, however, the calculated increase exceeds the observed increase; in such cases the assumption that the change in shares is attributable to substitution is obviously unfulfilled. But, on average, the calculation suggests that something of the order of 26–40% of the total increase in labour produc-tivity could be consistent with substitution between labour and capital.

Despite their shortcomings, these calculations do help to establish that our pattern of results are quite consistent with a significant amount of substitution accompanying improving technology. The basic reason is that changes in relative shares, or divergences between cost movements, are an insensitive indicator of the extent of factor substitution, and thus the observed changes in shares are consistent with substitution on an appreciable scale. Whether or not such substitution has actually taken place is quite uncertain in the absence of data about movements in the stock of capital. Relative shares may change for reasons quite independent of substitution: technical advances which involve unequal factor saving, changes in the degree of monopoly and short-term variations in profit margins at the beginning and end of the period. If, as is quite possible, the observed changes in shares are wholly attributable to such influences, then it could be that factor substitution has made a completely unimportant contribution. On the other hand, if the variation is attributable to substitution, then the contribution to the observed increases in labour productivity may have been considerable. We simply do not know which is the more likely alternative.[1]

The important point which this analysis does establish is that the pattern of results is quite consistent with factor substitution superimposed upon uneven rates of largely unbiased technical advance. Thus, the new techniques actually coming into use would save more labour than other factors, because labour was becoming dearer relatively to other factors; but because factor substitution induced in this way has a relatively small effect on cost movements, the movements of each type of costs could still be of a similar magnitude within each industry.

5. ECONOMIES OF SCALE

In addition to technical advances, economies of scale may also lead to simultaneous savings in all factors of production. Two types of scale economies are relevant: economies of firm and plant scale, and economies of industry scale. The first comprises such well-known economies as mass-production methods, standardisation of products, spreading of overheads, distribution outlets and so forth. While it could be argued that incomplete utilisation of such plant and firm economies is impossible under competition, the relevant equilibrium situation is very long run. In the developing historical situations to which our figures refer, the realisation of such economies must be considered in relation to the history of each industry. The process of concentrating output and ownership into optimum-sized plants and firms may be a lengthy one.

---

[1] One piece of evidence that suggests some substitution has taken place is the fact that the regression coefficient between changes in relative prices and output per head is below unity (-0.84). If technical advances which saved all factors were the only influence, one would expect this coefficient to be unity, but to the extent that substitution increases output per head without a proportionate decrease in relative total costs, this regression coefficient will fall below unity. However, to place overmuch significance on this coefficient would be to impute an unwarranted degree of accuracy to the figures.

A common case is where a number of small firms enter an industry at its birth—the classic case is the motor industry. Even though potential scale economies are very great, once such a situation has arisen, to realise these economies may be a slow and painful process. This is important in the context of our figures; for progress in realising such economies is likely to be much more rapid in an industry which is expanding. Progressive firms can realise economies by expanding as the market expands, rather than by relying solely on forcing under-sized firms out of business, their only alternative if output is constant or declining. The cotton textile industry in the United Kingdom provides a good example of the difficulty and slowness of such a readjustment in a declining industry.[1] Exactly the same argument is relevant (and probably more important) in non-competitive market situations. Scitovsky has shown in a detailed analysis that rapid expansion of the market is conducive to the realisation of potential plant and firm scale economies.[2] Thus, in all market situations, expanding output is conducive to realisation of firm and plant economies of scale.

Probably equally important, but more difficult to pinpoint, are economies of industry scale: the growth of specialist industries and services (such as materials and component suppliers), specialised education and training facilities, and the special cases where optimum plant scale is equal to or greater than industry output. A striking example of the importance of such economies is provided by the development of the grid system in electricity supply. Beginning in 1928, the grid system very quickly yielded substantial economies: the average running time of generating stations increased from 1127 hours per annum to 2701 hours per annum by 1939, and high-voltage transmission greatly reduced waste power.[3] There can be little doubt that such economies were one of the most important factors in the rapid rate of productivity increase in the electricity industry. Similarly, the emergence of specialist suppliers has certainly been a critical factor in the growth of the motor industry.

Given the existence of such potential economies of plant, firm and industry scale, it would be possible to explain the pattern of results as follows. First, the realisation of such economies is likely to increase the productivity of labour, materials and capital, and so could explain the general cost reductions which have accompanied increases in labour productivity. Secondly, inter-industry movements of costs and labour productivity could be explained in either one of two ways:

(i) All industries may be subject to the same potential economies of scale. The extent to which they are realised would then depend upon autonomous increases in output originating on the side of demand: population increase, rising real income, or even new wants created by

---

[1] See the *Report of the Cotton Textile Mission to the United States* (H.M.S.O., London, 1944), p. 33.

[2] 'Economies of Scale, Competition, and European Integration', *Amer. Econ. Rev.* vol. XLVI, no. 1 (March 1956), p. 71.

[3] See S. Lilley, *Men, Machines, and History* (London, 1948).

advertising. If the extent of such autonomous increases in output varied between industries, the largest increases would allow the greatest realisation of scale economies and so lead to inter-industry differences in increases in labour productivity and reductions in costs and relative prices.

(ii) The second case is the converse of the first. All industries receive the same external stimulus to increased output but differ in the extent of potential scale economies. As before, this could produce a pattern of inter-industry cost, price and productivity movements similar to that of the empirical data.

While a completely self-contained explanation of the results along the above lines is possible, it is much more plausible to think of technical progress and economies of scale as complementary to each other. Economies of scale may be regarded as reinforcing the inter-industry variation in cost and productivity originally attributable to the uneven impact of technical progress. Industries which, in the first instance, are expanding because of improvements in technology, receive an additional stimulus through the realisation of scale economies. Conversely, industries with little stimulus to expansion are handicapped in realising potential scale economies. The net effect could magnify the inter-industry differences originally attributable to technical progress.

If economies of scale are closely allied to technical progress, a number of more dynamic scale and growth economies become relevant. One of the more important relates to the analysis of chapter IV which pointed out the advantages of expanding industries in utilising new techniques of production. Because expansion of output is achieved by new capacity embodying modern techniques, this leads to a concentration of output in plants with relatively high productivity and low operating costs. This would tend to reinforce the associations between movements of output per head and labour costs, and movements of output per head and materials cost, which are in the main attributable to technical progress. Expanding output also favours utilisation of new techniques in other ways: an expanding industry has a high morale; there is a willingness on the part of labour and management to adopt new methods; finance is readily available; and the very success of the industry tends to attract progressive management. Finally, since an expanding industry provides a good market for capital equipment, machine-manufacturers (and engineers within the industry) find it worth while to develop special-purpose machinery and, in addition, to employ mass-production methods in its manufacture.[1]

6. THE EXPLANATORY HYPOTHESIS

To round off this chapter it is useful to draw together the threads of the argument, first, by restating the suggested explanation of the results of

---

[1] There seems to be some evidence that the lack of such an incentive has magnified the difficulties of the United Kingdom cotton textile industry. See the *British Cotton Industry*, U.S. Productivity Team Report, Anglo-American Council on Productivity, 1952.

the previous chapter and, secondly, by putting into perspective our findings as to the significant causes of increased productivity.

The analysis has suggested that the variation between industries in the extent of increases in labour productivity can be explained primarily by the uneven impact of three influences: (i) improvements in technical knowledge, (ii) potential economies of scale and the extent of their realisation, and (iii) factor substitution. Although analytically distinct, these three influences are highly interrelated: realisation of economies of scale depends upon increases in output which are in part induced by technical advances; while factor substitution is prompted by changes in relative factor prices which to some extent originate in technical change itself.

In the case of labour costs, the effect of such differential increases in labour productivity may be traced directly. Since the variation between industries in earnings movements has been relatively small—presumably through competition in the labour market—differential increases in labour productivity have led to an inverse movement of unit labour costs. The suggested explanation of the tendency for relative reductions in non-labour costs to accompany increases in labour productivity is based on the idea that technical advances and economies of scale tend to increase the productivity of materials and capital as well as that of labour. As we have seen, the observed cost behaviour is consistent with a significant amount of factor substitution. To what extent this has actually taken place is uncertain. However, the net result has been that general cost reductions have accompanied increases in labour productivity and thus made possible the association between changes in relative prices and labour productivity.

This explanation has several important shortcomings. First, it is quite mechanical. The theoretical analysis has shown that the relationships between industry-wide costs, prices and productivity are extremely complex. One cannot say that a reduction in the average costs of the industry leads to a fall in price in anything but an arithmetical sense, for these costs are themselves partly determined by price. A complete explanation should run in terms of the effect of new methods on best-practice costs and productivity, and from there to the industry-wide costs and productivity which we actually measure. The difficulty is the complete lack of data concerning best-practice costs and productivity. However, while it is impossible to trace through these relationships in terms of actual figures, it is at least possible to indicate the operation of these mechanisms. In the first instance we should think of technical advances, economies of scale and factor substitution as largely confining their impact to best-practice costs. This in turn leads to an expansion of output and a fall in price. Two mechanisms ensure these changes are reflected in industry-wide costs and productivity, the quantities we actually measure: the first is the effect of a fall in price in forcing the abandonment of high-cost obsolete methods; and the second is voluntary replacement which achieves the same result. The net result is that industry average costs fall through the addition of new low-cost capacity, and because of the abandonment of obsolete high-cost capacity. Similarly with the labour productivity of the whole industry.

While an interpretation along these lines adds little to the explanation, it does prevent one from taking a simplistic view of the causation involved. For example, it is tempting to say that differential changes in labour productivity 'cause' changes in relative prices. However, changes in relative prices also cause differential changes in labour productivity; the decline in the price of electricity has undoubtedly been one of the factors contributing to the large increase in labour productivity in that industry, for it has forced the abandonment of obsolete high-cost methods. In fact, the whole pattern of causation is far too complex to admit of any simple interpretation with the available data; one can only think of the observed figures as the result of a complicated interplay between new methods, costs, prices and productivity.

The second shortcoming of this explanation is that it is purely a hypothesis unsupported by direct evidence. No more can be claimed than that the hypothesis is consistent with the data and is plausible—and even this may be a matter of opinion. It is quite possible that an equally plausible explanation along quite different lines can be derived. For this reason, the suggested explanation must be regarded as highly tentative until detailed industry studies either confirm or deny its validity.

Finally, to summarise our findings as to the causes of increased labour productivity. The analysis has suggested that, to explain the data, primary emphasis must be placed on technical progress and economies of scale. These are causes of labour productivity which extend their influence to all factors and so can account for the behaviour of costs. Increases in the personal efficiency of labour and factor substitution cannot explain the data by themselves although, in the case of factor substitution at least, it is possible (and indeed likely) that an important contribution has been made to the observed increases in productivity.

These findings are by-products of the main inquiry and, for this reason alone, deserve to be treated with considerable reserve. Moreover, they refer to a particular group of industries over a particular period. Even apart from these qualifications, there is a need for great care in the implications which may validly be drawn from such findings. Consider our very tentative findings concerning the personal efficiency of labour. Although labour skills, effort and intelligence may be unimportant as a long-run direct cause of increased productivity, they could, nevertheless, be extremely important in making effective increases in productivity directly attributable to other causes. For example, to realise the benefits of improving technology the pattern of labour skills and responsibilities must be constantly changing—technical change requires that the craftsman weaver transform himself (or his son) into an electronic technician. Whether this implies more skill is difficult to gauge; but what is certain is that different skills are required if the process of technical change is not to be stultified.

The same considerations are relevant to the suggestion that substitution of capital for labour has played a secondary role. This in no way diminishes the need for saving.[1] Even if it were possible to demonstrate that all increases in productivity were entirely attributable to new techniques, the importance of investment is undiminished; for investment is of critical importance in realising the potential of this new knowledge. All new methods require investment outlays before they can be utilised, irrespective of whether they are more mechanised or not. The point that should be stressed is that the relevant concept is gross investment; all investment expenditures increase productivity, either by bringing the capital stock up to date, or by increasing the degree of mechanisation.

7. SUMMARY

1. The most appropriate means of deriving an explanation of the pattern of results of the previous chapter is to consider alternative causes of increases in productivity: increased personal efficiency of labour, factor substitution, technical change and economies of scale. Each such cause may be expected to involve a distinctive pattern of inter-industry cost and price behaviour; and by examining the observed data we may derive the explanation of the productivity movements which is most consistent with the results.

2. The hypothesis that the increases in labour productivity originate in greater personal efficiency of labour is rejected because of the lack of any association between movements of labour productivity and earnings, the extreme unevenness of productivity movements and the behaviour of labour and non-labour costs.

3. The hypothesis that the results are principally the product of factor substitution is unsatisfactory because the differential movements of labour and non-labour costs are positively correlated, whereas the hypothesis implies a negative association. Industries with the greatest increases in output per head—which the hypothesis would explain by the greatest increase in capital per head—have recorded the smallest, rather than the largest, increases in gross margin costs.

4. The results are consistent with uneven rates of technical advance between industries when these advances are of the type which tend to save labour, capital and materials. Since technical advance in the capital goods industries lowers the price of capital equipment relative to that of labour, we expect to find that there has also been, throughout the economy, some substitution of capital equipment for labour in the manner indicated in chapter III. There are no data to test this directly, but the data about the shares of labour, materials and gross margin costs in the various industries' selling prices are quite consistent with its having taken place on a substantial scale.

---

[1] Colin Clark draws this quite unjustified implication from evidence of a declining capital–output ratio. See 'The Declining Importance of Capital', *The Listener*, 10 March 1953, vol. LIII, no. 1358, p. 411.

5. The results may also be partially explained by the uneven impact of economies of scale. Such economies reinforce the inter-industry differences in cost and productivity movements originally attributable to technical change.

6. Because of the lack of data concerning best-practice costs, it is impossible to integrate the explanation with the analysis of chapters IV–VII. However, the causal processes which lead to the observed results may be shown to be both extremely complex and highly interrelated.

7. Although the suggested explanation places primary emphasis on technical change and economies of scale, this does not mean that factor substitution and the personal efficiency of labour are unimportant. Both are important elements in increasing productivity, if not directly, at least in making effective productivity increases originating in technical change.

CHAPTER XI

PRODUCTIVITY AND
STRUCTURAL CHANGE

ONE of the most striking features of the statistical results is the diversity in the experience of different industries. Labour productivity has increased by over 200 % in some industries and declined in others; prices have trebled in some industries and fallen in others; output has increased tenfold in the electricity industry and declined by 27 % in the coal industry. This chapter carries the analysis a stage further by relating these structural changes to the interpretation of the previous chapter. It considers some of the factors determining differences in the rates of growth of individual industries; the contribution made by rapidly growing sectors of the economy; and the relationship between structural change and aggregate productivity. The final sections examine the implications of these structural changes for the index-number problem.

I. THE PATTERN OF STRUCTURAL CHANGE

We have already noted that differential increases in costs and productivity are associated with major changes in the structure of relative prices. Equally important, at least over the period covered by the figures, are the complementary changes in the structure of output and employment. The following figures summarise the structural changes which have accompanied differential increases in labour productivity. The first column sets out the coefficient of variation of output, price and employment movements, while the second column records the extent to which such variation is associated with uneven productivity movements.

Table 23. *Coefficient of variation of changes in the structure of output, prices and employment, and coefficient of correlation with movement of output per head*

Changes in the	Coefficient of variation (%)	Correlation coefficient (r)
Output structure	87·2	+0·81
Price structure	29·1	−0·88
Employment structure	50·1	+0·61

Sources: Tables 15 and 16.

The output structure is the most variable and is closely associated with changes in labour productivity. Next in variability is the employment structure, although much less closely related to productivity movements. The structure of relative prices is the least variable but is highly correlated with productivity movements.

If these structural changes are interpreted along the lines suggested by our explanatory hypothesis, then the following picture emerges. At one extreme are industries with high rates of growth. Under the impetus of rapidly improving technology and allied economies of scale their costs are continually falling relative to other industries, making possible falling relative prices, rapidly expanding output and, in the majority of cases, increasing employment. These industries are the real pace-setters in the growth process, for not only do they outstrip industries with fewer technical opportunities but their very success generates demand and cost pressures which accentuate the difficulties of such industries. Consider first the demand pressures: since technically progressive industries are able to reduce the relative prices of their products, less fortunate industries are robbed of their markets as the prices of substitutes are reduced. Nylon displaces cotton, plastics invade markets formerly secure to steel, paper takes over the role of jute and timber as packing materials, and cement displaces bricks and timber as building materials. Similarly with the pressures generated by costs. These are most general in the case of labour costs: expanding industries which require an increasing labour force find it necessary to offer (or agree to) higher wages and, in order to retain their labour forces, the less progressive industries must, to some extent, follow suit. But while increased earnings are wholly or partially offset by increased labour productivity in progressive industries, they are a much more serious problem for industries with few opportunities for increasing productivity. In these industries increased earnings lead to higher labour costs which, although they can be passed on in the form of higher prices, diminish even further a slow rate of growth. Such industries are caught in a vicious circle. Few technical opportunities lead to a performance which compares unfavourably with the average of the economy as a whole and, since their relative costs and prices are rising, the decline in their relative importance in the output structure is accentuated.

In some cases, demand conditions may provide a measure of relief to this process. As real income rises, principally because of the achievements of progressive industries, declining industries benefit from the extra demand. For example, the decline of the textile industry has almost certainly been modified by increases in real income originating in other industries. A low price elasticity may also prove a powerful prop to an industry where productivity is lagging for, even though the relative prices of its products may be rising, the effect on output is small. Thus, either a low price elasticity or a high income elasticity may enable industries to grow even though they cannot match the average performance of the economy as a whole. The housing industry is perhaps the best example; despite a poor technological performance it grows in the train of progressive industries.

2. THE CONTRIBUTION OF RAPIDLY EXPANDING INDUSTRIES

This picture of the structural changes accompanying technical change places primary emphasis on the contribution of rapidly growing industries. The importance of this contribution is illustrated statistically in Table 24.

Table 24. *Changes in total output, employment, output per head and prices, twenty-eight industries, United Kingdom, 1924–50*

1924 = 100 (weight base = 1935)

	Output	Employ-ment	Output per head	Net prices
1. All industries in sample	185	94	196	158
2. Excluding the five industries with the largest increases in output	118	82	145	209
3. Excluding the ten industries with the largest increases in output	103	77	134	236

Note: These figures should not be taken as representative of all industry.

Line 1 represents index numbers of the total changes for all twenty-eight industries of output, employment, output per head and net prices (which are the appropriate prices for such aggregation). Line 2 refers to the changes for an aggregate of twenty-three industries, which excludes the five industries with the greatest increases in output: electricity, rubber, chemicals, cutlery and steel tubes. Comparison of lines 1 and 2 gives an approximate indication of the contribution made by these five rapidly growing industries to the total change. They have been responsible for most of the total increase in output, almost half the increase in output per head, and without their influence the increase in prices would have been much greater. Similarly, comparison of lines 1 and 3 indicates the contribution made by the ten most rapidly growing industries.

From another point of view, the contribution of rapidly growing industries can be illustrated by comparing their relative importance in 1924 and 1950. Within the aggregate of twenty-eight industries the electricity, cutlery, rubber, chemicals and steel tubes industries were relatively unimportant in 1924. By 1950 they had come to play a major role. Table 25 illustrates this change.

Table 25. *Relative importance of the electricity, cutlery, rubber, chemicals and steel tubes industries in 1924 and 1950*

Percentage of total sample represented by these industries with respect to	1924 (%)	1950 (%)
Employment	7·8	20·2
Volume of output (at 1935 prices)	10·5	42·6
Value of output (at current prices)	10·9	24·5

These industries have increased their relative contribution to the volume of output much more significantly than their contribution to the value of output. This arises out of the tendency noted earlier for increasing output to be accompanied by declining relative prices. Similarly, the smaller increase in their relative importance with respect to employment is attributable to the large increases in output per head achieved by such industries.

Even though it is possible these figures somewhat exaggerate the point,[1] the tendency revealed by these two tables is undoubtedly important. One has only to think of how large a fraction of British output is produced in industries with a significant history of only thirty years—motors, aircraft, household appliances, radio and electrical engineering, to name but a few. There can be little question that without such industries increases in productivity and real income would only be a fraction of what has been achieved.

It is useful to consider the exact way in which these progressive industries make their contribution to increasing aggregate labour productivity. In the first place, there is the obvious reason that the part of the labour force employed in such industries has increased its productivity much more rapidly than workers in other industries. Equally important are the structural changes that have increased the relative importance of these industries in the employment structure. For example, the economy has benefited not only because the 1924 workforce of the electricity industry have trebled their productivity, but also because the large numbers of workers who entered the industry between 1924 and 1935 have doubled their productivity, an achievement that would have been unlikely if they had remained in the mining or textile industries. The importance of such inter-industry shifts in employment may be illustrated by dividing the total increase in recorded labour productivity into two components, one measuring the contribution made by productivity increases within each industry and one measuring the contribution made by inter-industry shifts.[2] In Table 26, the first line sets out the increase in labour productivity which would have been recorded if the 1924 employment structure had remained constant. The

Table 26. *Components of changes in total labour productivity, twenty-eight industries, 1924–48*

	1924	1948
Internal	100	136
Shift component	100	133
Total change	100	181

[1] Examination of the adequacy of the sample (Appendix B, p. 188) suggests the possibility of a slight tendency to include an unduly high proportion of declining and rapidly expanding industries. If so, this would tend to over-emphasise the contribution of expanding industries.

[2] The division of the total change into two components is multiplicative since any additive division is impossible within the theory of index numbers. The method is considered in Appendix A, p. 184.

second line indicates the increase in labour productivity directly attributable to changes in the employment structure.[1] The striking fact which emerges is that the shift component is of almost equal importance to the internal component. This suggests that structural changes play a role equally important as increases in productivity within individual industries. While it is again possible that the sample exaggerates this point, the general tendency revealed by these figures is obviously of central importance. If we produced goods in exactly the same proportions today as in 1924, the total increase in productivity would almost certainly be very much less than that which has been achieved. Industries with a high productivity performance would remain of minor importance and be unable to influence significantly the growth of the economy as a whole. In fact, such industries grow rapidly and, by so doing, increase their relative importance and their contribution to increases in total productivity.

3. PRODUCTIVITY AND THE INDEX-NUMBER PROBLEM

From another viewpoint, these structural changes are manifestations of the fact that as we grow we tend to produce more of the goods we have learnt to produce at lower cost. Growth is much more than simply producing more of the same bundles of goods; the other half of the story arises out of changing patterns of consumption and output in response to changing patterns of technology. An economy which is able and willing to make extensive structural changes in the structure of its consumption in response to improving technology, will of necessity record a high rate of productivity increase. In the extreme case, an economy which is willing to consume only automobiles must record a higher rate of productivity increase than an economy that insists on consuming beer and textiles. If American consumers had proved unwilling to consume automobiles, household appliances and mass produced products, then the increase in productivity would be much less impressive than that which has been achieved.

Once the problem is put in these terms, the whole concept of aggregate productivity becomes ambiguous. The difficulty is that those goods we produce more of are the goods whose relative valuation falls the most. Yet it is in the production of such goods that improving technology

[1] The relative importance of the shift and internal components depends, of course, upon which year we select as the original employment structure. Set out below are the figures obtained by employing the 1935 and 1948 employment structures as the starting-point for the calculations:

	Component	1924	1948
1935 employment	Internal	100	150
	Shift	100	121
	Total	100	181
1948 employment	Internal	100	152
	Shift	100	119
	Total	100	181

provides the greatest opportunity for increases in purely physical productivity. In such circumstances, the concept of aggregate productivity is bedevilled with index-number ambiguities. Only when a precise system of valuation is stated—output per head at 1935 prices—does the concept have a clear-cut meaning. Although productivity can be measured and thought of in such terms to do so misses half the point, for these changes in valuation are themselves an integral part of the structural changes which contribute so much to increased productivity. How serious a difficulty is involved is illustrated by Table 27 which sets out measures of the total increase in output per head for the twenty-eight industries which are calculated on both 1924 and 1948 systems of valuation. (Net prices are employed as the basis of valuation in such an aggregation.[1])

Table 27. *Aggregate output per head movements: alternative weights, twenty-eight industries, 1924–48*

Weights	1924	1948
1924 net prices	100	181
1948 net prices	100	138

The divergence between these measures is very great.[2] If the performance of labour productivity is measured in terms of 1948 prices, it is less than half the figure obtained by measurement in terms of 1924 figures. The difference arises from the fact that although the physical quantity of goods per worker has increased, this has been accompanied by structural changes such that the greatest increases in output have accompanied the largest decreases in relative prices. Again, it is possible that the sample may exaggerate the divergence, but it is almost certain that the real divergence is important.[3] It is essential to recognise that this is not simply a problem of measurement, a problem that can be dismissed as irritating but basically unimportant. The index-number problem is part and parcel of the structural changes that are an essential ingredient in increasing productivity. Even if we are prepared to assume, somewhat illogically, that productivity has a meaning independent of index-number problems, analysis of aggregate productivity must take account of the accompanying structural changes that involve changing systems of valuation. Analysis that assumes away the index-number problem runs the danger of neglecting the very important role played by structural change.

[1] In this calculation products within each industry are summed on the basis of 1935 gross prices. Thus the divergence between the two measures refers to that caused by changes in the net price of a composite bundle of goods produced within each industry; not the divergence caused by changes in the relative price of individual products within each industry.

[2] Equally wide divergences result from a calculation (reported in chapter XIII, p. 170) based upon American data.

[3] It could be argued that index-number biases of this magnitude may be present in the measures for each industry. This, however, is unlikely for the changes in relative prices of the products of each industry is much less than that for the economy as a whole. This is confirmed by Table A (3), Appendix A, which compares the divergence between the output series of each industry calculated at 1935 and 1948 prices.

4. IMPLICATIONS

The close relationship between structural change and increasing productivity leads to several implications concerning public policies to raise productivity. Obviously it is not enough that such policies should simply encourage individual industries to become more efficient. Equally important is the contribution that may be made simply by ensuring an economic climate where structural changes can take place with a minimum of hindrance—a climate where expanding industries are not hampered in their growth nor declining industries artificially supported. This is not to suggest that structural changes should be consciously hastened; to do so would elevate productivity (as conventionally measured) to an undeserved status by making nonsense of demand, and would be as indefensible as the converse policy. What should be recognised, however, is that the problem of achieving a high rate of increase of productivity is intimately associated with the efficient allocation of resources. Artificial support of declining industries not only causes misallocations today, but, more important, retards the growth of productivity. The ideal is a highly flexible economy which allows resources to be moved with a minimum of friction from declining to expanding industries where technical change is currently progressing the most rapidly.

One of the more important ways by which public policy impinges on this process is through wages policy. Because wages play a major part in inducing such structural changes, it is particularly desirable that the market for labour should cut across inter-industry boundaries, thereby ensuring that comparable labour has the same price in expanding and declining industries. The argument that an industry cannot 'afford' higher wages is, in the long run, extremely dangerous. If it were accepted and wages were based on the 'capacity to pay', employment would be perpetuated (unless labour deserted them) in industries which should properly decline to make way for more vigorous industries. Equally dangerous is the argument that industries which are prosperous because of new techniques have the 'capacity to pay' high wages. This would penalise the expanding industries on which so much depends. Ideally, the only means by which the wage structure should be linked to the fortunes of particular industries are through skills and incentives to transfer from one industry to another. As industries decline, specialised skills become obsolete in the same way as capital equipment, and the relative valuation placed on them should properly decline; the point analogous to zero surplus is when the margin for skill disappears; for example, when a skilled weaver is of more value to the community as an unskilled vehicle-assembler than by continued employment in the textile trades. Closely related is the need of an expanding labour force in progressive industries. To overcome the inevitable frictions these industries may need to offer higher than average wages[1] (though not

---

[1] It is possible to overestimate the need for such differentials; a powerful force attracting labour to expanding industries may be simply the greater opportunities for personal advancement.

necessarily a higher than average rate of increase in wages, as has sometimes been suggested).[1]

A second important requirement for a flexible economy is a high rate of gross investment. At any one time the existing physical capital stock consists of equipment that is specialised not only in terms of techniques but also in terms of a particular structure of production. In effect, the product-structure is fossilised in the capital stock. The rate at which structural change can proceed is accordingly limited by the rate of gross investment, for this determines the rate at which equipment appropriate to new industries comes into existence. For example, the speed with which labour can be transferred from textiles to engineering is limited by investment in the engineering industries. A high rate of gross investment makes possible a flexible structure of production which allows an economy to adjust its distribution of resources to take maximum advantage of changing patterns of technical advance. For both types of productivity increase, those due to improvements within each industry and those arising out of changes in inter-industry structure, a high rate of gross investment is an essential prerequisite to high levels of productivity.

5. SUMMARY

1. Since 1924, very considerable changes have taken place in the structure of output, employment, and relative prices. An interpretation based upon the explanatory hypothesis of the previous chapter suggests that such structural changes originate in the uneven impact of technical change and associated economies of scale. Industries enjoying rapid rates of technical advance and the realisation of economies of scale are able to achieve falling relative prices and high rates of increase of output. Less fortunate industries are not only unable to match this performance but, depending upon their price and income elasticities of demand, may be faced with shrinking markets as the prices of substitute goods fall, and increasing labour costs as wage rates rise to meet the demand for labour of expanding industries.

2. The role of expanding industries may be illustrated with the sample data. The five industries with the greatest increases in output are responsible for most of the increase in total output of the twenty-eight industries, and almost half the total increase in output per head; without their influence, the total increase in selling prices would have been very much greater. Such industries make their contribution to aggregate increases in productivity both through their high individual rates of productivity increase, and through their increasing importance in the employment structure. In fact, almost half of the total increase in output per head recorded for the sample industries has originated in such shifts in the inter-industry distribution of employment.

[1] For example, Dunlop, 'Productivity and the Inter-industry Wage Structure' in *Essays in Honor of Alvin H. Hansen* (New York, 1948), p. 350).

3. Such structural changes are a response to the changing pattern of costs and prices resulting from uneven rates of technical change. Since they are partly determined by demand conditions, the concept of aggregate productivity is rendered ambiguous and its measurement is bedevilled by the index-number problem. This is illustrated by alternative index-number measures of the total increase in output per head of sample industries: the index employing 1924 prices as weights records double the increase in output per head compared to the measure based upon 1948 prices.

4. Even though the sample may exaggerate its importance, structural change obviously plays an important part in increasing productivity. Policies to raise productivity should therefore ensure a climate where expanding industries are not hampered in their growth and declining industries are not artificially supported. One requirement for such a climate is a market for labour which cuts across industry boundaries; another is a high rate of gross investment, for this allows the flexibility in the capital stock necessary for rapid structural change.

CHAPTER XII

THE DISTRIBUTION OF THE GAINS

ALL discussion of measures to increase productivity inevitably involve some consideration of the way in which the benefits will be distributed. This is quite natural; no group has any interest in increased productivity unless they are convinced they will share in the gains. Unions, particularly, insist on a 'fair share' of the gains as the price of their co-operation.[1] However, in what proportions, and by what means, productivity gains should be distributed are matters of dispute. What is a 'fair share' depends first of all on the way in which productivity is defined; if productivity means labour efficiency, a fair share to labour is all the gains. Even if labour productivity is defined in its output per head sense, an appropriate distribution depends in part upon the causes of increased labour productivity. The distribution appropriate to increases originating in factor substitution is very different to that appropriate to increases due to improving technology. Moreover, the economically appropriate distribution may be distorted by the activities of monopolistic business and strong unions which appropriate the gains of productivity to themselves.

The statistical analysis enables some light to be thrown on these problems, at least in so far as past experience is relevant to the present. This chapter examines the results with three questions in mind: (i) to whom are the gains distributed, (ii) by what method are they distributed, and (iii) are the results consistent with the marginal productivity theory of distribution?

I. THE SHARE OF LABOUR

From one point of view, the problem of the distribution of the fruits of increasing productivity is simply that of the distribution of a growing product and, as such, must be approached in terms of the economy as a whole. An overall answer to the first question, to whom are the gains distributed, can be derived from the empirical fact that the share of labour has remained relatively constant. Given this, it follows almost as a mathematical necessity[2] that the percentage increase in labour productivity in the economy as a whole (including services, etc.) has been equal to the percentage increase in real wages. And, if increases in labour productivity have been accompanied by increases in the pro-

---

[1] See *Productivity: Report of a Conference of Trade Union Executives, T.U.C.* (London, 1948).

[2] This statement is not quite a mathematical necessity, since it requires that the prices of total output move over time in exactly the same way as the prices of consumption goods. Thus the prices of consumption and capital goods must move together, and the prices of goods exported must move parallel with prices of goods imported (i.e. constant terms of trade).

ductivity of non-labour factors, then constant shares imply that their real rate of reward has increased or decreased proportionately with their productivity. In the United Kingdom, where the share of wages and salaries in gross national product is approximately 65 %, of each £1 increase in output per head approximately two-thirds has gone to labour in the form of increased real wages and one-third to swell gross trading profits (which may or may not imply an increase in real rates of return depending upon changes in the aggregate productivity of non-labour factors, particularly capital). But, beyond stating the bald fact, this does not help very much. It does not indicate whether this distribution is fair in any sense, or economically appropriate. Neither does it indicate the means of distribution; we do not know whether the gains have been distributed by means of factor incomes or prices. For a more comprehensive picture we must probe behind these aggregative figures and examine the increases in productivity at their source, that is, at industry level.

A significant statistical result in this context is the lack of any correlation between inter-industry movements of earnings and labour productivity.[1] This suggests that increases in productivity have not resulted in higher relative earnings of the labour employed in the industries where the increases have taken place. This result is heartening for two reasons. In the first place it suggests that there is no significant tendency for productivity gains to be appropriated at their source by strong trade unions. If this had been the case, workers in industries where the greatest productivity gains had occurred would have fared better than their colleagues in less progressive industries. Fortunately, there is no evidence of such a narrow division of the gains. The second reason why this result is heartening concerns the sources of increased productivity. Businessmen have no direct interest in increased productivity for its own sake; to them increased productivity is simply a means of reducing costs. If strong unions (or some statutory agreement) led to a situation where increases in productivity in each firm or industry were automatically accompanied by increased earnings, the incentives to increased productivity would thereby be weakened; for the effect on costs of increased productivity would be much less. A similar argument applies to those increases in productivity which originate in structural change. If wages and productivity were linked together in each industry, the inter-industry structure of costs and prices would be less responsive to unequal productivity movements. This would seriously inhibit the structural changes which make such an important contribution to increases in aggregate productivity.[2]

[1] See chapter IX, p. 115.
[2] These arguments are relevant to proposals to link wages and productivity at industry level. Such proposals are not only unfair but self-defeating for they strike at the sources of increased productivity.

2. THE SHARE OF PROFITS

The alternative to the gains being appropriated at their source by labour is that they have been channelled into enhanced profits in progressive industries; the reductions in labour costs would simply be offset by increased gross trading profits. If this had taken place, the inter-industry analysis would reveal above-average increases in unit gross margins in those industries where labour productivity increased the most. However, as pointed out in our analysis of factor substitution,[1] this has not been so. The tendency is for unit gross margins to decline the most in those industries where the greatest increases in labour productivity have taken place. This finding warrants two observations. First, it is quite inconsistent with the gains of increased labour productivity being appropriated in the form of increased profits. If this were so, rising relative gross margins would have accompanied the largest increases in labour productivity, and vice versa. In fact, gross margins have declined in such industries, presumably because of increases in capital productivity. Secondly, this result implies that the distributive problem is not simply to account for the gains of increased labour productivity, but in addition to account for the gains of increased capital productivity.

A similar situation arises when we ask whether these savings have been offset by increased materials cost. Again the correlation analysis[2] shows that savings in labour costs have been accompanied by large savings in materials cost, and these have augmented rather than offset the gains of increased capital and labour productivity. This is the distributive aspect of the phenomenon whereby all costs have declined as labour productivity has increased. We must account for the gains of increased productivity of all factors, labour, capital and materials.

3. THE ROLE OF PRICES

The key to this distributive puzzle is, as we have seen, the behaviour of relative prices. The correlation between increases in labour productivity and changes in relative prices[3] is such that the observed price changes exceed those made possible by differential increases in labour productivity, and include the accompanying savings in materials and gross margin costs. The implication to be drawn from this result is that the gains of increased productivity of all factors have, by and large, been passed on to consumers. It appears, therefore, that the fear often expressed that productivity gains may be appropriated by monopolistic groups in society is largely groundless. Over the period under consideration the evidence suggests that the economy has functioned as we should hope it would, by distributing the gains to consumers. Price reductions or, rather, smaller increases in prices than would otherwise have occurred, have been the means of distribution; not abnormal increases in rewards to factors of production in the industries where the large gains have originated.

---

[1] Chapter IX, p. 117.   [2] Chapter IX, p. 118.   [3] Chapter IX, p. 119.

This distributive pattern is consistent with our analysis of the probable causes of increases in productivity. Economies of scale and improving technology are not the product of any particular group. They arise out of basic research and natural conditions in which all society has an interest and are certainly not the creation of the particular industries where such advances are implemented. No particular group has any economic or ethical right to appropriate the fruits of productivity increases of this nature; and, if the statistical data are reliable, they have not in fact been successful in doing so.

The accompanying changes in the structure of production are an integral part of this distributive process. Because productivity movements are uneven between industries, a necessary condition for distribution via prices is a changing composition of output. It is only because output has expanded in those industries where increased productivity has reduced relative costs that relative prices have fallen.[1] If this had not been the case and the output structure were constant, differential productivity increases could only reflect themselves in the inter-industry structure of factor rewards, and not in the structure of relative prices. From this viewpoint, freedom from restrictions to structural change is as essential for an economically appropriate distribution of productivity gains as it is for their creation.

On the surface, the distributive pattern we observe is consistent with an economy which is basically competitive, at least in the long run. The pattern of results is analogous to that implied by a competitive general equilibrium model if it were set in motion by a flow of new techniques in each industry. However, to assume that the economy is in fact competitive is unjustified for two reasons. First, the analysis is only concerned with *movements* of prices, costs and output. A substantial degree of monopoly may have existed both in 1924 and 1950, and while the proportionate movements of costs and prices are similar to those of competition, their absolute values may be influenced by monopoly elements.[2] If this is so, the only implication we are entitled to draw from the figures is that if the consumer were exploited by monopolies in 1924, he appears to be exploited to approximately the same extent in 1950. Secondly, it is quite possible (and even probable) that the result of monopoly has been to slow down the rate at which new techniques have been introduced and so retard the rate of increase of productivity. The theoretical sections[3] have shown that control of price

---

[1] Chapter IX, p. 122.

[2] The formal condition for equal proportional movements is that the degree of monopoly (in the Lerner sense) should remain constant. Under competition, price (P) equals marginal revenue (MC), and thus

$$\frac{\Delta MC}{MC} = \frac{\Delta P}{P}.$$

In non-competitive situation $MC = P(1 - 1/n)$, where n is the elasticity of demand and $1 - 1/n$ is the degree of monopoly. Thus

$$\frac{\Delta MC}{MC} = \frac{\Delta P(1 - 1/n)}{P(1 - 1/n)} = \frac{\Delta P}{P} \quad \text{when } 1 - 1/n \text{ is constant.}$$

[3] Chapter VII, p. 92.

enables a monopolist to dispense his own discipline with respect to replacement; consequently price and costs may be higher, and productivity lower, under monopoly than competition. With industry-wide cost data, such cost and price behaviour cannot be distinguished from that of competition. It is, therefore, quite possible that a greater degree of competition may have led to greater increases in productivity and larger changes in relative prices.

4. LABOUR PRODUCTIVITY AND PRODUCT WAGES

An interesting form of summary of the distributive pattern emerges from a comparison of inter-industry movements of labour productivity and product wages and salaries—money wages and salaries divided by the price of each industry's products. Fig. 23 compares the movements of output per operative with product earnings per operative and output per head with product wages and salaries.

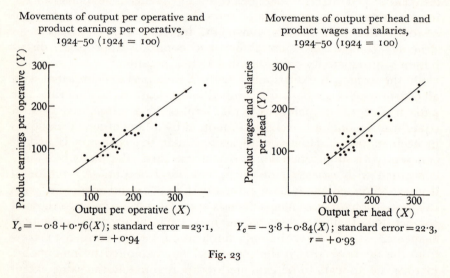

Movements of output per operative and product earnings per operative, 1924–50 (1924 = 100)

Movements of output per head and product wages and salaries, 1924–50 (1924 = 100)

$Y_c = -0.8 + 0.76(X)$; standard error $= 23.1$, $r = +0.94$

$Y_c = -3.8 + 0.84(X)$; standard error $= 22.3$, $r = +0.93$

Fig. 23

Both comparisons reveal a high degree of association ($r = +0.94$ and $r = +0.93$). This is to be expected for these results are obtained by combining two previous observations: (i) that money wages and salaries have increased by approximately the same extent in all industries; and (ii) that movements of labour productivity and relative prices are inversely correlated. The procedure of expressing money wages and salaries as product wages and salaries transfers the variation in prices to the wage variable, and so leads to the above association.

When cast in this form, the statistical results suggest a parallel with the traditional proposition that the product wage determines, and is determined by, the marginal product of labour. Our findings may be summarised by stating that differential increases in product wages are associated with differential increases in the *average* product of labour.

However, while it is possible that this association may have arisen because differential movements of average and marginal products of labour are correlated, this is not necessarily the case. The association is simply another means of stating: (a) that unequal movements of output per head are not reflected in corresponding variations in the share of wages; and (b) that there are differences between industries in the extent of increases in output per head. The share of wages is equivalent to the ratio of product wages to output per head, and if changes in this ratio are not correlated with differential movements of output per head, differential movements in output per head must, to some extent, be correlated with differential movements of product wages.

On the other hand, the result is not inconsistent with the marginal productivity proposition, for it is quite possible that differential movements of average and marginal products are correlated. Indeed the explanatory hypothesis of chapter x implies this; for the set of conditions necessary to explain the behaviour of costs—that uneven technical advances have tended to save all factors, and that elasticities of substitution are not greatly in excess of unity—are conditions which would lead to a correlation between movements of average and marginal products. If, therefore, the results are interpreted in this way the association does arise, because movements of average and marginal products are correlated. From another viewpoint, we have found that the results may be interpreted in a way consistent with competition, and it is not therefore surprising that this derived result may also be interpreted in a way consistent with one aspect of competition, the marginal productivity theory. However, as has been pointed out, this explanatory hypothesis has little independent support, and it is quite possible that an alternative hypothesis, inconsistent with the marginal productivity schema, may explain the data equally well. For this reason, the association between movements of product wages and labour productivity, while a useful form of summary, has little bearing on the validity of the marginal productivity theory.

5. SUMMARY

1. While the stability of shares in the total product provides some information concerning the overall distribution of productivity gains, it does not indicate either the means of distribution, or whether it is economically appropriate. A more detailed analysis must examine productivity increases at their source, at industry level.

2. The lack of any correlation between differential increases in earnings and labour productivity implies that productivity gains have not been distributed directly to workers in the industries where the gains have originated. This finding also suggests that strong unions have not been successful in capturing a direct share in productivity increases.

3. The finding that differential increases in gross margins are negatively correlated with differential increases in labour productivity also

implies that productivity gains have not been directly appropriated in the form of increased profits.

4. The implication to be drawn from the analysis of costs of chapter x and the high inverse correlation between movements of relative prices and labour productivity is that the gains of increased productivity (including capital and labour productivity) have been distributed to consumers by means of price reductions—or smaller increases in prices than would otherwise have occurred. This is consistent with the hypothesis that technical change and economies of scale are the major causes of increased productivity; for productivity increases of this nature are not the product of the industries in which such advances are actually implemented.

5. The distributive pattern may be summarised in terms of the movements of output per head and product wages (earnings in each industry divided by the prices of each industry's products). These are highly correlated ($r = +0.94$) implying that unequal increases in output per head have been reflected in unequal increases in product wages. The basic reason for this association is that changes in the share of wages are not correlated with differential increases in output per head. This association, therefore, does nothing to confirm or deny the marginal productivity theory of distribution, although it is not inconsistent with it.

CHAPTER XIII

THE AMERICAN SCENE

A NUMBER of important conclusions have emerged from the three preceding chapters: technical change and allied economies of scale are the causes of increased productivity most consistent with the behaviour of costs and prices; the gains of increased productivity have been distributed by means of prices; and structural changes not only play an important part in increasing productivity but inevitably surround the whole concept with index-number ambiguities. As they stand, these conclusions must be highly tentative for they are based on figures which may contain large errors and are drawn from a small sample which is confined to a particular period. We should be entitled to much more confidence in the results if they could be confirmed by another set of observations based upon a different sample of industries operating in different circumstances. This is the purpose of this chapter; it reports the results of a complementary survey of the experiences of twenty-seven American industries over the years 1923–50. This survey provides a check on the United Kingdom survey in two respects: the first is the narrow statistical sense of an alternative sample and, more important, the use of independent data which is free from the worst dangers of spurious correlation due to errors. The second is the wider sense of ascertaining whether associations which lead to the same interpretive conclusions are to be found in the United States as well as the United Kingdom.

I. THE BASIC DATA

The statistical analysis is basically similar to that of the United Kingdom survey. The experiences of twenty-three industries with respect to movements of the volume of output, output per man-hour, hourly earnings, unit labour costs and selling prices, have been compared over the years 1923–50. The data for output, man-hours and earnings are based upon the careful productivity studies of the Bureau of Labor Statistics. In order to allow comparisons to be made over a sufficiently long period, in some cases these data have been supplemented with material prepared by the Bureau of the Census, and the Federal Reserve Board. These figures are not completely independent, with the result that the danger of spurious correlation has not been wholly removed from correlations involving output per man-hour, output, earnings and unit wage cost. The price data, however, are derived from wholesale price statistics and are completely independent. This is a distinct advantage, for there is no danger of spurious correlation through errors in the important associations involving prices. The errors which arise from the use of data derived from independent sources—

differences in product-coverage, industrial classification and methods of valuation—are errors which we can be certain will reduce rather than increase the correlation coefficients. Table 28 sets out the basic figures.

Table 28. *Changes in output per man-hour and related quantities for twenty-seven industries, United States, 1923–50*

(1923 = 100)

Ranked according to increases in output

	Output	Man-hours	Output per man-hour	Hourly earnings	Unit labour cost	Whole-sale price
1. Rayon and allied products	3602	296	1217	339	28	32
2. Electricity	564	168	335	281	84	61
3. Petroleum refining	383	132	290	302	104	138
4. Glass products	326	137	238	296	125	97
5. Rubber tyres and tubes	319	102	312	275	88	65
6. Paint and varnishes	306	167	183	289	158	139
7. Pulp and paper mills	296	161	184	285	155	159
8. Canning and preserving	287	144	200	318	159	—
9. Fertilisers	240	121	198	309	157	97
10. Iron and steel	240	88	273	294	107	147
11. Icecream	225	66	341	227	67	85
12. Confectionery	202	79	256	292	114	—
13. Hosiery	173	100	172	343	199	—
14. Bread, etc.	171	146	117	258	220	170
15. Cement	163	70	234	263	112	127
16. Cotton goods	146	72	203	310	152	168
17. Meat packing	143	115	125	270	216	299
18. Footwear	140	83	168	213	127	193
19. Coke	130	101	131	218	167	191
20. Cane sugar refining	125	79	158	281	177	128
21. Non-ferrous metals	122	68	180	256	142	140
22. Woollen and worsted	113	55	214	295	137	151
23. Tobacco products	108	37	289	309	107	32
24. Leather	92	56	164	278	169	181
25. Flour, etc.	90	70	130	266	205	175
26. Bituminous coal	88	53	167	252	151	171
27. Clay construction products	79	52	154	213	138	163
Median	171	88	198	281	142	139
Upper quartile	296	137	256	302	167	171
Lower quartile	122	68	164	258	107	85

Notes: (*a*) Figures for electricity refer to 1923–48 only, and for confectionery for the period 1925–50.

(*b*) Prices for icecream and glass products are based on unit values.

(*c*) Iron and steel refers to the blast furnaces and melting and rolling trades only.

Sources: See Appendix A.

As in the United Kingdom, the figures reveal a very great diversity in the experiences of different industries. Table 29 summarises the salient features of this variation.

Table 29. *Means, standard deviations and coefficients of variation of inter-industry changes in the United States, twenty-three industries, 1923–50*

Changes in	Mean	Standard deviation	Coefficient of variation (%)
Output	203	111	55·0
Man-hours	97	38	39·5
Output per man-hour	208	64	30·8
Earnings	276	32	11·7
Unit wage cost	144	39	27·3
Price	142	54	37·9

Source: Table 28.

The pattern is similar to that revealed by the United Kingdom sample. Output movements show the greatest diversity, ranging between increases exceeding 300 % in six industries and declines up to 20 % in four industries. Movements of output per man-hour are also extremely uneven: four industries have more than trebled output per man-hour and four have recorded increases of less than 50 %. In this context it is interesting to note that the median increase for the United States data is approximately 100 %, compared to 51 % for increases in output per head in the United Kingdom data. Table 30 compares the experiences of eleven broadly similar industries in both countries.

Table 30. *Movements of labour productivity in selected industries in the United Kingdom and the United States*

Industry	United States. Changes in output per man-hour, 1923–50		United Kingdom. Changes in output per head, 1924–50	
	1923 = 100	Rank	1924 = 100	Rank
Electricity generation	335	1	311	1
Rubber products	312	2	294	2
Iron and steel	273	3	148	7
Glass products	238	4	211	4
Confectionery	256	5	199	5
Cement	234	6	239	3
Paper mills	184	7	173	6
Paint and varnish	183	8	128	9
Footwear	168	9	125	10
Leather	164	10	111	11
Coke	131	11	137	8

Sources: Tables 14 and 28.

While both the very small number of industries, and the great differences concealed by similar titles, make it unwise to infer overmuch from this table, the comparison is suggestive for two reasons. First, with the exceptions of the coke and cement industries, the increase in labour productivity in each United States industry has outstripped that of its British counterpart—although not always by a large margin. This, combined with the difference in the median increases, supports the findings of Rostas[1] and others that the rate of productivity increase is generally higher in the United States than in the United Kingdom. Secondly, there is a striking similarity in the inter-industry variation (the rank correlation coefficient is +0·83). This lends support to the hypothesis that such differences originate in unequal rates of technical advance; for differences which arise out of the uneven incidence of improvements in technical knowledge might reasonably be expected to appear in both countries.

As in the United Kingdom, earnings movements show a relatively small inter-industry variation compared to price, cost and output movements. This again supports the idea of a semi-unified market for labour which cuts across industry boundaries.

Table 31 summarises the results of correlation analysis similar to that of the United Kingdom survey.

Table 31. *Product-moment coefficients of correlation between changes in output per man-hour and related quantities for twenty-seven industries, United States, 1923–50*

	Output	Man-hours	Output per man-hour	Hourly earnings	Unit labour cost	Wholesale price
Output	—	+0·80	+0·62	—	—	−0·46
Man-hours	—	—	+0·05	+0·13	—	—
Output per man-hour	—	—	—	+0·22	−0·90	−0·76
Hourly earnings	—	—	—	—	−0·09	—
Unit labour cost	—	—	—	—	—	+0·76
Wholesale price	—	—	—	—	—	—

Notes: (*a*) Coefficients between output and output per man-hour and other quantities exclude observations for the rayon and allied products industry.

(*b*) Coefficients between wholesale price changes and other changes refer to only twenty-four industries.

A glance is sufficient to indicate that the results are basically similar to those of the United Kingdom survey.[2] Three features, however, deserve special attention: the higher correlation coefficient between movements of earnings and output per man-hour; the correlation between unit labour cost and wholesale prices; and the low correlation coefficient between changes in employment and output per man-hour.

2. EARNINGS AND LABOUR PRODUCTIVITY

Whether an association exists between movements of labour productivity and earnings and, if so, what are its implications, are questions which have aroused considerable controversy in the field of labour economics in the United States. Fabricant's pioneering study[3] yielded

[1] *Comparative Productivity in British and American Industry* (Cambridge, 1948).
[2] The corresponding rank correlation coefficients are set out in Appendix A, Table A (6). p. 187.
[3] *Employment in Manufacturing, 1899–1939*, p. 100.

a rank coefficient of -0.05 between movements of unit labour content and earnings per head over the years 1909–37. Dunlop,[1] using Bureau of Labor Statistics data of changes in hourly earnings and output per man-hour over the years 1923–40, records a rank coefficient of $+0.47$ which, with some adjustments (the appropriateness of which may be questioned), he raises to the undoubtedly significant level of $+0.72$. Subsequent studies[2] have yielded coefficients ranging between $+0.10$ and $+0.60$ depending upon the sample and the time period involved; while the figures of Table 30 yield a coefficient of $+0.22$. Because of these very different results, and since few of the coefficients are statistically significant, the evidence for such an association must be regarded as inconclusive.

Even if such an association does exist, differential productivity movements are almost certainly only a minor influence on the inter-industry wage structure. The regression coefficient between movements of earnings and output per man-hour is only 0.11;[3] this implies that a 10 % differential increase in output per man-hour leads, on average, to a 1 % increase in comparative earnings. From another point of view, the inter-industry variations in earnings movements are much less than those of output per man-hour (the coefficients of variation are 11.7 and 30.8 % respectively). Both these results suggest that the influence of differential productivity movements on the inter-industry wage structure is very weak.[4] But, if there is such an influence, our previous analysis suggests two possible explanations: uneven improvements in the personal efficiency of labour; or strong unions which have succeeded in directly capturing a minor share of the productivity gains of progressive industries. In terms of the latter explanation, the difference between American and British experience (which could well be illusory) may be associated with the fact that the normal unit for collective bargaining in the United States is the firm or industry, compared to nation-wide craft unions in the United Kingdom.

Apart from this slightly higher correlation between earnings and productivity movements, American experience parallels that for the

[1] John T. Dunlop, 'Productivity and the Wage Structure in Income, Employment and Public Policy', *Essays in Honor of Alvin H. Hansen* (New York, 1948), p. 341. Dunlop adjusts the original coefficient by removing two small industries, and then calculating a weighted coefficient. However, in the present context, no distinction should be drawn between large and small industries, for the regularity in behaviour should be expected in all industries, irrespective of size.

[2] Joseph Garbino, 'A Theory of Inter-industry Wage Structure Variations', *Quart. J. Econ.* vol. LXIV (1950), p. 282; W. Goldner and A. M. Ross, 'Force Affecting the Inter-industry Wage Structure,' *Quart. J. Econ.* vol. LXIV (1950), p. 254; F. Myers and R. Bolby, 'The Inter-industry Wage Structure and Productivity', *Industrial and Labour Relations Rev.* vol. VII, no. 1 (October 1953), p. 97; and Richard Perlman, 'Value Productivity and the Wage Structure', *Industrial and Labour Relations Rev.* vol. x, no. 1 (October 1956), p. 26.

[3] The regression equation is $Y_e = 235.58 + 0.11 (X)$, where $X =$ the change in earnings and Y the change in output per man-hour (1923 = 100). The standard error is 31.5.

[4] This view is supported by the investigations of Clark Kerr who suggests that 'variations in productivity create few effective pressures focused in the wage-setting process' ('The Short-Run Behaviour of Physical Productivity and Average Hourly Earnings', *Rev. Econ. and Statist.* vol. XXXI (1949), p. 229).

United Kingdom. The high correlation coefficient between movements of output per man-hour and unit labour costs ($r = -0.90$) confirms that the main impact of uneven increases in labour productivity has been on labour costs; and, as will be shown, this is reflected in movements of relative prices.

3. LABOUR PRODUCTIVITY AND RELATIVE PRICES

Two of the most important results in confirming the United Kingdom survey are the correlations between movements of unit labour cost and wholesale prices, and output per man-hour and wholesale prices. Fig. 24 sets out these associations.

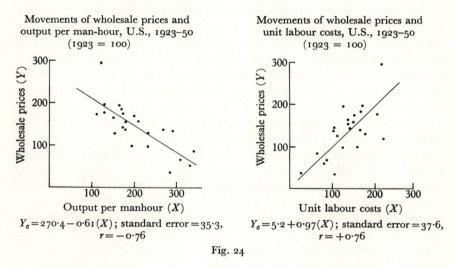

Movements of wholesale prices and output per man-hour, U.S., 1923–50
(1923 = 100)

Movements of wholesale prices and unit labour costs, U.S., 1923–50
(1923 = 100)

$Y_c = 270.4 - 0.61(X)$; standard error $= 35.3$,
$r = -0.76$

$Y_c = 5.2 + 0.97(X)$; standard error $= 37.6$,
$r = +0.76$

Fig. 24

Although the correlation coefficients are not as high as those recorded in the United Kingdom survey, this does not necessarily imply a weaker underlying association; for the price data contains many errors and incomparabilities which, by themselves, would tend to record a lower correlation. Equally as important as the correlation coefficients is the regression coefficient of $+0.97$ between movements of unit labour costs and wholesale prices. This implies that differential movements of unit labour costs have, in general, been paralleled by equal movements of relative prices and, as chapter IX has pointed out, this is only possible if non-labour costs—unit material costs and unit gross margin costs— have also increased or decreased parallel with labour costs. Thus, we find exactly the same phenomenon as in the United Kingdom: all costs have declined as output per man-hour has increased, making possible changes in relative prices greatly in excess of those which can possibly be attributed to savings in labour.

This finding provides three important checks upon the United Kingdom analysis. In the first place it shows that increases in labour productivity in the United States are also part of a wider process that extends to all factors of production. Since the observed inter-industry cost behaviour is only possible if differential savings of labour are accompanied by differential savings of materials and capital, this finding supports our conclusion that causes of increased productivity which have this characteristic—such as technical advances and economies of scale—are likely to be the major elements in productivity movements. Secondly, these results confirm the important role of uneven productivity movements in shaping the changing pattern of relative prices. It should be noted, however, that both the association between output and price movements, and the association between output and output per man-hour movements, are less clear-cut than in the United Kingdom. Finally, these associations support our conclusions concerning the distribution of productivity gains. The association between movements of output per man-hour and relative prices implies that the gains of increased productivity have been distributed to consumers by means of price changes; and that, apart from the weak association between movements of earnings and output per man-hour, the gains from differential increases in productivity have not been appropriated at their source by strong unions.

The broad picture revealed by the British and American surveys is therefore basically similar. Both suggest that growth has been accompanied by constant adjustment to the structure of output and prices. Both imply that such structural changes reflect the need to adapt to the uneven incidence of technical change. And, in each case, adjustment to the structure of output and relative prices have provided the mechanism whereby productivity gains have been distributed to consumers.

4. LABOUR PRODUCTIVITY AND EMPLOYMENT

One respect in which the United States results are quite different to those for the United Kingdom is the low correlation coefficient between changes in employment (measured in man-hours) and output per man-hour ($r = 0 \cdot 05$).[1] This means that there has been no tendency for above-average increases in employment to accompany above-average increases in productivity, and vice versa. It appears, therefore, that the expansive effect has been much weaker in the United States than in the United Kingdom. Why this should be so is something of a problem. A possible explanation is that because overseas trade is relatively more important in the United Kingdom, elasticities of demand are generally higher, and so allow greater scope for the expansion of progressive industries. But, whatever the reason for this difference, it implies that changes in the structure of employment have probably contributed much less to increasing aggregate productivity in the United States than in the United Kingdom.

---

[1] Fabricant (p. 88) and Garbino (p. 285) also report low coefficients.

5. ALTERNATIVE INDEX-NUMBER MEASURES

The data of Table 28 are inconvenient for checking our findings with respect to index-number ambiguities, for the price and output data are not wholly consistent in terms of weighting systems and coverage. For such a check Fabricant's data are more appropriate; they also provide a larger sample covering thirty-eight industries which contribute approximately 50 % of manufacturing value added. Measures of changes in output and output per head over the period 1909–37 have been computed on both systems of valuation. As in the United Kingdom calculations, the alternative weighting systems do not refer to the weights of individual products within each industry, but only the weights (net output prices) employed to aggregate output between industries.

Table 32. *The effect of alternative weighting systems on measures of changes in output and output per head, thirty-eight industries, United States, 1909–37*

(1909 = 100)

Index numbers for changes in	1909 weights	1937 weights
Output	382	209
Output per head	278	152

Source: Computed from Table 8 (p. 101) of Fabricant, *Employment in Manufacturing, 1899–1939*, and Appendix C (p. 603) in *The Output of Manufacturing Industries, 1899–1937*, also by Fabricant.

Again we find a striking divergence between measures based on the two weighting systems: the comparison based on 1909 prices yields an increase in productivity of 178 %; while that based on 1937 prices yields an increase of only 52 %. This is by no means due to chance: it arises out of the correlation between price and output movements[1] which, as chapter XI has shown, is an essential part of the growth process—the tendency for technically progressive industries to expand output and reduce their relative prices. If such ambiguities are a general phenomenon—and the two calculations suggest that they could well be—this underlines the necessity for great care in interpreting long-run measures of output and productivity. The index-number problem is not simply a problem of measurement, but a reflection of the continuous adjustment in the structure of output necessitated by uneven rates of technical change.

6. SUMMARY

1. The chief purpose of the United States survey is to provide an independent check on the United Kingdom analysis. It does this in two ways: first, by providing an alternative sample which is free from

[1] Fabricant records a −0·66 rank correlation between changes in net prices and output over the years 1899–1937 (*The Output of Manufacturing Industries*, p. 109), and a −0·66 rank correlation between changes in wholesale price and output over the years 1909–39 (*Employment in Manufacturing*, p. 109).

the worst dangers of spurious correlation through errors; second, by confirming the interpretive conclusions which have been derived from the United Kingdom analysis concerning the nature and impact of technical change.

2. The statistical approach is similar to that for the United Kingdom. Movements of output, employment, output per man-hour, hourly earnings, unit labour costs and wholesale prices, are compared for twenty-three industries over the period 1923–50. The wholesale price data, although, not entirely comparable with the output data, are completely independent, thereby removing the danger of spurious correlations through errors in the correlations involving prices.

3. The data reveal a very great diversity in movements of output and output per man-hour, as in the United Kingdom. Earnings movements again show a relatively small dispersion compared to price and cost movements. Inter-industry correlation analysis yields the same broad pattern of associations as the United Kingdom survey.

4. Differential increases in output per man-hour and hourly earnings show some small degree of correlation ($r = +0.22$). This result should be interpreted in relation to other studies of United States data which have revealed associations ranging between $r = +0.10$ and $r = +0.72$. In view of these results the evidence for such an association must be regarded as inconclusive. But, even if there is such an association, the quantitative influence of unequal productivity movements on the inter-industry wage structure is certainly small.

5. There is a high inverse correlation ($r = -0.90$) between movements of output per man-hour and unit labour cost; this confirms that the primary impact of unequal increases in labour productivity has been on the inter-industry structure of labour costs rather than earnings.

6. Movements of relative wholesale prices and output per man-hour are also inversely correlated ($r = -0.76$); also the regression coefficient is close to unity. As in the United Kingdom, these results are only consistent with productivity increases which include materials and capital—such as technical change and economies of scale. They also imply that productivity gains have been distributed to consumers by means of price changes.

7. In contrast to the United Kingdom survey, the United States figures reveal a low correlation ($r = +0.03$) between differential increases in output per man-hour and employment. This implies that changes in the employment structure have not made as important a contribution to aggregate productivity in the United States as in the United Kingdom.

8. Calculations of aggregate output and output per head movements over the period 1909–37 based upon thirty-eight industries, covering almost 50% of the manufacturing sector, reveal very large differences between alternative weighting systems. These differences originate in an association between price and output movements which is the consequence of uneven rates of technical change.

STATISTICAL SOURCES AND METHODS

I. SOURCES OF THE UNITED KINGDOM SURVEY

The basic series for the United Kingdom survey have been derived from the following sources.

(i) *Volume of gross output at 1935 prices*

For the years 1924–35, series of this definition are available from the Final Reports of the Vth (1935) Census of Production. By linking these series with the preliminary tables of 1948 gross output at 1935 prices,[1] prepared by Mr B. C. Brown of the Board of Trade, a continuous series from 1924 to 1948 can be obtained for census years (1924, 1930, 1935 and 1948), and in some cases for Import Enquiry Years (1933, 1934 and 1937). The figure for 1937, however, is current weighted, and has been incorporated into the series by means of the 1937–48 comparison also prepared by Mr Brown.

To ensure accuracy as far as possible, the component series have been examined for the following features.

(a) *Quality changes*

The degree of detail in the product classification of the volume measure for 1924–35 has been examined for its ability to distinguish between products of different quality.

(b) *Coverage*

As far as possible, only those industries have been included in the sample where the output measures have a high coverage and little output included in such measures is produced in other trades. Such details are set out in Table A (1) below.

(c) *Scope*

Significant discrepancies due to changes in classification and inconsistent treatment of Northern Ireland were regarded as sufficient to warrant exclusion from the sample.

(d) *Uncovered output*

The 1924–35 series treat uncovered output by making the quantity assumption, whereas the modern approach prefers the price assumption. In most cases it has been possible to recalculate the series on the basis of the price assumption. In few cases were significant differences to be observed. The 1935–48 series are based on the price assumption.

---

[1] Final Tables published in the *Bulletin of the London and Cambridge Economic Service* under the title: 'Industrial Production in 1935 and 1948' (December 1954).

Table A (1). *Coverage of the indexes of output, 1924–48*

	1924–35		
Industry	Approximate coverage of gross output in detail in 1935 (%)	Approximate percentage of the index components produced in other trades in 1935 (%)	1935–48. Approximate coverage of gross output in 1935 (%)
Coal mines	100	—	99
Brick and fireclay	95	2	95
Glass (containers and other)	96	2	70
Cement	96	—	91
Coke ovens and by-products	68	25	98
Chemicals	65	11	70
Paint and varnish	97	—	89
Matches	99	—	97
Blast furnaces	92	5	99
Iron and steel	98	4	87
Tinplate	93	5	98
Wrought iron and steel tubes	80	8	97
Cutlery	99	5	74
Wire and wire working	87	3	86
Cotton spinning and doubling	99	3	98
Jute	97	—	94
Hosiery and other knitted goods	100	8	99
Leather (tanning and dressing)	97	—	84
Boots and shoes	100	1	93
Cocoa and confectionery	97	4	93
Brewing and malting	95	—	94
Spirit distilling	89	1	99
Paper and board	89	—	96
Wallpaper	98	1	95
Rubber	79	3	77
Linoleum and oilcloth	99	2	96
Brushes and brooms	97	1	89
Electricity	91	—	88

Table A (2). *Series and sources, output measures, 1948–50*

Industry	Source type	Description of series
Coal mines	C	Saleable mined coal produced
Brick and fireclay	C	Bricks produced
Glass	A	Deflation of gross value of output by price index for glass containers
Cement	C	Cement produced
Coke ovens	A	Production of coke from coke works
Chemicals	B	Weighted output of principal products
Paint and varnish	—	No measure
Matches	C	Gross boxes produced
Blast furnaces	A	Output of pig-iron (unweighted)
Iron and steel	B	Weighted output index
Wrought iron and steel tubes	A	Deliveries of tubes, pipes and fittings
Tinplate	A	Output of tinplate, ternplate and black plate
Cutlery	B	Knives produced
Wire and wire working	A	Output of steel wire
Cotton	B	Weighted output by counts
Jute	A	Home consumption of raw jute
Hosiery and other knitted goods	B	Weighted output of principal products
Leather	C	Weighted quantities of finished leather sold
Boots and shoes	C	Weighted output of principal products
Cocoa and confectionery	C	Weight of chocolate and sugar confectionery produced
Brewing and malting	B	Proof bulk barrels of beer
Spirit distilling	A	Proof spirit produced
Paper and board	C	Paper produced weighted by 1948 net output values
Wallpaper	—	No measure
Rubber	B	Weighted rubber consumption for various uses
Linoleum and oilcloth	C	Principal products weighted by 1948 net output values
Brushes and brooms	C	Principal products weighted by net output values
Electricity	A	Electricity sent out

Sources: A = Annual Abstract of Statistics.

B = C. F. Carter, 'Index Numbers of the Real Product of the United Kingdom', *J. Roy. Statist. Soc.* vol. cxv (1952), part i, pp. 82–125.

C = L. Rostas, 'Changes in the Productivity of British Industry, 1945–51', *Econ. J.* vol. lxii (March 1952), p. 15.

Table A (3). *Changes in the volume of gross output from 1935 to 1948 based on 1935 and 1948 prices: selected United Kingdom industries*

(1935 = 100)

Industry	1935 prices	1948 prices	Industry	1935 prices	1948 prices
Coal mines	85·5	84·8	Jute	154·0	155·7
Brick and fireclay	79·6	77·9	Hosiery and knitted	105·1	107·2
Glass (containers only)	181·3	180·2	goods		
Cement	138·2	137·1	Leather (tanning and	107·1	102·9
Coke ovens	128·7	128·2	dressing)		
Chemicals (general only)	266·2	240·9	Cocoa, chocolate, etc.	82·2	81·9
Paint and varnish	172·9	162·1	Boots and shoes	92·9	95·2
Blast furnaces	71·2	73·5	Brewing and malting	134·2	134·2
Iron and steel (excluding	167·4	172·4	Spirit distilling	139·2	127·4
steel sheets)			Paper and board	104·6	127·2
Tinplate	101·3	101·3	Wallpaper	50·7	50·5
Wrought iron and steel	160·9	157·2	Matches	122·5	123·7
tubes			Rubber goods	187·6	183·5
Cutlery	157·2	143·3	Linoleum	92·9	93·0
Wire and wire manu-	155·0	150·8	Brushes and brooms	138·7	130·7
factures			Electricity supply	252·8	252·5
Cotton spinning and	85·5	85·3			
doubling					

Sources: Preliminary Tables of 'Industrial Production in 1935 and 1948' by B. C. Brown (Board of Trade) published in *The Bulletin of the London and Cambridge Economic Service* (December 1954).

(ii) *Total employment and numbers of operatives*

From Census Tables with some adjustment for individual industries. See notes by industry.

(iii) *Wages and salaries*

In general the wages bill in each industry for pre-war census years was estimated from the sample earnings inquiry conducted in conjunction with each census. The total wages bill for each industry was derived on the basis of net output and employment characteristics of the sample in relation to the totals for the industry. Where significant discrepancies resulted from these alternative procedures, the mean of the two estimates was taken. For some groups of industries (chemicals and cotton) more hazardous methods were used (see notes on individual industries). For post-war years, complete totals are available from the census tables.

Estimates of the salary bill in each industry for 1924, 1930 and 1935 were prepared by multiplying the number of salaried staff by the average salaries implicit in Miss Chapman's estimates of wages and salaries.[1] These in turn are based on the Marley–Campion survey but have the advantage of a finer industry classification not available in the

[1] Agatha L. Chapman, *Wages and Salaries in the United Kingdom in 1920–1938* (Cambridge, 1953).

published data.[1] The industry grouping is, however, broader than for this survey; the most appropriate classification to each industry has been used. For post-war years, complete data are available from the census tables.

These estimates in conjunction with the output and employment series yield estimates of changes in earnings per operative, unit wage cost, unit salary cost, and the two combined, unit labour cost.

(iv) *Gross margins*

Estimates of the residual element in net output are derived by deducting the estimates of the wage and salary bill from net output. This is a particularly hazardous procedure since errors in the wage and salary estimates may be compounded. Moreover, the exact content of the residual is not known; certain minor costs are included, the treatment of repairs and maintenance, and work given out on contract, is uncertain for pre-war years.

Unit gross margin cost has been derived by division with the output series.

(v) *Unit materials cost, unit net price and gross price*

These estimates have been obtained by dividing census data by the output series.

Notes on individual industries

1. Coal mines

   (*a*) Small discrepancy with Ministry of Fuel and Power estimates.

   (*b*) 1948 and 1935 output not precisely comparable because of differences in treatment of free and concessionary coal.

   (*c*) Output series for 1933, 1934 and 1937 from *Ministry of Fuel and Power Statistical Digest*.

2. Brick and fireclay

   (*a*) 1924–35 output series adjusted to price assumption.

   (*b*) Possibility of considerable errors in the earnings movements.

3. Glass (containers and other)

   Two industries have been combined. For the part that produces glass products, quality changes may be considerable.

4. Cement

   (*a*) Arbitrary downward adjustment of 3500 workers in 1924 to allow for employment in quarries not included in following years. Similarly for 1924 wage and salary bill.

   (*b*) Adjustment for change in classification 1935–48.

5. Chemicals

   To avoid incomparabilities, three census trades have been combined: general chemicals, dyes and dye-stuffs, and coal-tar products. The 1924 numbers of operatives (not employment) have been estimated on the basis of the employment in these trades. Similarly for wages bill.

6. Blast furnaces

   A considerable discrepancy exists in the employment figures from census sources and the *Statistical Bulletin of the Iron and Steel Federation*.

7. Iron and steel

   Although the melting, rolling and steel sheets sections of the industry have been combined, small discrepancies remain that impair year to year comparability.

[1] Joan A. Marley and H. Campion, 'Changes in Salaries in Great Britain, 1924–1939', *J. Roy. Statist. Soc.* vol. CIII (1940), part IV, p. 524.

8. Wrought iron and steel tubes

1935–48 output movements from special calculation from detailed output data in the 1948 report.

9. Cotton spinning and doubling

Wages bill for 1924, 1930 and 1935 estimated for the whole cotton industry and allocated on the basis of employment figures.

10. Jute

Earnings estimates in some doubt.

11. Leather

1948 gross margins include £7 m. appreciation of government-owned stocks.

12. Boot and shoe manufacturing

(a) 1924 figures include some repair work.
(b) 1930 figures include some production of umbrellas, etc.

13. Brewing and malting

Some incomparability due to bottling activity in 1924 and 1930; appears to be minor.

14. Paper and board

Small incomparabilities in 1935 and 1948 reports for 1935 figures.

15. Electricity supply

(a) Material cost estimates do not check with those of the Ministry of Fuel and Power for fuel consumed.
(b) Some incomparability between 1935 and 1948 due to meter rents and some capital formation. See 1948 Report.
(c) Addition of 1500 persons (1400 operatives) to 1924 employment to meet incomparability caused by persons employed in railway generating stations.

Table A (4). *Changes in output, employment, output per head, earnings, costs and prices, for selected United Kingdom industrial industries, selected years 1924–50*

(1924 = 100)

Standard industrial classification	Volume of gross output	Total employment	Output per head	Output per operative	Earnings per operative	Unit wage cost	Unit salary cost	Unit gross margin cost	Unit materials cost	Gross price	Net price
Order II											
10				Coal mines							
1924	100	100	100	100	100	100	100	100	100	100	100
1930	92	78	118	118	82	64	88	78	74	72	72
1933	78	65	119	—	—	—	—	—	—	—	—
1934	83	65	127	—	—	—	—	—	—	—	—
1935	83	64	130	131	86	54	86	83	72	70	69
1937	91	65	138	—	—	—	—	—	—	—	—
1948	71	64	118	115	282	246	392	218	279	250	244
1949	73	64	115	119	289	243	298	253	286	255	250
1950	73	61	120	124	302	243	399	245	280	253	248

Table A (4) *(cont.)*

Standard industrial classification	Volume of gross output	Total employment	Output per head	Output per operative	Earnings per operative	Unit wage cost	Unit salary cost	Unit gross margin cost	Unit materials cost	Gross price	Net price
Order III											
20 and 29 (3) Part					Brick and fireclay						
1924	100	100	100	100	100	100	100	100	100	100	100
1930	117	110	106	104	98	94	85	91	85	90	92
1933	128	110	117	117	—	—	—	—	78	83	86
1934	156	123	126	126	—	—	—	—	76	80	81
1935	168	134	125	125	98	78	72	92	74	80	83
1937	179	140	128	127	—	—	—	—	88	88	88
1948	134	105	127	132	246	187	262	181	218	198	189
1949	152	109	140	145	259	181	257	159	228	193	178
1950	158	111	142	147	270	185	265	162	244	201	182
22 and 23					Glass (containers and other)						
1924	100	100	100	100	100	100	100	100	100	100	100
1930	116	107	108	111	98	89	112	85	94	91	89
1933	132	108	123	126	—	—	—	—	86	82	80
1934	150	118	127	130	—	—	—	—	84	83	83
1935	161	125	129	132	95	72	97	92	83	82	82
1937	197	134	147	152	—	—	—	—	78	80	81
1948	317	168	189	200	236	118	171	136	139	134	129
1949	340	171	199	211	247	117	172	132	155	134	127
1950	369	174	211	226	259	115	177	135	148	136	128
24					Cement						
1924	100	100	100	100	100	100	100	100	100	100	100
1930	149	110	136	136	107	79	75	106	68	68	89
1933	139	96	144	156	—	—	—	—	63	64	83
1934	165	101	163	176	—	—	—	—	62	66	87
1935	175	102	172	189	108	57	101	98	65	69	93
1937	220	131	168	179	—	—	—	—	73	78	97
1948	242	109	221	234	240	93	179	135	198	150	141
1949	262	112	233	243	253	94	182	138	198	152	145
1950	276	116	239	251	266	102	200	143	206	158	150
Order IV											
30					Coke ovens and by-products						
1924	100	100	100	100	100	100	100	100	100	100	100
1930	101	83	122	124	91	73	98	30	70	64	51
1933	84	62	136	140	—	—	—	—	61	57	46
1934	102	71	144	147	—	—	—	—	64	62	54
1935	106	76	140	144	92	64	100	49	66	64	57
1937	132	83	160	164	—	—	—	100	85	85	85
1948	137	99	138	151	211	139	372	145	256	226	150
1949	138	102	136	149	219	147	397	152	270	238	158
1950	137	100	137	165	223	147	426	164	274	244	165

Table A (4) (cont.)

Standard industrial classification	Volume of gross output	Total employment	Output per head	Output per operative	Earnings per operative	Unit wage cost	Unit salary cost	Unit gross margin cost	Unit materials cost	Gross price	Net price
29 (3) Part, 31 (3), 31 (4), 31 (1)					Chemicals						
(including general chemicals, dyes and dyestuffs and coal-tar products)											
1924	100	100	100	100	100	100	100	100	100	100	100
1930	106	103	102	111	104	95	131	91	78	86	96
1935	168	118	146	159	101	64	100	105	61	72	90
1937	198	129	154	168	—	—	—	—	119	75	—
1948	435	250	174	208	240	116	275	129	142	140	137
1949	436	256	170	204	246	120	308	111	146	140	131
1950	528	272	194	236	257	109	286	143	141	142	143
34					Paint and varnish						
1924	100	100	100	100	100	100	100	100	100	100	100
1930	116	115	100	102	99	97	97	104	98	100	101
1935	131	134	98	107	97	91	119	119	71	120	113
1948	227	178	128	124	203	141	246	184	141	207	206
35 (2) and 199 (3) Part					Matches						
1924	100	100	100	100	100	100	100	100	100	100	100
1930	99	82	120	123	100	81	100	88	84	98	87
1935	106	77	138	140	109	78	87	84	74	93	83
1948	130	79	165	176	200	114	233	70	160	153	89
1949	124	81	154	164	205	125	256	85	160	205	104
1950	124	79	156	169	217	128	272	87	171	218	107
Order V											
40					Blast furnaces						
1924	100	100	100	100	100	100	100	100	100	100	100
1930	84	72	116	117	86	74	92	203	76	78	90
1933	55	42	129	136	—	—	—	—	56	63	96
1934	78	55	142	144	—	—	—	—	61	65	87
1935	87	59	148	151	102	67	87	167	62	66	89
1937	111	72	152	154	—	—	—	—	84	89	116
1948	122	101	121	131	246	185	354	647	191	205	294
1949	125	104	120	130	251	192	372	645	216	227	302
1950	127	104	122	132	260	197	391	648	229	240	307
41, 43 (1)			Iron and steel: melting, rolling and steel sheets								
1924	100	100	100	100	100	100	100	100	100	100	100
1930	83	86	96	97	103	109	123	50	79	84	96
1933	79	72	109	113	—	—	—	—	67	74	91
1934	97	80	121	123	—	—	—	—	70	77	97
1935	108	86	125	127	118	93	93	117	72	79	99
1937	158	106	149	151	—	—	—	—	80	86	102
1948	180	139	129	139	251	180	275	346	178	190	228
1949	185	142	131	142	259	186	288	461	198	209	260
1950	198	142	140	152	275	181	289	482	199	220	261

Table A (4) (*cont.*)

Standard industrial classification	Volume of gross output	Total employment	Output per head	Output per operative	Earnings per operative	Unit wage cost	Unit salary cost	Unit gross margin cost	Unit materials cost	Gross price	Net price
43 (2)					Tinplate						
1924	100	100	100	100	100	100	100	100	100	100	100
1930	95	90	106	106	91	86	102	77	69	73	84
1933	89	84	107	107	—	—	—	—	60	67	83
1934	85	81	105	106	—	—	—	—	66	71	85
1935	83	79	105	106	86	79	109	98	67	74	94
1937	110	94	117	117	—	—	—	—	84	89	100
1948	84	59	142	149	208	139	349	308	176	180	190
1949	85	60	141	148	219	147	380	323	199	200	201
1950	86	61	144	152	229	150	409	362	214	214	215
44					Wrought iron and steel tubes						
1924	100	100	100	100	100	100	100	100	100	100	100
1930	123	104	119	118	102	86	82	86	74	78	85
1933	127	83	152	154	—	—	—	—	62	65	71
1934	163	100	163	164	—	—	—	—	63	67	81
1935	179	111	161	164	96	58	69	90	64	66	71
1937	214	127	169	172	—	—	—	—	69	76	89
1948	303	152	199	214	242	112	137	177	142	140	138
1949	372	162	231	248	258	103	129	159	150	140	125
1950	402	167	240	259	282	106	128	187	172	153	136

Order VIII

Standard industrial classification	Volume of gross output	Total employment	Output per head	Output per operative	Earnings per operative	Unit wage cost	Unit salary cost	Unit gross margin cost	Unit materials cost	Gross price	Net price
90 (2)					Cutlery						
1924	100	100	100	100	100	100	100	100	100	100	100
1930	138	104	132	134	109	81	83	69	64	64	79
1933	179	97	181	180	—	—	—	—	40	45	65
1934	212	103	206	204	—	—	—	—	36	40	60
1935	238	109	212	220	95	43	44	118	37	36	64
1937	276	117	237	236	—	—	—	—	37	44	64
1948	374	132	284	293	228	78	96	332	71	92	141
1949	396	131	303	316	232	73	98	355	77	96	144
1950	434	140	312	324	237	73	95	373	80	99	147
93					Wire and wire working						
1924	100	100	100	100	100	100	100	100	100	100	100
1930	100	88	114	115	122	106	94	23	82	78	70
1933	104	80	130	131	—	—	—	—	64	66	67
1934	121	86	141	141	—	—	—	—	66	67	67
1935	133	94	140	141	122	86	73	57	67	68	72
1937	162	109	148	150	—	—	—	—	91	88	81
1948	207	141	147	158	228	144	221	197	182	179	174
1949	242	142	171	186	243	131	206	151	174	164	145
1950	254	143	178	194	255	131	213	170	199	184	155

Table A (4) *(cont.)*

Standard industrial classification	Volume of gross output	Total employment	Output per head	Output per operative	Earnings per operative	Unit wage cost	Unit salary cost	Unit gross margin cost	Unit materials cost	Gross price	Net price
Order X											
110					Cotton spinning and doubling						
1924	100	100	100	100	100	100	100	100	100	100	100
1930	78	75	104	104	90	87	105	20	51	51	54
1933	88	73	121	122	—	—	—	—	37	39	47
1934	89	73	123	123	—	—	—	—	38	41	49
1935	91	72	126	126	92	73	80	22	40	42	47
1937	100	74	136	136	—	—	—	—	44	47	57
1948	78	61	127	131	249	190	380	163	153	160	183
1949	78	63	124	127	264	207	417	166	300	170	193
1950	83	64	129	133	278	209	437	227	324	204	225
110					Jute						
1924	100	100	100	100	100	100	100	100	100	100	100
1930	80	83	96	97	91	95	109	29	88	84	75
1933	83	65	127	129	—	—	—	—	56	61	68
1934	93	68	136	138	—	—	—	—	51	58	73
1935	98	69	140	142	101	72	100	54	54	58	67
1937	98	70	140	142	—	—	—	—	63	59	65
1948	62	50	125	130	224	174	404	334	252	246	233
1949	55	46	119	125	242	194	505	386	300	290	266
1950	65	49	134	140	262	186	478	368	324	303	254
118					Hosiery and other knitted goods						
1924	100	100	100	100	100	100	100	100	100	100	100
1930	99	111	91	90	92	102	122	117	86	94	109
1933	134	116	116	117	—	—	—	—	61	68	81
1934	139	120	116	117	—	—	—	—	60	67	80
1935	143	121	118	120	95	79	88	78	57	65	79
1937	157	126	125	126	—	—	—	—	59	67	81
1948	150	99	151	157	220	140	229	268	157	171	197
1949	168	110	164	158	241	152	234	258	179	183	200
1950	183	119	153	159	255	160	242	324	202	212	230
Order XI											
130 (1)					Leather (tanning and dressing)						
1924	100	100	100	100	100	100	100	100	100	100	100
1930	100	94	107	108	94	87	93	86	86	86	87
1933	102	95	108	108	—	—	—	—	55	71	80
1934	103	97	107	107	—	—	—	—	67	70	79
1935	114	100	115	115	89	78	78	78	68	71	78
1937	125	106	117	117	—	—	—	—	83	81	76
1948	123	111	111	113	211	187	322	421	196	225	307
1949	125	111	112	116	221	191	336	300	222	230	254
1950	125	112	111	115	231	200	360	393	261	273	304

Table A (4) (*cont.*)

Standard industrial classification	Volume of gross output	Total employment	Output per head	Output per operative	Earnings per operative	Unit wage cost	Unit salary cost	Unit gross margin cost	Unit materials cost	Gross price	Net price
Order XII											
148, 149					Boots and shoes (manufacturing)						
1924	100	100	100	100	100	100	100	100	100	100	100
1930	104	89	116	116	95	82	83	96	86	86	86
1933	115	87	131	131	—	—	—	—	63	65	69
1934	112	86	130	130	—	—	—	—	63	65	69
1935	122	89	137	136	94	69	68	74	61	65	70
1937	124	90	137	137	—	—	—	—	66	68	71
1948	113	85	133	136	216	158	185	360	231	224	216
1949	117	91	128	132	226	171	205	315	254	237	214
1950	112	90	125	129	218	181	224	313	276	253	222
Order XIII											
156					Cocoa, chocolate and sugar confectionery						
1924	100	100	100	100	100	100	100	100	100	100	100
1930	113	94	121	123	97	78	93	90	76	80	86
1935	147	95	154	160	98	61	78	77	56	62	71
1937	161	98	164	168	—	—	—	—	65	65	64
1948	121	69	174	187	230	123	171	162	212	185	148
1949	164	80	204	214	241	113	138	138	196	166	128
1950	171	86	199	211	250	120	150	146	217	182	136
163					Brewing and malting						
1924	100	100	100	100	100	100	100	100	100	100	100
1930	94	94	101	100	98	97	100	107	80	97	105
1935	81	85	97	98	98	99	117	120	78	96	116
1948	109	109	101	104	187	180	278	172	200	272	180
1949	102	111	92	95	193	204	329	154	240	284	173
1950	97	108	91	93	198	214	346	151	254	280	173
168 (1) Part					Spirit distilling						
1924	100	100	100	100	100	100	100	100	100	100	100
1930	84	74	112	114	105	92	101	76	76	78	81
1935	118	66	177	183	99	54	69	77	42	53	71
1948	164	94	174	182	196	107	172	111	181	156	113
1949	195	105	185	197	175	89	176	57	155	136	105
1950	201	106	191	205	209	102	188	122	175	155	120
Order XV											
180					Paper and board						
1924	100	100	100	100	100	100	100	100	100	100	100
1930	125	104	120	121	104	86	97	78	82	83	82
1933	146	104	140	143	—	—	—	—	57	63	72
1934	170	113	150	154	—	—	—	—	60	62	69
1935	170	117	145	149	108	73	93	79	58	65	77
1937	197	123	160	165	—	—	—	—	65	69	77
1948	177	129	137	146	241	166	355	195	203	198	189
1949	204	134	152	162	256	158	333	122	195	179	149
1950	239	139	173	184	269	146	313	229	183	187	196

Table A (4) (*cont.*)

Standard industrial classification	Volume of gross output	Total employment	Output per head	Output per operative	Earnings per operative	Unit wage cost	Unit salary cost	Unit gross margin cost	Unit materials cost	Gross price	Net price
181					Wallpaper						
1924	100	100	100	100	100	100	100	100	100	100	100
1930	116	126	91	90	100	110	101	86	94	96	96
1933	121	117	104	115	—	—	—	—	76	85	93
1934	131	126	103	122	—	—	—	—	72	86	99
1935	143	134	107	130	102	93	111	121	70	81	89
1937	149	141	103	136	—	—	—	—	70	83	91
1948	72	86	84	82	229	261	418	246	254	259	264
Order XVI											
190					Rubber						
1924	100	100	100	100	100	100	100	100	100	100	100
1930	192	110	175	174	102	56	62	73	62	63	64
1933	226	109	208	215	—	--	—	—	38	45	52
1934	250	116	216	221	—	—	—	—	40	44	49
1935	263	117	225	231	101	44	47	49	43	50	47
1937	301	124	246	252	—	—	—	—	54	48	41
1948	494	183	269	276	260	94	81	94	125	109	92
1949	484	181	268	279	260	93	92	76	120	103	85
1950	568	193	294	302	277	91	86	84	151	120	87
191					Linoleum and oilcloth						
1924	100	100	100	100	100	100	100	100	100	100	100
1930	99	104	95	96	84	87	117	57	90	80	70
1933	121	98	124	130	—	—	—	—	55	56	58
1934	135	98	137	145	—	—	—	—	54	56	59
1935	139	101	138	146	88	66	108	60	54	58	64
1937	143	103	139	148	—	—	—	—	58	64	64
1948	129	98	131	155	209	134	438	102	241	188	129
1949	172	105	164	194	222	114	364	83	191	152	107
1950	176	119	154	184	238	129	381	92	218	171	118
192					Brushes and brooms						
1924	100	100	100	100	100	100	100	100	100	100	100
1930	95	100	95	109	99	91	216	96	95	103	111
1933	110	102	108	111	—	—	—	83	79	85	92
1934	116	104	112	128	—	—	—	80	80	86	92
1935	127	108	117	134	93	70	163	93	81	86	91
1937	160	119	134	153	—	—	—	—	94	90	86
1948	176	142	124	129	220	171	206	410	296	274	251
1949	178	134	132	139	226	163	205	323	280	250	219
1950	197	131	151	160	233	145	196	291	257	228	198
Order XVIII											
211					Electricity						
1924	100	100	100	100	100	100	100	100	100	100	100
1930	211	153	138	143	86	60	78	88	68	73	77
1935	370	204	181	196	81	41	70	91	39	58	71
1948	936	296	316	365	159	44	76	67	67	63	60
1949	980	329	298	350	163	47	87	72	67	66	65
1950	1094	351	311	372	170	46	91	70	66	67	64

2. RANK COEFFICIENTS OF CORRELATION

Table A (5). *Coefficients of rank correlation with respect to changes in output per head and related quantities, selected United Kingdom industries, 1924–50*

	Volume of output	Output per head	Output per operative	Earnings per operative	Unit wage cost	Unit wage and salary cost	Unit gross margin cost	Unit material cost	Gross price	Net price	Total employment
Volume of output	—	+0·83	—	—	—	—	—	—	−0·86	—	+0·91
Output per head	—	—	—	—	—	−0·92	−0·585	−0·82	−0·91	−0·77	+0·60
Output per operative	—	—	—	+0·13	−0·93	—	—	—	—	—	—
Earnings per operative	—	—	—	—	+0·11	—	—	—	—	—	—
Unit wage cost	—	—	—	—	—	—	—	+0·80	+0·87	+0·83	—
Unit wage and salary cost	—	—	—	—	—	—	+0·63	+0·69	—	—	—
Unit gross margin cost	—	—	—	—	—	—	—	+0·42	+0·56	—	—
Unit material cost	—	—	—	—	—	—	—	—	+0·80	—	—
Gross price	—	—	—	—	—	—	—	—	—	—	—
Net price	—	—	—	—	—	—	—	—	—	—	—
Total employment	—	—	—	—	—	—	—	—	—	—	—

Source: Data from Table 14.

3. THE DIVISION OF OUTPUT PER HEAD MOVEMENTS INTO SHIFT AND INTERNAL COMPONENTS

For many purposes it is desirable to separate changes in aggregate output per head which are due to changes within each industry from changes caused by employment movements between industries. This can be achieved by the following approach.

Let O equal the output of each industry valued at some set of prices that need not be specified. Then $\Sigma O_n / \Sigma O_o$ is the change in aggregate output from time o to n. Applying the identity output = output per head times employment, this expression becomes

$$\frac{\Sigma(O_n/E_n)\,E_n}{\Sigma(O_o/E_o)\,E_o}.$$

Let $O/E = P$ = output per head so that this expression becomes

$$\frac{\Sigma P_n E_n}{\Sigma P_o E_o} \quad \text{in the new notation.}$$

Overall output per head changes, including both shifts between industries and internal changes, are then

$$\frac{\Sigma P_n E_n}{\Sigma P_o E_o} \cdot \frac{\Sigma E_o}{\Sigma E_n}.$$

This expression resolves into two pairs of components. The first pair is

$$\frac{\Sigma P_n E_n}{\Sigma P_n E_o} \cdot \frac{\Sigma E_o}{\Sigma E_n} \cdot \frac{\Sigma E_o P_n}{\Sigma E_o P_o}.$$
$$\quad\text{(a)}\qquad\text{(b)}\qquad\text{(c)}$$

The first component (a) is an index of employment, or more usefully a current weighted index of output subject to the restriction that output per head in each industry does not change. It measures the increase in output caused solely by an increasing labour force and shifts in employment between industries. Division by a measure of the overall increase in employment (b) removes the effect of an increasing labour force so that (a) and (b) together measure the increase in output, when output per head is constant in each industry and the total labour force does not increase, that is, the increase in output due to inter-industry shifts in employment. The component (c) is a base-weighted index of output per head subject to the restriction that employment in each industry does not change. Index numbers of this form enable the total increase in output per head to be resolved into two components which distinguish the output per head increases caused by inter-industry shifts in employment, and increases in output per head within each industry.[1]

The second pair of components is

$$\frac{\Sigma P_o E_n}{\Sigma P_o E_o} \cdot \frac{\Sigma E_o}{\Sigma E_n} \cdot \frac{\Sigma E_n P_o}{\Sigma E_n P_o}.$$

These components have the same meaning as the previous ones except that the shift component is now base weighted and the internal component is current weighted.

4. THE CALCULATIONS OF CHAPTER IX

These calculations, which are illustrative only, are based upon relationships derived from the definitions of the elasticity of substitution. They assume that this elasticity does not vary with factor proportions.

The equation relating changes in the input of one factor to changes in relative factor prices is (6) in the Appendix to chapter III.

The equation relating changes in shares to changes in relative factor prices and the elasticity of substitution is derived as follows:

Let α be the relative share of factor a,

Let β be the relative share of factor b.

[1] This approach to distinguishing the two influences results in measures that stand in a multiplicative, not an additive, relationship. Within the theory of index numbers, an additive break-up of the total change is impossible except as a residual form which cannot be given a precise meaning. The reason lies in the weighting problem; shifts of employment from one industry to another not only change overall output per head by reason of the shifts but, if a current weighted index is used for the internal component, also increase that component. For a careful discussion of the problem see Irving H. Siegel, 'Concepts and Measurement of Production and Productivity', *The Bureau of Labor Statistics* (Washington, 1952), p. 86.

Since $r = Pa/Pb$ and $r = -db/da$, which for equilibrium points is Pa/Pb,

$$\frac{b}{a} = r\frac{\beta}{\alpha},$$

$$d\left(\frac{b}{a}\right) = rd\frac{\beta}{\alpha} + \frac{\beta}{\alpha}dr,$$

$$\sigma = \frac{\left(rd\dfrac{\beta}{\alpha} + \dfrac{\beta}{\alpha}dr\right)\dfrac{\alpha}{\beta}\dfrac{1}{r}}{dr/r},$$

$$\sigma = \frac{dr + rd\dfrac{\beta}{\alpha}\cdot\dfrac{\alpha}{\beta}}{dr},$$

$$\frac{\alpha}{\beta}d\frac{\beta}{\alpha} = (\sigma - 1)\frac{dr}{r},$$

and since $\alpha = 1 - \beta$, $d\beta = \beta(1 - \beta)(\sigma - 1)\dfrac{dr}{r}$.

5. SOURCES AND METHODS FOR THE UNITED STATES SURVEY

(a) Output, man-hours and output per man-hour

Although the Bureau of Labor Statistics has prepared careful estimates of changes in output per man-hour,[1] these estimates only span the period 1923–50 in a handful of cases: canning and preserving, cane sugar, tobacco, cane-sugar refining, cement, clay construction products, coke, confectionery, paper and pulp, icecream, rayon and allied products, flour and other grain-mill products, and non-ferrous metals. These industries are too few for a comparative analysis, and thus it has been necessary to extend the Bureau of Labor Statistics estimates to additional industries where the period is only partially covered.

The Bureau of Labor Statistics estimates have been extended beyond 1939–50 for the following industries: tyres and tubes, hosiery, paints and varnish, petroleum refining, woollen and worsted, cotton goods, slaughtering and meat-packing, and iron and steel. Output measures for these industries over the period 1939–47 have been derived from the indexes prepared by the Bureau of the Census.[2] For the period 1947–50, the sub-indexes of the Federal Research Board have been employed.[3] Estimates of changes in man-hours over this period have been derived from Bureau of Labor Statistics data, supplemented by employment and man-hour data from the Census of Manufactures.

[1] The Bureau of Labor Statistics data is located in the following publications: *Productivity and Unit Labor Cost in Selected Manufacturing Industries, 1919–1940* (February 1942); *The Handbook of Labor Statistics, 1947 and 1950 editions, Productivity Trends in Selected Industries, Index through 1950* (Bulletin 1046).

[2] *Census of Manufactures, Indexes of Production* (U.S. Govt. Printing Office, Washington, 1952).

[3] 1953 Revision of the Monthly Index of Industrial Production, *Federal Reserve Bulletin* (December, 1953).

Extensions over the period 1947–50 have been necessary for the following industries: fertilisers, footwear, leather, glass products, and bread and other bakery products. In such cases the sub-indexes of the Federal Reserve Index have provided the basis for the extension of the output series, while the employment data have been derived from the 1947 and 1950 Census of Manufactures.

In the case of the bituminous coal industry the series have been taken back from 1935 to 1923 by means of estimates prepared by the National Research Project.[1] To extend the Bureau of Labor Statistics estimates beyond 1948 for the electric light and power industry proved impossible because of incomparabilities in the employment data.

(b) Earnings and labour cost

The earnings data are from Bureau of Labor Statistics sources, principally *The Handbook of Labor Statistics*, 1936, 1939, 1947 and 1950. Unit labour cost has been derived by dividing changes in earnings by movements of output per man-hour.

(c) Prices

The majority of the price measures are sub-indexes of the Bureau of Labor Statistics wholesale price index.[2] In the case of the bread, cane-sugar refining and flour industries, individual price relatives, or un-weighted averages of price relatives, constitute the price estimates. For the icecream and glass-products industries, satisfactory price data are not available from this source, and unit values have been derived from Census data. No reliable estimates of price changes could be derived for the canning and preserving, confectionery, and hosiery industries.

(d) Product-moment correlation coefficients are set out in Table 31, p. 166

Table A (6). *Coefficients of rank correlation between relative changes in output per man-hour and related quantities for twenty-seven industries, United States, 1923–50*

	Output	Man-hours	Output per man-hour	Hourly earnings	Unit labour cost	Wholesale-price
Output	—	+0·84	+0·64	—	—	−0·56
Man-hours	—	—	+0·18	+0·36	—	—
Output per man-hour	—	—	—	+0·46	−0·90	−0·85
Hourly earnings	—	—	—	—	—	—
Unit labour cost	—	—	—	—	—	+0·71
Wholesale price	—	—	—	—	—	—

Notes: (*a*) The coefficients are Spearman's rank coefficients.

(*b*) Coefficients between changes in wholesale prices and other changes refer to only twenty-four industries.

[1] *Production, Employment, and Productivity in Fifty-nine Manufacturing Industries* (National Research Project, Report S-1, Philadelphia, 1939).

[2] *Monthly Releases of Average Wholesale Prices and Index-Numbers of Individual Commodities* (U.S. Department of Labor.)

APPENDIX B

THE RELIABILITY OF THE SAMPLE

Although the sample covers approximately 30 % of the industrial sector, it could give a false impression of the impact of technical change by recording misleadingly high coefficients if it contains an undue proportion of either rapidly expanding or declining industries. Undue weight would be given to exceptional cases.

To evaluate such dangers is not easy. The usual sampling tests are inapplicable because the sample has not been randomly selected. The only alternative is to compare the characteristics of the sample with the

Frequency distribution of percentage increases and decreases in output per head, 1935–48.
Sample industries compared with the total industrial sector

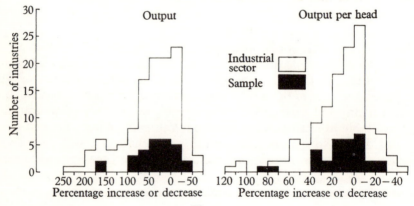

Fig. 25

characteristics of the whole industrial sector; and this is difficult because industries outside the sample are those where measures of characteristics such as output and employment movements are the least reliable. However, three such tests have been carried out.

The first compares output and output per head movements of the sample and the whole industrial sector between 1935 and 1948. From the tables prepared by Mr B. C. Brown, measures of changes in output and output per head are available for almost all industries in the industrial sector. Many of these estimates are extremely hazardous, for low coverage and susceptibility to quality changes (as in the engineering industries) make measurement of output almost impossible. Despite this, frequency distributions of movements of output and output per head have been prepared and compared with those for sample industries. The results are set out graphically in Fig. 25 and in tabular form in Table B (1).

Table B (1). *Frequency distributions of percentage increases in output and output per head, industrial sector, 1935–48, by numbers of industries*

Output			Output per head		
Percentage increase	Population	Sample	Percentage increase	Population	Sample
225–250	1	—	Over 110	1	—
200–225	1	—	100–110	2	—
175–200	4	—	90–100	—	—
150–175	6	2	80–90	1	1
125–150	4	—	70–80	2	1
100–125	5	—	60–70	2	—
75–100	8	3	50–60	6	—
50–75	17	4	40–50	5	—
25–50	21	6	30–40	9	4
0–25	21	6	20–30	12	2
−25 to 0	23	5	10–20	18	5
−50 to −25	8	2	0–10	23	5
−75 to −50	3	—	−10 to 0	27	6
			−20 to −10	8	2
			−30 to −20	7	2
			−40 to −30	3	—
			−50 to −40	1	—

The distribution of changes in output over the period 1935–48 suggests that the experience of sample industries has not been significantly different from that of all industries, and the proportion of either rapidly expanding or declining industries in the sample does not appear to be unduly high. But, comparison of the movements of output per head does suggest a slight tendency for the sample to include an excessive number of medium increases. If this is so, the effect is slightly to overemphasise the diversity of output per head movements. This reservation, as has been noted, is important in relation to consideration of structural change.

While these distributions do not reveal any marked bias, the years 1935–48 are only a part of the period under analysis. Moreover, changes over these years are distorted by the war years and the postwar recovery. A comparison between employment movements over the whole period 1924 to 1950 is useful to overcome this deficiency. Fig. 26 and Table B (2) set out the distributions of the sample and industrial sector.

The measurement of employment changes for non-sample industries is complicated by changes in classification. These tend to be concentrated in rapidly expanding industries, and so render the distribution of the 'population' suspect. For example, the electrical engineering industry is excluded because of changes in classification; in 1924 the industry was classified as a single census trade, and in 1950 embraced six trades and employed over half a million workers.

Despite the exclusion of such cases, no great differences are apparent between the two distributions. There is a slight tendency for the sample to include too high a proportion of industries with small declines in

Table B (2). *Frequency distribution of percentage increases in total employment, industrial sector, 1924–50, by numbers of industries*

Percentage increase	Population	Sample
Over 180	4	1
160–180	3	1
140–160	2	—
120–140	1	—
100–120	2	—
80–100	4	1
60–80	7	3
40–60	9	2
20–40	7	8
0–20	15	4
−20 to 0	8	4
−40 to −20	6	1
−60 to −40	6	—
Below −60	1	—

Note: Excludes industries where major changes in classification have occurred.

Frequency distribution of percentage increases and decreases in employment, 1924–50. Sample industries compared with the total industrial sector

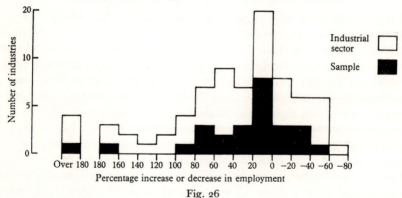

Fig. 26

output. The probability of such a bias is reinforced by Table 13, p. 104, which shows that the proportion of total employment represented by the sample has fallen slightly since 1924.

To sum up these tests, it does not appear likely that the sample is misleading. While it is unrepresentative in one or two respects, in general, the tests reveal an approximate reflection of the characteristics of the population. In addition, Fabricant's study and the American survey of chapter XIII give some grounds for believing that the tendencies revealed by correlation analysis of the sample data are likely to be duplicated for the economy as a whole.

APPENDIX C

THE INFLUENCE OF ERRORS ON THE PRODUCT-MOMENT CORRELATION OF RATIOS

I. THE NATURE OF THE PROBLEM

In chapter VIII reference was made to the effect on the observed correlation of certain ratios, such as output per man employed with unit wage and salary costs, of errors of measurement in either the numerator or denominator of the ratios. The problem here must be distinguished from related problems which concern the correlation of ratios and which have been treated, for example, by Pearson[1] as long ago as 1897 and more recently by Kuh and Meyer.[2] Pearson showed that if three quantities, X, Y and Z, are in fact distributed independently of each other the product-moment correlation coefficient between such ratios as X/Z and Y/Z is nevertheless likely to be quite high (between 0·4 and 0·5), merely because the denominator is common to both ratios. Kuh and Meyer considered the conditions in which the same correlation coefficient could be regarded as a good estimate of the *partial* correlation between X and Y (assuming now that such a relation exists) with the influence of the third variable Z held constant. In both these cases it will be noted that from the standpoint of the writers the variables X, Y and Z are in some sense fundamental whilst any ratios calculated from them are regarded as derivative measures; consequently, any relationship observed to hold between such ratios is regarded as spurious unless it reflects a similar relationship between the fundamental variables.

The present context is different. Here, for example, unit labour cost is regarded as a fundamental variable, and the fact that it must be estimated by dividing the total wages bill by the total number employed is a mere arithmetical necessity dictated by the form taken by the published statistics. Or, more correctly, this would be the case if it could be assumed that the published statistics contained no errors of measurement; for it is these errors which introduce the specific difficulty with which this appendix is concerned. Consider, for example, the relationship between output per man employed and the level of output, which has a valid meaning in its own right. If the level of output is written X and output per man employed is written X/Y to indicate that it is estimated by dividing total outputs X by numbers employed Y; and if we further assume that whilst employment statistics are accurate

---

[1] K. Pearson, 'On a Form of Spurious Correlation which may arise when Indices are used in the Measurement of Organs', *Proc. Roy. Soc.* (1897).

[2] E. Kuh and J. R. Meyer, 'Correlation and Regression Estimates when the Data are Ratios', *Econometrica* (October 1955).

output statistics are not, the following problem arises. Instead of working with the true series X/Y and X we work with series x/Y and x, where $x = X+e$. The symbol e represents an error of measurement which is common to both the series whose correlation we are considering and is, therefore, capable of leading to a spurious estimate of the true correlation between X/Y and X. This appendix therefore considers the relationship between the calculated product-moment correlation coefficient $r(x/Y, x)$ and the 'true' coefficient $r(X/Y, X)$ on the assumption that e is a random variable defined by an assumed probability distribution, and other variants of the same problem.

2. NOTATION AND METHOD

We shall work with three true variables X, Y and Z and three observed variables x, y and z which correspond respectively to the upper-case variables except that they may be subject to random errors of measurement. The operator E when applied to a random variable will denote its mathematical expectation, but when applied to a fixed variable the same operator will denote the variable's arithmetic mean value in the series considered; similarly the operator V will denote the variance of a random variable, and also the mean-squares deviation of a fixed variable about its mean value. Finally the operator C will denote the covariance of two random variables as well as the analogue for fixed variables. Thus

$$V(u) = E(u^2) - \{E(u)\}^2, \tag{1}$$

$$C(u, v) = E(uv) - E(u)\,E(v). \tag{2}$$

The product-moment correlation coefficient between two variables or variates will be written $r(u, v)$ and is defined:

$$r(u, v) = C(u, v)/\sqrt{\{V(u)\,V(v)\}}. \tag{3}$$

The method of analysis will be to compare the expected values of correlation coefficients calculated between various ratios of the lower-case variables x, y and z with coefficients calculated between corresponding ratios derived from the upper-case variables X, Y and Z. The assumptions with regard to errors of measurement will be that these are located in the measurement of X above and are multiplicative in form.

3. ANALYSIS

We assume

$$x = X(1+e), \tag{4}$$

$$y = Y, \tag{5}$$

$$z = Z, \tag{6}$$

where ϵ is a random variable rectangularly distributed in the range $(-k, k)$, where $k < 1$. We shall require the following simple results:

$$E\left(\frac{1}{1+\epsilon}\right) = \frac{1}{2k} \log\left(\frac{1+k}{1-k}\right); \tag{7}$$

$$E\left(\frac{1}{1+\epsilon}\right)^2 = \frac{1}{1-k^2}; \tag{8}$$

and
$$V(\epsilon) = \tfrac{1}{3}k^2. \tag{9}$$

Correlation type 1: $r(x/y, x)$

$$r(x/y, x) = \frac{r(X/Y, X)(1+q_1)}{\sqrt{\{(1+q_2)(1+q_3)\}}}, \tag{10}$$

where
$$q_1 = \tfrac{1}{3}k^2 E(X/Y, X) \div C(X/Y, X), \tag{11}$$

$$q_2 = \tfrac{1}{3}k^2 E(X^2/Y^2) \div V(X/Y), \tag{12}$$

$$q_3 = \tfrac{1}{3}k^2 E(X^2) \div V(X). \tag{13}$$

For exact results equations (11)–(13) may be rewritten in terms of the observed variables x, y, z and the postulated error bounds k; alternatively for approximate results the observed values x, y and z may be inserted in (11)–(13) in place of the true values X, Y and Z.

Correlation type 2: $r(x/y, z/x)$

We obtain for $r(x/y, z/x)$ an expression of the same form as (10) but with the following definitions for q_1, q_2 and q_3:

$$q_1 = -E(X/Y)E(Z/X)\left\{\frac{1}{2k}\log\left(\frac{1+k}{1-k}\right) - 1\right\} \div C(X/Y, Z/X), \tag{14}$$

$$q_2 = \frac{k^2}{3} E(X^2/Y^2) \div V(X/Y), \tag{15}$$

$$q_3 = \left\{E(Z^2/X^2)\frac{k^2}{1-k^2} + (EZ/X)^2\left[1 - \left(\frac{1}{2k}\log\frac{1+k}{1-k}\right)^2\right]\right\} \div V(Z/X). \tag{16}$$

Again, observed values x, y and z may be substituted in these equations for approximate results, whilst for exact results (14)–(16) must be rewritten in terms of x, y, z and k.

Correlation type 3: $r(y/x, z/x)$

Analysis again yields an expression of the form of (10) with, this time,

$$q_1 = \left\{\frac{k^2}{1-k^2}\, E(Y/X, Z/X) + \left[1 - \left(\frac{1}{2k}\log\frac{1+k}{1-k}\right)^2\right] E(Y/X)\, E(Z/X)\right\}$$
$$\div C(Y/X, Z/X), \quad (17)$$

$$q_2 = \left\{\frac{k^2}{1-k^2}\, E(Y^2/X^2) + \left[1 - \left(\frac{1}{2k}\log\frac{1+k}{1-k}\right)^2\right] (EY/Z)^2\right\} \div V(Y/X),$$
$$(18)$$

$$q_3 = \left\{\frac{k^2}{1-k^2}\, E(Z^2/X^2) + \left[1 - \left(\frac{1}{2k}\log\frac{1+k}{1-k}\right)^2\right] (EZ/X)^2\right\} \div V(Z/X).$$
$$(19)$$

4. CONCLUSIONS

Exact results have been calculated along the lines indicated in paragraph 3, and are given in Table 17 of chapter VIII. It should perhaps be emphasised that the arguments given in this Appendix are constructed entirely in terms of the mathematical expectation of the observed correlation coefficients compared with the true correlation coefficients which would result if the variable X (here taken to indicate output) contained no errors of measurement. Two qualifications must therefore be made. First, the results of Table 17 have been calculated on the assumption of a particular form of the probability distribution of the errors in measurement; namely that a rectangularly distributed error has entered the measurement in a multiplicative form. This is not an unreasonable assumption, and it is unlikely that the results of Table 17 would be seriously upset by the substitution of any reasonable alternative.

Secondly, the results of Table 17 should be interpreted as showing a general tendency to bias in the calculated correlation coefficients. We have not examined the problem of the distribution of individual estimates about their expected values as would arise in a series of sets of observations. Thus, in a particular case, very different figures from those given in Table 17 would be consistent with the data if errors of the size postulated had in fact happened to be distributed in a particularly perverse way on this occasion.

THE POST-WAR SCENE

Addendum by W. B. Reddaway

THE title for this addendum has been chosen to emphasize the similarity of its role, in relation to the main book, to that of Chapter XIII on 'The American Scene'. In the words used at the opening of that chapter: 'We should be entitled to much more confidence in the results if they could be confirmed by another set of observations based upon a different sample of industries operating in different circumstances'.[1] And again, adapting slightly the text which follows, 'This post-war survey provides a check on the earlier survey . . . in the wider sense of ascertaining whether associations which lead to the same interpretive conclusions are to be found in the post-war period as well as in the earlier one'.

I. THE BASIC DATA

The statistical analysis is basically similar to that in the main survey. Owing to changes of statistical classification it was not possible to use exactly the same list of industries as Salter took, but in general a broadly similar industry has been used to replace one which had to be dropped. Some detailed notes on problems connected with the statistical data are given at the end of this addendum, but it may be useful to draw attention to some of the important points here.

Period. The period taken for the main comparisons was 1954 to 1963, because these are the earliest and latest years respectively for which it is possible to get Census of Production data on a sufficiently comparable basis. For 1963 the information is provisional and does not, at the time of writing, include details of output and input; but it is (just) sufficient to enable the job to be done.

There is something to be said for starting with a year in which most of the post-war transitional problems were already well behind us (raw material controls, etc.), so that the omission of the years before 1954 from the period covered is no real loss. 1963 is not however as 'comparable' a year to 1954 as 1964 would be: it started with the great frost and the aftermath of the restrictive policies applied in 1962, which were still depressing the output of certain industries (e.g. steel). The influence of the cyclical factors, as contrasted with secular growth, is often exaggerated in relation to the post-war period, but we thought that it might be more important in an analysis which rests on *differences* in movements between one industry and another than in studies of growth in broad aggregates. We therefore used some rather hazardous

[1] See p. 163.

methods to extend our series from 1963 to 1964 on a strictly provisional basis, and re-calculated the correlation coefficients using the movements over the decade 1954–64. The differences between these results and the ones for 1954–63 were not however big enough to justify publishing a separate set of figures.

Volume and Price Calculations. Salter's calculation of the movement in the *volume* of output for each industry between 1924 and 1948 rested fundamentally on the quantity statistics for the output of individual commodities recorded in the censuses of production; the implied price index was then found by dividing this volume index into the index for the movement in the value of gross output. The figures were then extended to 1950 by less comprehensive data.

For 1954–63 this method was not available to us, since the detailed output statistics of the 1963 census had not yet been compiled. We had therefore to bring in from non-census sources an indicator for each industry either of the price movement or of the movement in the volume of output. In fact both were available in nearly all cases, coming respectively from the components of the index-number of wholesale prices and the data collected for the index of industrial production. We therefore used both, by averaging the relevant whole-sale price index with the implied price-index obtained by combining the value figures and the index of production data; these 'compromise' price index-numbers were then used to deflate the value figures, so as to give a 'compromise' volume index for each industry's output.

With the aid of these volume index-numbers it was possible to produce a complete set of 'compromise' figures; these are given in Table 33, which shows for 1954–63 data comparable to those for 1924–50 given on page 107. Although the two basic approaches gave substantially different answers for some individual industries[1] the median index for the volume of output was not very greatly affected: a calculation based on the index of production data alone gave 125, against the compromise figure of 123 shown in Table 33.

2. DIVERSITIES AND SIMILARITIES

Salter's technique of statistical analysis is much concerned with the *differential* movements recorded for particular industries, as compared

---

[1] The industries where the two methods gave substantially different results are indicated by an asterisk or a dagger in Table 33. An asterisk implies that the 'compromise' figure for the volume of production shown in the table is significantly higher than would have been derived from the data collected for the index of production and correspondingly, the 'compromise' figure shown in the table for the price movement is significantly higher than that derived from the index of wholesale prices. Conversely, a dagger implies that each of these 'compromise' figures is significantly lower than the corresponding direct measure.

It follows that industries marked in the table with an asterisk show higher figures, and those industries marked with a dagger, lower figures, for output per head and output per operative than would have been obtained by using index of production data; also that the price found by combining the figures shown for unit labour cost, unit materials cost and unit gross margin cost would be higher than the wholesale price index for those industries marked with an asterisk and lower for those marked with a dagger.

Table 33. *Changes over the period 1954–63 for selected United Kingdom industries*

(Index numbers 1954 = 100)

Industry (1958 S.I.C.) ranked according to increases in output	Gross output	Total employment	Output per head	Output per operative	Earnings per operative	Unit wage cost	Unit labour cost	Unit gross margin cost	Unit material cost	Net price	Gross price
1. Electricity	209.5	118.0	177.5	179.8	172.5	95.9	98.2	163.6	102.0	136.5	114.5
2. Chemicals (general)*	186.9	117.2	159.5	171.9	153.4	89.2	99.7	140.5	91.1	123.8	106.5
3. Toilet preparations*	155.3	146.2	106.2	109.1	159.7	146.4	149.8	148.4	121.6	148.7	139.3
4. Fertilisers, etc.	154.3	100.5	153.5	171.3	164.2	95.9	110.8	127.8	93.7	120.4	101.9
5. Misc. paper manufactures	147.1	109.3	134.6	139.0	162.8	117.1	118.7	136.0	100.3	127.1	113.0
6. Glass	146.8	111.0	132.3	140.6	160.1	113.8	124.0	128.3	115.7	125.8	119.5
7. Paper and board	139.4	120.5	115.7	121.1	156.3	129.1	133.9	87.1	99.5	105.0	103.9
8. Hosiery and knitted goods	136.0	98.6	137.9	142.0	145.9	102.8	105.4	101.1	87.0	103.5	94.7
9. Linoleum, leathercloth, etc.	135.9	120.5	112.8	123.3	167.5	135.8	141.2	183.4	107.0	161.9	126.9
10. Wire and wire manufactures	132.9	112.2	118.4	122.0	163.4	133.9	136.9	130.2	110.5	133.9	117.8
11. Rubber	126.5	108.7	116.4	124.6	170.7	137.0	145.7	151.3	102.1	148.3	124.0
12. Non-ferrous metals	125.9	102.6	122.7	125.8	155.4	123.6	129.8	131.3	94.8	130.4	103.8
13. Steel tubes	125.7	119.3	105.4	107.5	153.0	142.3	147.5	142.2	130.3	145.0	134.1
14. Brewing and malting	123.4	111.1	111.1	112.6	179.9	159.8	154.6	160.2	119.3	158.5	136.5
15. Paint and printing ink†	122.8	94.4	130.1	140.2	157.3	112.2	171.0	115.0	93.2	115.9	103.2
16. Cement	117.2	111.9	104.7	108.7	160.4	147.5	154.3	133.6	111.3	140.2	123.8
17. Footwear†	113.2	84.8	133.5	135.7	159.5	117.5	118.6	128.4	88.2	122.3	102.6
18. Iron and steel (general)	109.6	103.7	105.7	112.1	155.7	139.0	148.1	116.4	128.7	132.4	128.6
19. Bricks, fireclay, etc.†	106.1	84.6	125.4	128.0	151.3	118.2	122.1	147.9	114.6	131.0	121.9
20. Dyestuffs	105.6	83.8	126.0	129.9	153.3	118.0	120.1	130.7	88.9	125.5	104.7
21. Cutlery†	103.6	95.2	108.8	115.8	160.0	138.2	149.7	87.4	110.5	108.6	110.4
22. Jute	101.0	89.8	112.5	114.9	157.7	137.2	141.7	108.7	95.0	127.1	110.7
23. Cocoa and confectionery	97.5	93.7	104.1	108.6	164.9	151.9	155.3	126.3	82.1	138.8	106.7
24. Brushes and brooms	93.3	79.3	117.7	128.5	162.0	126.0	133.4	144.8	124.4	138.4	133.4
25. Coal mining	86.9	77.4	112.3	114.8	139.2	121.3	125.8	253.3	153.0	146.7	150.4
26. Coke ovens	86.4	90.5	95.5	98.9	159.7	161.6	165.6	123.0	169.9	142.6	163.0
27. Leather	85.9	71.8	119.6	118.3	150.3	127.0	122.9	154.1	105.5	135.3	112.3
28. Cotton spinning, etc.	69.2	55.0	125.8	129.1	150.7	116.8	121.5	92.2	90.2	110.1	98.3
Median	122.7	101.6	118.1	124.0	159.6	126.5	133.7	131.0	103.8	131.7	113.8
Upper quartile	143.1	114.7	132.9	139.6	163.8	140.7	149.8	149.9	120.5	143.8	131.0
Lower quartile	102.3	87.3	110.1	113.7	153.4	117.0	120.8	119.7	93.5	123.1	104.3

* ⎱
† ⎰ See footnote on page 196

Sources: Based principally on Census of Production Reports.

with the average movement. It is useful to start with a quick look at what these average movements were in the post-war period, as compared with those from 1924–50. Using the median index-numbers from Tables 14 and 33 for convenience, and expressing the movements as annual (compound) growth rates, the main figures are as shown in Table 34.

Table 34. *Annual rates of increase of median values for certain indicators, 1924–50 and 1954–63*

Indicator	Percentage rate of increase	
	1924–50	1954–63
Volume of output	2·17	2·30
Employment	0·44	0·17
Output per head	1·60	1·84
Earnings per operative	3·59	5·33
Unit labour cost	1·87	3·28
Unit material cost	2·81	0·42
Unit gross margin cost	2·38	3·05
Net price	2·14	3·11
Gross price	2·78	1·44

Sources: Based principally on Census of Production Reports.

Table 34 shows relatively small changes in the growth-rates for the 'physical' series: in the post-war period output rose slightly faster, employment even more slowly, and hence output per head rather faster. Where money and prices are involved, however, there are more striking changes. Earnings per operative rose a good deal faster, and so, in consequence, did unit labour cost. As unit gross margin cost (a poor statistical approximation to gross profits per unit of output) also rose more rapidly, the same inevitably applied to net price, which is compounded of these two. Unit materials cost, on the other hand, rose very much more slowly, and this sufficed to keep the rise in the gross price to a slower pace than in 1924–50.

As in the earlier period, a leading feature of Table 33 is the wide diversity of movement between the various industries, which shows itself for every series with, once again, the important exception of 'earnings per operative'. A simple measure of the scatter of movements may be obtained by taking half the difference between the upper and lower quartiles for each series, and dividing by the median for that series: broadly speaking, this measure tells us that the central half of the observations lie within the range given by the mid-point, plus or minus $x\%$. Table 35 gives the values of x for each series, both for 1924–50 and for 1954–63.

One point should be noted immediately in relation to Table 35: since the period over which the post-war comparison stretches is only 9 years, against 26 for the previous one, the amount of scatter is bound to be smaller, whether or not there was a weaker basic tendency for the industries to show different movements. Allowing for this, the figures in Table 35 do not point to any clear tendency for the scattering process to have worked faster or more slowly.[1]

Table 35. *Dispersion measures* for each series, 1924–50 and 1954–63*

Series	1924–50	1954–63
Volume of output	46·9	16·6
Unit gross margin cost	46·2	11·5
Unit wage cost	26·2	9·4
Net price	25·7	7·9
Employment	25·4	13·5
Output per operative	24·7	10·4
Output per head	21·9	9·7
Unit material cost	20·9	13·0
Gross price	20·8	11·7
Unit labour cost	20·1	10·8
Earnings per operative	8·6	3·3

* The figures express half the difference between the upper and lower quartiles as a percentage of the median.

Sources: Based principally on Census of Production Reports.

Two important points of similarity between the new data and that used by Salter emerge from Table 35:

(a) In each case, the dispersion is *greatest* for the volume of output: it is the large differences in the movements of output for different industries which make analysis of Salter's kind so powerful.

(b) In each case, the dispersion is much smaller for earnings per operative: the tendency for all industries to show much the same movement of earnings—or at least for the differences in these movements to be almost trifling compared with differences in the industries' experience in every other respect—plays a key role in Salter's explanation of many correlations.

Apart from these two extreme cases, nearly all the series had shown much the same amount of dispersion in the period 1924–50. The

[1] The effect on the dispersion measure of having a longer period, taken by itself, is somewhat complex. Speaking very broadly, if the movement of the average or median in any year tends to be about the same throughout the whole period, we can say two things:

(a) *Random Scatter.* If there is no tendency for the increases (or decreases) of above-average size in any year to be concentrated on the same industries as showed them in other years, then the index of scatter will increase through purely random forces in proportion to the *square root* of the number of years in the period: for 26 years it would then be about 1·7 times as big as for 9 years.

(b) *Systematic Dispersion.* If, at the other extreme, each industry showed much the same percentage increase each year (so that some fast-growing industries systematically went further ahead of the median, and other slow growing ones systematically fell further behind), then the dispersion index would increase almost proportionately to the number of years in the period: for 26 years, it would then be 2·9 times as big as for 9.

For the type of series which we have, one would clearly expect the second simplifying condition to be much more nearly fulfilled than the first in most cases. Over 26 years, however, one would not expect exactly the same industries to serve as pace-makers or laggards throughout the period.

changes in ranking order to be seen in Table 35 are not of much importance.

Finally, so far as this section is concerned, it is interesting to ask the question whether the *same* industries have shown the fastest (and slowest) growth-rates in 1954–63 as in the earlier period. For the 23 industries which are common to the two lists, Table 36 gives a comparison of the ranking order in the two periods, both for output and for output per head.

Table 36. *Comparison of ranking order of 23 industries for movements over the period 1924–50 and 1954–63 in* (a) *output and* (b) *output per head*

Industry	Ranking order			
	(a) *Output*		(b) *Output per head*	
	1924–50	1954–63	1924–50	1954–63
Electricity	1	1	2	1
Chemicals (general)	3	2	8	2
Hosiery and knitted goods	13	5	12	3
Footwear	19	13	20	4
Glass	6	3	6	5
Paint and printing ink	10	11	19	6
Cotton spinning, etc.	21	23	18	7
Bricks and fireclay	16	15	14	8
Leather	18	22	22	9
Wire and wire manufactures	8	7	9	10
Brushes and brooms	12	19	13	11
Rubber	2	8	3	12
Paper and board	9	4	10	13
Linoleum	14	6	11	14
Jute	23	17	17	15
Coal mining	22	20	21	16
Brewing	20	10	23	17
Cutlery	4	16	1	18
Iron and steel	11	14	15	19
Steel tubes	5	9	4	20
Cement	7	12	5	21
Cocoa and confectionery	15	18	7	22
Coke ovens	17	21	16	23

Note: The industries are arranged in descending order of their output per head index for 1954 to 1963.

It will be seen that for *output*, there is a broad similarity in the ranking order. Only one industry—cutlery—shows a difference of more than nine places, which is about the average movement to be expected if there is no correlation between the rankings; the Spearman coefficient of rank correlation is indeed 0·67, so that one can *broadly* say that fast-growing industries in the earlier period continued to grow fast, declining or slow-growing industries continued to fare badly.

In terms of *output per head*, however, the short answer is that correlation coefficient between the two rankings is negligible. The lists are not in a truly random relationship to one another: there are more industries with almost the same ranking than one would expect on such a basis, but there are also more really large discrepancies, and these reduce the correlation coefficient effectively to zero. A few of the big discrepancies may be accounted for by the production difficulties in 1963 (e.g. cement and steel tubes would be considerably higher up the list if 1964 had been taken as terminal year, and so nearer to their position in the earlier period). But there are—to say the very least— far more exceptions than there were in the case of output to any generalisation that the previous period's star performers remain stars, and the laggards remain laggards.[1]

3. COMPARISON OF CORRELATION COEFFICIENTS

Perhaps the most interesting question on which this addendum can throw light is the extent to which 'the Salter correlations'—given in Table 16 on p. 110 for the United Kingdom and in Table 31 on p. 166 for the United States—are repeated in the post-war period. An overall view of the comparison with earlier United Kingdom experience is provided in Table 37.

We must consider the meanings of the similarities and differences for related groups of series in the succeeding sections. One general observation may however usefully be made here. The basic hypothesis which Salter advanced for explaining the nature of progress and so the relationships to be expected between variables was essentially a *long-term* one. On the whole, if the theory suggests a fairly high value of a correlation coefficient, then a rather lower value is to be expected over a period of nine years than over twenty-six, because chance and trade-cycle factors are more likely to 'spoil' the correlation. On the other hand, where theory suggests an *absence* of correlation (as with the movements in earnings per operative and output per operative) chance might produce a small correlation over a short period.[2]

In the light of this general presumption, the post-war results seem on the whole to support Salter's fundamental analysis: there are some striking differences in certain correlation coefficients, but we shall see that the leading examples are ones where the theory gave little or no presumption of a high correlation.

4. OUTPUT PER HEAD, EARNINGS, LABOUR COSTS

One very important result may be quickly noted: there is once again a negligible correlation between output per operative and earnings per operative. Table 19 on p. 126 gives this correlation for five different periods, and the figures range from +0·18 for 1924–30 to −0·18 for 1935–48. The new figure of +0·10 fits neatly into the picture by

---

[1] In Table 36 industries are arranged in descending order of their increase in output per head from 1954 to 1963, so that the stars and laggards can be easily identified, and the values of all three of their other index-numbers easily seen.

[2] These tendencies are clearly visible in the figures given for sub-periods of 1924–48 in Table 19, on p. 126. The lower correlations shown between output and output per head for the sub-periods are particularly noteworthy; they are much lower than for 1924–50 even when 1924–35 is taken—for which the terminal years might be thought fairly 'similar'.

Table 37. *Product-moment coefficient of correlation with respect to changes in output per head and related quantities: selected United Kingdom industries, 1924–50 and 1954–63*

	Volume of output	Output per head	Output per operative	Earnings per operative	Unit wage cost	Unit labour cost	Unit gross margin cost	Unit material cost	Gross price	Net price	Total employment
Volume of output		+0·69 / *+0·81*	+0·69 / *+0·86*						−0·19 / *−0·84*	+0·01 / *−0·63*	+0·75 / *+0·93*
Output per head	+0·69 / *+0·81*					−0·80 / *−0·91*	−0·01 / *−0·37*	−0·49 / *−0·79*	−0·53 / *−0·88*	−0·36 / *−0·73*	+0·04 / *+0·61*
Output per operative	+0·69 / *+0·86*			+0·10 / *−0·09*	−0·91 / *−0·89*		−0·01 / *−0·37*		−0·52 / *−0·89*	−0·37 / *−0·75*	
Earnings per operative			+0·10 / *−0·09*		+0·30 / *+0·27*						
Unit wage cost			−0·91 / *−0·89*	+0·30 / *+0·27*				+0·48 / *+0·78*	+0·59 / *+0·86*	+0·54 / *+0·80*	
Unit labour cost		−0·80 / *−0·91*					−0·11 / *+0·39*	+0·39 / *+0·74*	+0·56 / *+0·45*	+0·72 / *+0·83*	
Unit gross margin cost		−0·01 / *−0·37*	−0·01 / *−0·37*			−0·11 / *+0·39*		+0·43 / *+0·10*	+0·56 / *+0·45*	+0·72 / *+0·83*	
Unit material cost		−0·49 / *−0·79*			+0·48 / *+0·78*	+0·39 / *+0·74*	+0·43 / *+0·10*		+0·94 / *+0·90*	+0·49 / *+0·63*	
Gross price	−0·19 / *−0·84*	−0·53 / *−0·88*	−0·52 / *−0·89*		+0·59 / *+0·86*	+0·56 / *+0·45*	+0·56 / *+0·45*	+0·94 / *+0·90*		+0·73 / *+0·76*	
Net price	+0·01 / *−0·63*	−0·36 / *−0·73*	−0·37 / *−0·75*		+0·54 / *+0·80*	+0·72 / *+0·83*	+0·72 / *+0·83*	+0·49 / *+0·63*	+0·73 / *+0·76*		
Total employment	+0·75 / *+0·93*	+0·04 / *+0·61*									

Sources: Data from Table 14 and Table 33.

Figures in italics relate to the period 1924–50.

equalising the numbers of positive and negative values. All of them are negligibly small, and their sign is immaterial: the result is exactly what Salter's analysis leads one to expect, though it can also be explained in other ways.

The American statistics, discussed on p. 167, suggested a weak positive association between unusually large (or small) rises in output per head, and unusually large (or small) rises in average earnings. Even there this association was of negligible quantitative importance for explaining differential movements in earnings. In the United Kingdom there seems to be no significant tendency for industries in which output per head rises at more than the average pace to have wage increases which are either more or less than the average.

This result would, in itself, automatically mean that output per operative and unit wage costs must be negatively correlated, since the latter is simply the reciprocal of the former, with an allowance for wage movements. If, however, movements in earnings per operative had shown very large variations between one industry and another, these might have spoiled the correlation quite a lot, even though the variations were random with respect to movements in output per operative.

In fact, however, we have seen from Table 35 that variations in the movement of earnings per operative are much smaller than those for any other series. It follows inevitably, therefore, that there is a very high negative correlation between output per operative and unit wage cost (-0.91, against -0.89 for 1924–50).

The third pair which can be selected from these three variables—average earnings and unit wage costs—is not very interesting. Unit wage costs can be expressed as *average earnings* divided by *output per operative*: as the numerator and denominator of this fraction are uncorrelated, the answer is bound to be positively correlated with the numerator (average earnings). The correlation is however bound to be weak, because the denominator varies so much more than the numerator that the automatic correlation is largely 'spoiled'. It is not surprising, therefore, to find the correlation much the same as in 1924–50 at $+0.30$.

5. OUTPUT PER HEAD, COSTS AND PRICES

The high negative correlation between movements in output per head and those in unit labour costs, noted in the last section, was an inevitable corollary of the tendency for wages to show much the same movement in all industries, and for such variations as there are to be uncorrelated with variations in the rise in output per head. No such 'automatic' link exists, however, between movements in output per head and those in the other elements which make up the industry's selling price—unit materials cost and unit gross margin cost.

Salter's fundamental analysis provided some presumption that there would be a negative correlation in these cases also, on the grounds that industries which were being more than averagely successful in saving labour (per unit of output) were also likely to be more than averagely successful in reducing (at least in real terms) the other cost elements, since the 'success' largely depended on introducing new techniques, and these would be aimed at reducing all kinds of cost. The correlations could not however be expected to be as high as in the case of labour costs, for two main reasons. Firstly, our statistical measures are so imperfect—'unit gross margin cost', in particular, is a very poor measure of the cost of capital per unit of output. And secondly, the variations between industries in the movements of the prices which they have to pay for their materials are much greater than the corresponding variations for the price of a week's labour: if—as is perhaps plausible—these movements in the relative prices of industries' materials are uncorrelated with the industries' success in saving materials in physical terms, then they tend to reduce (but not destroy) the correlation between movements in output per head and in unit materials cost.

The figures given in Table 37 for 1954–63 show that there was again a substantial negative correlation between movements in output per head and in unit materials cost. The coefficient is not so high as in 1924–50 (−0·49 against −0·79), and the difference is perhaps bigger than one would expect merely from the general presumption in favour of smaller coefficients in shorter periods, mentioned above. But the height of the correlation in 1924–50 was rather a surprise both to Salter and to me: when it emerged from the calculations we both described it as 'almost too good to be true'. The value of −0·49 for 1954–63 is more nearly what we were expecting, and is quite high enough to show that there is a real tendency for industries which have achieved above-average reductions in the amount of labour needed per unit of output *also* to achieve a differential reduction in material costs. The results certainly do *not* support the view that the abnormal saving in labour was achieved by (for example) using electricity in place of human energy, or buying more highly fabricated components, since such processes would tend to produce a differential *rise* in unit materials costs in industries where output per head had risen most.

For unit gross margin costs, Table 37 shows no correlation with output per head in 1954-63, against a weak one ($r = -0.37$) in 1924–50. As gross margin cost is a statistically uncertain residual, found by subtracting the other costs from price, and does not correspond exactly with any economic concept, it is perhaps best to incorporate comment on this result mainly in the comments on the correlations with gross and net price. But one negative point again emerges: if differential increases in output per head had reflected mainly the fact that certain industries had done more in the way of substituting capital for labour than others, then one would expect to find a significant *positive* correlation, and of this there is no trace.[1]

[1] See the discussion on pp. 130–32.

As movements in output per head are negatively correlated with those in unit labour cost and unit material cost, and uncorrelated with those in unit gross margin cost, it is not surprising that they are negatively correlated with those in price: the industries which have raised labour productivity most have, on the whole, raised their price least. The correlations are lower than in 1924–50, but still clearly significant: −0·53 for gross price, and −0·36 for net price (i.e. excluding the materials).

The figures in Table 33 for individual industries enable one to examine the question whether the value of these or other correlation coefficients are likely to have been seriously depressed by a single industry showing results which are entirely contrary to those which a high correlation would imply. So far as these two correlations are concerned, it is readily apparent that electricity provides a marked exception to the rule, especially for net price: it has the highest index for output per head, and so 'should' have a low index for price, but in fact its index is above the median for both net and gross price (well above for the former). This is in marked contrast to the picture for 1924–50, when the electricity industry was also virtually at the top of the table for output per head, but duly showed the lowest index for both types of price-movement.

The proximate explanation of the above results is to be found largely in the figures for unit gross margin cost. Electricity showed the lowest index for this in the earlier period, so contributing to the low index for the price-movement, but in 1954 to 1963 it showed one of the highest. This is not the place to discuss how far the index for the former period was reduced by an 'artificially' low price of electricity in 1950 (when load factors were very high, partly as a result of load-spreading into the night, and when plant was largely valued at pre-war cost, with the price of electricity being deliberately fixed so as to give a gross return to capital in line with that valuation and with low gilt-edged rates); nor can we discuss here the extent to which the big rise in gross margin per unit of electricity between 1954 and 1963 was due to each of such possible factors as the following:

(a) a deliberate, Government-inspired policy of raising prices in order to secure higher gross profits, partly with the object of paying for a bigger part of the capital expenditure out of revenue;

(b) higher advertising expenditure (which is included in gross margin cost), so as to compete with other fuels now that the supply position was stronger;

(c) a higher cost of capital per unit through the provision of bigger safety margins.

It is clear that there are enough 'special' factors about electricity in both periods to make it interesting to see what the correlation coefficients would have been if electricity were omitted from the calculations. The figures are as follows:

Series correlated	Correlation, excluding electricity	
	1924–50	1954–63
Output per head/net price	−0·67	−0·50
Output per head/gross price	−0·88	−0·62

The effect of excluding electricity is to bring the two periods' figures for the correlation with net price much closer together; for 1954–63 the correlation with net price is raised from 0·36 to 0·50 by the exclusion of this single industry. For the correlation with gross price the post-war figure is raised appreciably, from 0·53 to 0·62, but the earlier one remains at the very high level of 0·88.

6. OUTPUT, OUTPUT PER HEAD, EMPLOYMENT

One of the most striking correlations observed in Salter's work was that between movements in output and movements in output per head: industries which showed the biggest rises in output, also showed the biggest rises for output per head, and correspondingly for the least progressive industries. For the whole period 1924–50 the correlation coefficient between these two movements was +0·81, though shorter periods had lower values ranging from 0·66 to 0·77 (as shown on p. 126).

The new information for 1954–63 fits quite nicely into this picture, with a coefficient of 0·69 (Table 37): the reduction in the value might reasonably be attributed to the shortness of the period. Nevertheless, it is interesting to look at the figures for individual industries in Table 33 to see whether anything can be learnt from the exceptions to the general rule; the process is made easier by the fact that the industries are arranged in descending order of their output index.

Such a scrutiny readily yields three interesting observations:

(a) If one takes the top quarter of the list—which by definition comprises the seven industries which have the highest index-numbers for output—we see that five of the seven are in the top seven for output per head, and there is only one (toilet preparations) which has a really low index for output per head. On the whole, therefore, the rule works well at the top of the table, and little is likely to be learned from a study of the exceptional case of toilet preparations.[1]

(b) At the bottom of the table, however, the rule works much less well: of the last seven (in terms of output), only two fall in the bottom seven for output per head—a number which might well be expected if the distribution were purely random.

(c) As an extreme case of (b), cotton-spinning etc., comes at the

[1] Perhaps rising incomes and rising expenditures on advertising have produced a large increase in demand, which has led to a large increase in output, but not in output per head, and has not produced lower relative prices.

very bottom of the table, with an index for output of only 69·2; but for output per head its index of 125·8 would put it in tenth place.

The tendency for movements in output and output per head to be much less closely correlated at the bottom of the table than at the top did not apply in the 1924–50 period. It is tempting to ascribe the change to the much tighter position in the labour market in post-war years. Whatever the state of the labour market, it is easy to see how an exceptional rise in the demand for the product and an exceptionally rapid improvement in its technology are likely to combine to put an industry well above the average for both output-increase and productivity-increase. 'Nothing succeeds like success', and success on one of these two fronts helps to produce success on the other by many inter-acting processes.[1]

At the bottom end of the output table, however, the state of the labour market seems likely to have more influence. In pre-war days, an industry for which demand was declining did not usually suffer from labour shortage, even if the work-force attached to it (including the unemployed) might show some reduction. Each firm was of course under pressure to get down its costs, so as to avoid losses and be able to quote lower prices. But profits were liable to be particularly low, because so many firms were scrambling for whatever orders were going, without any fear of inadequate labour to execute them: these low profits made it hard to finance capital expenditure in a declining industry, even if it seemed to the managers to promise a good reduction in costs, and such expenditure was certainly not necessary to enable the orders obtained to be executed in face of a labour shortage. 'Nothing fails like failure' would be too dramatic as a description of the declining industries, but it conveys some of the reasons why a fall in demand led to a poor performance on output per head as well as on output.

In the post-war period, however, industries whose labour requirements were declining often found that they nevertheless suffered from 'labour shortage' just as much as the expanding industries. Firms in such industries could not assume that labour would always be available to execute such orders as they secured, so that they had a more direct and compelling interest in improving labour productivity; moreover they generally had the financial means to meet the necessary expenditures, because there was not the same competive pressure in the product market—some of their rivals had switched their plant to other types of production, others were short of labour. 'Failure' of the industry, in terms of the amount of output which could be sold, did not provide so strong a presumption of 'failure' in terms of output per

---

[1] See the analysis in Chapter X. Personally I attribute rather more importance than Salter did to the influence of exceptional increases in demand, attributable to factors other than prices—i.e. exceptionally large outward shifts of the demand curve, caused by rising incomes or by consumers becoming familiar with a new product. These help to make increases in output and in output per head mutually stimulatory.

head. Particularly in industries with a good number of competing firms, the pressures in favour of 'modernisation' expenditures which would lower costs generally (and reduce labour requirements per unit of output in particular) were quite strong even if aggregate demand for the industry's products was stagnant: the fact that such schemes often raised the firm's capacity was not a serious objection.[1]

The special case of cotton-spinning would provide material for a fascinating special study, centred presumably around the Government-inspired reorganisation scheme at the end of the 1950's. In the main it is an extreme illustration of what has just been said, with deliberate rationalisation applied to aid natural forces.

Table 33 shows that all the price and cost columns for cotton conform to what one would expect for an industry in which output per head has risen by more than the average, and *not* to what one expects, in the ordinary way, for an industry which has suffered an outstandingly great fall in its output. In consequence the inclusion of cotton-spinning tends to spoil correlations between any of the price or cost indicators and *output*,[2] but not their correlations with *output per head*.

Cotton naturally tends to spoil the positive correlation between output and output per head: if it is excluded, the coefficient is increased from 0·69 to 0·75. This is perhaps a better figure to regard as representing what happens in the absence of special reorganisation schemes, the direct effect of which is to concentrate the reduced amount of production on mills which are above average in efficiency and which will thereafter be able to make fuller use of the reduced labour force.

Output and Employment.   Salter's statistics showed a very high positive correlation between movements in output and movements in employment ($r = + 0·93$). For 1954–63 the correlation coefficient is $+0·75$, which is again substantial, though not so high. It is perhaps worth devoting some attention to this matter, if only to see whether one should be more impressed by the *reduction* in the coefficient, or by its repeated large size.[3]

At first sight it may seem 'obvious' that there would always be a substantial correlation between movements in output and movements in employment. If one thinks of the industries in which output has risen substantially more than the average, it seems 'too much to expect' that their output per head should have shown such abnormal increases that their employment need rise by no more than the average

---

[1] Agriculture in the post-war period provides an excellent example of a large rise in output per head with a modest rise in output, for just these reasons.

[2] One of the features of Table 37 is the much smaller (negative) correlation in the post-war period between movements in output and in price. Both cotton and electricity tend to spoil this, for reasons which may perhaps be considered 'special'. If both are excluded, the correlation coefficient changes from −0·19 to −0·33; this is still well below the 1924–50 figure of −0·84, but the contrast is less marked, and in part it may well be due to the post-war period being shorter.

[3] If some of what follows seems rather obvious, I must plead in mitigation my experience as a teacher, whose pupils did *not* find it obvious until it was explained.

percentage (which in fact would mean very little increase indeed). Or—to take a slightly different approach—it is fairly natural to think of 'a rapidly expanding industry' as growing rapidly both in output and in employment.

These approaches rest, however, on tacit assumptions about what is in fact likely to happen to movements in output and in output per head, as between industries which operate under different conditions. Thus without considering problems of causation, the first approach would be invalid, at a 'statistical' level, if movements in output per head showed enormous variations between industries, and movements in output only small ones: it would then be inevitable that quite a number of industries which showed above-average increases in output would show *below*-average increases in employment[1]—which would in effect mean decreases in employment. This would also reduce the second approach to little more than a slovenly failure to be clear as to the meaning of 'a rapidly expanding industry'.

Since it is a fact that inter-industry variations in the movement of output are bigger than those for output per head, the natural approaches to the matter have some validity: if movements in these two were uncorrelated, there would be bound to be some positive correlation between movements in output and those in employment, because the employment index can be thought of as the quotient when the output index is divided by the index for output per head.[2] The variations in the output per head index are big enough, however, to ensure that in these circumstances the correlation coefficient would be kept down to a more modest figure than our observed one of $0 \cdot 75$ (let alone Salter's $0 \cdot 93$). To obtain a high positive correlation we *also* require that there should be a high correlation between movements in output and those in output per head.

It is worth noting that this last sentence does *not* require that the correlation between movements in output and output per head should be *positive*; a high negative correlation will do just as well—or even, in a sense, better. One can see this rather easily with the aid of Table 33, in which the industries are lined up in descending order of output-increases. A high negative correlation between output and output per head would mean that the column for the latter would show low values at the top and high ones at the bottom; the 'employment' column, being obtainable by dividing the output index by that for output per head, would then show figures systematically declining as one went down it. The order of the industries would thus be the same for employment as for output, but the range of values would be greater for employment: 'the concertina would be stretched out'. It does not matter, in this case, whether the dispersion of the index-numbers for

---

[1] Unless one is prepared to believe that the above-average increases in productivity mostly occurred in industries for which output was expanding more *slowly* than the average—i.e. a *negative* correlation between movements in output and those in output per head.

[2] *Cf.* the argument at the end of section 4 above.

output per head is greater or less than that for output: the dispersion for employment would be greater than for either of them.

By way of contrast, the actual picture in Table 33 is that the output per head column shows, on the whole, high figures at the top and low ones at the bottom: the correlation is positive, but not perfect. If this correlation had been perfect, then dividing these index-numbers into the output ones would have produced an employment column in which the index-numbers were again in strict descending order of magnitude; but the *range* or *dispersion* of the employment column would be less than that for the output one—the concertina would be compressed. Since the correlation between the output movement and that for output per head is high but not perfect, we get an approximation to this result.[1]

The analysis may usefully be taken a little further by bringing in the regression equations, for which the particulars are given in Table 38. The regression of the employment index (y) on the output index (x) has equation

$$Y_c = 44 \cdot 1 + 0 \cdot 46x \qquad (1)$$

In words, this tells us that an industry for which the output index is 10 points above the output average, is likely to have an employment index which is 4·6 points above its average.[2]

Table 38. *Parameters and standard errors in regression equations for 1954–63*

Dependent variable	Independent variable	Parameters a	b	Standard error	Correlation coefficient
Unit wage cost	Output per operative	235·0	−0·85	8·0	0·91
Unit labour cost	Output per head	236·8	−0·84	11·6	0·80
Unit materials cost	Output per head	174·1	−0·54	17·9	0·49
Unit materials cost	Unit labour cost	53·7	0·41	18·9	0·39
Gross price	Output per head	176·0	−0·47	14·3	0·53
Output per head	Output	72·3	0·41	13·6	0·69
Employment	Output	44·1	0·46	12·5	0·75

Note: Figures are not given for those regression equations where the correlation coefficient was less than 0·2. The form of the equation is in all cases $Y_c = a + b(X)$, where Y_c is the computed value of the dependent variable and X is the actual value of the independent variable.

[1] If the dispersion for movements of output per head had been greater than for output movements, then a high positive correlation between these two would mean a *negative* correlation between output and employment: the concertina would, as it were, be not merely compressed but turned inside out. (The danger of getting results of this kind explains why we referred to a negative correlation as 'better'.)

[2] I would like to take this opportunity of stressing that the figures are *index points*—i.e. percentages of the figures for output and employment in the *base* period. Both as supervisor of Salter's original research and as reader of the draft of his book I failed to point out that his unqualified reference to them as 'percentages' was likely to be taken as meaning percentages of the value in the later period. (See for example pp. 122–23.) Where the mean value in that period is much higher for one variable—e.g. output—than for the other—e.g. employment—this can be important. In many ways it would be more logical to use the logarithmic regression and correlation analysis—which Salter also prepared (see foot of p. 112).

The corresponding regression of the output per head index (y) on the output index (x) has equation

$$Y_c = 72 \cdot 3 + 0 \cdot 41x \qquad (2)$$

In words, the explanation is the same as above, but for the assumed output index the output per head index is likely to be rather fewer index points above its average than was the case with employment (4·1, against 4·6). As the median index in 1963 was 118·1 for output per head, against 101·6 for employment, the contrast is rather more marked when expressed as a percentage of the current level.

In effect, if we observe that an industry has shown a greater-than-average rise in output, we expect rather more of this to be due to a greater-than-average rise in employment than is explained by a greater-than-average rise in output per head.

Employment and Output per Head.   In the two preceding sub-sections we have been examining relationships which were in no sense statistically inevitable, but which Salter's analysis of the workings of the economy in general—and of technical change in particular—gave us good economic reason to expect. Such an analysis did not predict a correlation coefficient of any particular size—certainly not a perfect correlation —but it did predict a fairly high one. The fact that the correlation coefficients have turned out rather lower on this occasion is not as important as the fact that they are again high.

With employment and output per head, however, the analysis provides no clear-cut expectations. Salter discussed the matter on p. 123, where he explained that two opposing forces would be at work, and in such a case the net outcome may clearly differ in different periods or different countries. His actual results were a rather high positive correlation in the United Kingdom (+0·61), but a negligible correlation in the United States (+0·05).

For 1954 to 1963 the new statistics for the United Kingdom follow the American pattern, with a coefficient of as little as +0·04; even the exclusion of cotton—an obvious maverick—raised this only to +0·07.

This change from the results previously found for the United Kingdom seems to me to have no real bearing on the validity or usefulness of Salter's fundamental analysis. In itself, the new result means that there is no systematic tendency for industries in which productivity is rising at more than the average pace to show either a bigger or a smaller rise in employment than the average. This negative result is of some limited help in combating fears of technological unemployment, but of course individual industries may show big falls in employment accompanying big rises in output per head: the really important thing remains the adoption of measures which keep the general demand for labour high and which facilitate transfers from industries where employment opportunities are falling—whatever the reason for the fall.

7. TECHNICAL NOTES ON STATISTICS

The most important points about the statistics have been mentioned in the first section of this addendum. The function of this section is to deal with more technical matters.

Industrial Classification. Basically, the statistics used in this addendum relate to industries as defined by the 1958 Standard Industrial Classification, with adjustments to exclude purchases and sales of merchanted goods (and the associated figures for employment, wages, etc.). This exclusion was necessary because the 1954 Census forms instructed manufacturers to exclude merchanting activities from all sections of their return, so that comparability could only be secured by excluding an allowance for these from the 1963 figures.

Apart from the question of merchanted goods, the adjustments necessary to make the 1954 Census comparable with the 1963 one had been made (as far as possible) in the figures for 1954 published in the Report on the 1958 Census.

Industries Covered. The 1958 S.I.C. did not distinguish as separate industries five which had been used by Salter, namely:

> Tinplate
> Blast furnaces
> Spirit distilling
> Matches
> Wallpaper

To keep the number of industries at twenty-eight, five additional industries were included in our study, as follows:

> Non-ferrous metals
> Toilet preparations
> Fertilisers and chemicals for pest control
> Dyes and dyestuffs
> Miscellaneous manufactures of paper and board.

The scope of an industry as defined by the 1958 S.I.C. is not necessarily the same as that of an industry bearing a similar name used in Salter's calculations. For example, Iron and Steel now includes Tinplate and Blast Furnaces, which had been treated by Salter as separate industries, but General Chemicals now excludes Dyes and Dyestuffs, which we have used as one of our replacement industries. This does not, however, affect the usefulness or validity of doing calculations with the post-war figures.

Adjustment to Exclude Merchanting from 1963 Figures. The 1963 Census called on firms to report sales of merchanted goods (including canteen sales) separately from sales of goods which they had produced or processed themselves, but did not call for any further information about merchanting activities: in particular *purchases* of goods for resale were not distinguished from purchases of materials for use in manufacture, so that it was not possible to calculate directly a figure for the net output of manufacturing separately from merchanting.

As a matter of statistical logic, all sorts of procedures were possible for constructing plausible figures to represent the purchases, employment, wages and salaries which should be regarded as 'corresponding with' the single available figure for an industry's sales of merchanted goods. We experimented with several of them, and found that, although they gave (in some cases) markedly different answers for the size of the adjustment, nevertheless this size was itself usually so small that the proportionate difference in the adjusted figure was not great. We therefore decided to adopt a procedure which had the great advantage of being simple to apply; it also had a certain logic, in that it regarded the activity of 'merchanting' in one industry as likely to have ratios of (say) employment to net output which were more similar to those in merchanting activities carried on in other industries, than they were to those in the production activity of the industry in question. Any conventional procedure which worked largely on the basis of the figures for the industry in question, without reference to figures in other industries, was liable to produce ratios for the activity of merchanting which varied quite unjustifiably from one industry to another.

The first key assumption was, then, that the sales of merchanted goods should be split as to five-sixths for 'cost of purchases', and one-sixth for 'net output of merchanting'. From this figure for net output, we obtained an estimate of the numbers employed in merchanting by assuming a figure of £1,700 per annum for the net output per head in that activity; an assumption that they earned, on average, £700 a year gave the figure for wages and salaries. Both the employment and the remuneration were then divided equally between operatives and other staff.

The figures used for the above calculations were arrived at after considering a number of sources, notably the 1950 Census report on Wholesale Distribution and the subsequent movements, as inferred from figures in the 1965 National Income and Expenditure Blue Book. They do not pretend to be more than broad orders of magnitude, but as mentioned above the object was not to arrive at figures for merchanting which would be useful in themselves, but rather to arrive at adjusted figures for the productive side of the industry.

Two facts provide some consolation in considering how far one needs to worry about these adjustments. Firstly, there was only one industry (Fertilisers) in which the adjustment to the employment figure amounted to more than 5%. Unless, therefore, the adjustments ought really to have been much bigger—which seems very unlikely—any reasonable alteration in them would have little affect on the adjusted figures even for individual industries.

Secondly, some preliminary calculations made for another purpose enabled us to see what effect there would be on some of the correlation coefficients if one made the drastic assumption that merchanting has no net output or employment at all, as compared with the value of the coefficients when adjustments had been made for merchanting on the lines finally adopted. (Such an assumption might be taken as corresponding to a practice whereby one manufacturer invoiced his goods through a second manufacturer, with the latter never touching them or drawing any commission, but nevertheless including them as purchases and sales at the same value on his Census return). The test did not, unfortunately, extend to cover correlations involving unit materials cost, which might have been more noticeably affected, but for all the correlations where the test could be applied the effect of this drastic change in the assumptions was insignificant.

Brewing and Malting. A rather special consideration arose in relation to the Brewing industry, since the 1958 S.I.C. introduced the principle that the bottling of purchased beer was to be regarded as a part of distribution, rather than of production. In 1954, bottling had counted as production, and indeed there was a separate trade in which bottlers who did not produce their own beer made their returns; brewers who also bought some beer and bottled it returned that activity to the Census, since bottling was regarded as a productive activity. Brewers were, however, told to exclude 'merchanting', in accordance with the general practice of the 1954 Census, and this led to the exclusion of quite substantial sales of goods purchased from other firms (including bottles of alcoholic liquor).

If we had followed strictly our general principle of excluding from the 1963 figures whatever was regarded in 1963 as 'merchanting', then we would have had to make a large adjustment to the 1963 figures to exclude the bottling of purchased beer by brewers, as well as their straightforward merchanting activities. We would also, in the interest of comparability between 1954 and 1963, have had to eliminate from the 1954 figures everything which related to the bottling of purchased beer by the brewers, since this activity was then included as being 'productive'.

Rather than make these two substantial adjustments, we decided to seek a common basis on the lines of the 1954 treatment, whereby merchanted goods proper were excluded, but bottling of purchased beer was included. This meant that no adjustment to the 1954 figures was necessary, but before we could apply our normal procedure we had to estimate what part of the single figure given in the preliminary results of the 1963 Census for 'sales of merchanted goods' represented sales of beer which the brewers had purchased and bottled. This was done by using the proportion shown in the detailed tables for the 1958 Census.

Brewing presented a further problem, since the preliminary report did not show how much excise duty had been paid by the brewers, and this large item had to be subtracted for our purposes from both gross output and net output. As the Census Office were unable to provide this figure for us in advance of the publication of the more detailed tables, we had to derive it from the Annual Report of the Commissioners of Customs and Excise.

INDEX